REMEMBER ME AS LOVING YOU

A DAUGHTER'S MEMOIR

KIMBERLY CHILDS

swp

SHE WRITES PRESS

Published 2017
Printed in the United States of America
Print ISBN: 978-1-63152-157-7
E-ISBN: 978-1-63152-158-4
Library of Congress Control Number: 2017940408

For information, address:
She Writes Press
1563 Solano Ave #546
Berkeley, CA 94707

Cover design © Julie Metz, Ltd./metzdesign.com
Interior design by Tabitha Lahr

She Writes Press is a division of SparkPoint Studio, LLC.

Dedicated to all children and their ability to grow, heal, and nurture themselves and others.

INTRODUCTION

*They are kids, they are dumb, all they know is they are
innocent, they would never hurt anybody.
I want to go up to them and say Stop,
Don't do it—she's the wrong woman,
he's the wrong man, you are going to do things
You cannot imagine you would ever do,*

—SHARON OLDS

My mother, Wilma Jean Gibson, was born in 1928 in the Appalachian Mountains of Eastern Kentucky, a place of women who wore faded housedresses and sat on sagging porches worn down by the bare feet of too many flaxen-haired children. The men worked in the coal mines and scrabbled a few crops from ribbons of clay that settled in the valleys between the mountains.

Although she loved mountain men, the drudgery of a Kentucky coal miner's wife was not for my dazzling, vivacious mother. At age eighteen, she galloped out of Hazard, scattering all claims of allegiance save to her own hungry dreams. Her sights were set on Manhattan and beyond. Her parents, eight siblings, and husband were all left behind, destined to deal with the aftermath of her passage.

She had the classic good looks of Grace Kelly combined with the seductive charm of Marilyn Monroe. Manhattan quickly embraced her as one of its own. In short order, she changed her name to Jeanne, became a fashion model, a Miss Subways (her photo in the trains), and a tabloid darling. My father, Justin Gilbert, who was a reporter for the *New York Daily Mirror*, met her at a publicity shoot and was enthralled. He squired her to glamorous dining establishments like the Stork Club and introduced her to exciting stars like Charlton Heston. They spent the night at the exclusive Waldorf Astoria Hotel, where Jeanne drank too much and threw up all over the room. This should have been a tip-off about a drinking problem, but Justin didn't get it. Despite his penchant for the high life, he was unable to do much drinking or smoking. He had suffered from asthma and a weak constitution since childhood.

After a quickie divorce from Jeanne's first husband, they married, and Jeanne's belly almost immediately grew big. The sky was a radiant September blue the day her water broke at Jones Beach with Justin and some friends. She had braided her fine brown hair into tiny pigtails and wrapped her breasts in silk scarves. The Atlantic waves were buoyant and soothed her sunburned skin. A cool breeze was foretelling autumn. She refused to leave. Why should she cut short her pleasure to be driven in hot misery to a New York City hospital where she would labor? But biology took over, as it always does.

Except, in her case, nature left out the maternal gene.

My father paced the halls of the hospital. At thirty-two, he was on his second marriage, and this was his first child. He was jubilant as he carried me down in the elevator. He expected his new wife to settle down and become a homemaker.

Jeanne wasn't putting aside her bright dreams to cook dinner and change diapers. She asked her mother to send her two youngest sisters, Clara Belle, age eight, and Sue Ellen, age six, to come care for the baby. New York public schools would round out their education. In the meantime, she enjoyed New York nightlife with my father as he covered it for the paper. When her sisters had homework to do, and she was dining out, Jeanne counted on her friend, Kitty the hatcheck girl. The infant slept among the minks and mohair in the coatroom.

Here the story becomes suspect, because I have only my father's rendition, and he wrote for a tabloid newspaper and did like to dramatize. They drove to California to give Jeanne a shot at Hollywood. This took months longer than my father anticipated, so he returned to New York alone. He was typing his column for the paper one day when he received a call from a Mrs. Upchurch.

"I've been babysitting for months and haven't seen Jeanne once. I wonder if I could adopt Kim, because she would be the perfect sister for our little boys."

Justin emphatically said *no* and demanded his wife come home. On her way back, my mother dropped me in Kentucky with my grandparents. Some time later, my father drove the steep mountain roads and discovered me eating a caterpillar while the Gibson clan sat swinging on the front porch.

Reuniting his family back in New York, Justin hoped life would calm down. One sweltering summer day Jeanne said, "The sidewalks are hot enough to fry an egg. I want to take Kim to England, where it's cooler." Once there, she sent a letter to Kitty, the hatcheck girl. In it, she said, "Justin pricks my bubbles. I don't want trouble, but please mail Kim's winter clothes." She was breaking off the marriage and on a path that would lead her to becoming publicity director of the Savoy Hotel of London and the darling of Fleet Street, as well as to meeting David Merrick.

Chapter 1

A PROPER ENGLISH SCHOOL GIRL

~§§§~

It does not do to leave a live dragon
out of your calculations, if you live near him.
—J. R. R. TOLKIEN

My mother's scarlet fingernails dig into my wrist as she drags me through Harrods's heavy doors. With her free hand holding a lit cigarette, she shoves at anyone getting in her way. Straining to keep up, I dodge shoppers in the crowded London store.

"Oh, do hurry up. I have to get back to the office and on to the gala tonight." She takes a quick puff, and her icy blue eyes glitter down at me through bitter-smelling smoke.

As she strides past the perfume counter, a craggy-faced man with black hair calls out, "Jeanne, you are just the person I want to see."

Instantly, she pauses in her headlong rush, her full lower lip curves into a smile, and she drops her clutch on my wrist and curls her arm around his. "Darling boy, here I am."

Mother gazes up at him adoringly, offering her face like a flower. His eyes buzz all over her turquoise eyes, sculpted cheekbones, full lips, and winking cleavage. This is what happens between men and my mother. I watch; proud of her beauty yet frustrated because it's never directed at me.

Cascades of words flow from her, and he responds with his deep rumble. All around us the low roar of conversation bounces off the displays, racks of clothing, and high ceiling. I am forbidden to speak. But then the man's dark eyes shift to me.

"Well, hello, Miss Kimmie!" I am enchanted when he takes my hand and bows over it. I stick one foot behind the other and drop a curtsy, as I have been taught in school.

"Don't you remember me? I'm Victor Mature. We slept together at my place when your mommy went out of town. I wore a red-and-white-striped night shirt and cap." He bends down so we are eye to eye and makes a funny face. "You didn't wake me once."

"You saw him in *The Robe*," Mother prompts. I meet so many people, they all blur together. Suddenly I recall sharing a small bed with him in a book-lined room. I'd hoped he might be my new daddy, but I didn't see him again. Now I feel shy having his magnetic black eyes on me and can't think of anything to say. Mother tightens her grip on his arm, and they resume talking. It's my cue to disappear.

The glass display case is cool as I lean my forehead against it. I notice sample perfume bottles and reach up to squeeze the bulbs. Out puffs the sugary scent of honeysuckle, which grows near the outhouse on my grandparents' farm. Inhaling, I am there with my cousins, licking a drop of dew from the petals. I squeeze the perfume onto my finger and taste it. It's so awful I stick out my tongue. My mother gives me a look and sweeps the bottles out of reach.

I'd better entertain myself. Across the aisle a mother and

little girl are looking at dresses. The woman has mousy brown hair, and her stomach bulges over her waistband. She never dips her comb in stale beer to set her dyed blonde hair into a chignon, as my mother does. She never spits into a tiny tub of mascara and sweeps it over her eyelashes. She never slithers into a girdle and a black party dress. This woman is a real mother. I'd trade my mother for her in a heartbeat.

I move closer and peer at them from behind a mannequin. The girl has brown braids like me and is about my age, six years old. As the mother presses a frock to her daughter's shoulders, they speak with British accents. The mother rubs her daughter's shoulder blades, and they continue looking through the dresses. It's clear they still have their magnets. I learned in school how magnets pull things toward them. But Mother and I must have lost ours somewhere between New York, where we used to live, and here in London.

"Papa!" The girl cries when a man appears out of the crowd and puts his hand on her head and his arm around the woman. The mother beams and looks surprised. They are together, unlike my parents. I love my daddy more than anything, but he works for a newspaper in faraway New York. As I cling to the mannequin's legs, it topples with a crash of stiff limbs.

"Are you lost, little girl?" A man wearing a badge looms over me. The British family and everyone else in the store are staring at me. But I don't see Mother. I guess I *am* lost. This is nothing new. It has happened at the beach, at the airport, and at parties. My face crumples in on itself and I sob out, "They're by the perfumes." He takes my hand and leads me there. Mother and Victor are still deep in flirtation.

"Where have you been?" she asks angrily when she sees me. "I've been looking all over for you."

She pulls me onto the escalator, whose steps disappear just as I place a foot on them. I wipe my teary eyes so I can see. Mother is taking a long drag on her cigarette, so I breathe in as well. At last we ascend high above the other shoppers' heads.

"He wants publicity for another one of his terrible movies—I couldn't get away from him," she mutters. I know this is the only explanation I'll get.

"I thought you liked him."

"He's just a grade-B movie actor." She waves her cigarette dismissively. "But he did buy me a bottle of perfume." I never understand my mother. Her words have no connection to what she does.

We pause in an empty room lined with floor-to-ceiling drawers. A woman in gray walks from the back with a long white tape measure draped across her shoulders.

"My daughter will be attending Lady Eden's school at Fritham," Mother says in a British accent that shows no trace of her hillbilly roots. "Make sure she gets the proper uniform. Can she get riding clothes here? I want her to learn how to ride a horse."

"She's very small, madam, I have to measure her to see if we have her size." The woman kneels beside me and draws the tape around my middle and from knee to shoulder. It tickles, but I don't dare say anything.

"She's six years old, old enough," says Mother as she lights a new cigarette. "Actually, Lady Eden herself suggested it. She seems to think she could adopt you, but your father nixed that. So you're going to her boarding school, which has chandeliers, I might add."

I don't understand any of this. "I already go to Lady Eden's school here in London, Mommy. Why am I going someplace else?" Then I have a memory of elegant Lady Eden, looking dismayed when I arrived at school late with the wrong clothes and my hair in tangles. And another time when Mother forgot to pick me up and the staff had to make up a bed for me in the boarding section.

"The boarding school at Fritham has girls with titles, and you'll learn to be properly English there. You should take piano lessons as well." She grins at the idea and takes a puff of her cigarette. She glances at her wristwatch, and her eyebrows rise.

"If I get back to the office now, change, and grab that guest list, I can be at the gala before they arrive," she mutters to herself before turning to the saleslady her accent lapsing. "Say, as one working girl to another, can you help me out? Get her what she needs and put her in a taxi when she's done?"

"But, madam," the woman protests and rises, "you can't leave your child here! To whom shall I charge it, and what about the nametapes? Every item of clothing needs to have her name sewn on it."

"Have someone sew the tapes on, 'cause I'm not going to do it. You understand what it's like to punch a clock. I've simply run out of time. Put it on my account. I'll forward the bill to her father." Mother rummages in her purse and hands over a card. "Oh, have her delivered to this address." To me she says, "You've flown across the ocean by yourself, so this isn't a big deal. Here's money for the taxi. Love you, bye." She pats my shoulder, and her raincoat swings around.

My voice rises high in my throat. "Mommy, don't leave." She turns and cuts me off with a slicing motion of her cigarette and is gone.

I cross my arms around myself to squelch the sounds trying to erupt. It isn't being left at Harrods that bothers me so much. It is coming home to an empty rented house where I must pass a wooden, leering, half-human-half-goat creature whose outstretched hand might grab me. To be safe, I have to run straight up to bed and pull the sheets over my head. Sometimes I even leave my shoes on.

The saleslady looks in the direction my mother has disappeared. "Well, I never . . . these Americans. . ." She pats my shoulder, gives me a moment to collect myself, and gets on with business. She slides from the drawers a gray pleated skirt, blue flannel shirt, long gray knee socks, and a gray sweater. On a rack, she finds a gray worsted jacket with Lady Eden's school insignia on the pocket. It fits perfectly. On my head she places a round gray hat.

"You are the picture of a British schoolgirl," she says with an approving smile as I look at my reflection in the mirror.

"What name shall I have written on the nametapes?" Out of my mouth comes "Mary," the name of a normal British girl. With the right clothes and right name, I might be adopted by the English family downstairs or even Lady Eden herself.

Then into the riding department I go to purchase jodhpurs, a smart fitted jacket, the special hardhat, and proper boots with heels to hold the stirrups. Finally, a mound of bags is placed beside me in a black London taxi. I am all fitted out to be a proper English schoolgirl, even though inside I'm a sad little American.

❧

"You're a lucky, lucky girl and are going to have tons of fun," Mother had said at the train station, "so don't you dare cry." The tears I've been swallowing since then are erupting now that I'm in bed at school. Pressing my face into the pillow, I try not to waken the other students with my shuddering sobs that make the iron bedsprings squeak. *Why have you banished me to this strange place? I promise to be good. I'll never whine or wake you early in the morning, and I'll eat snails without complaint when you order them for me at a Parisian restaurant. I'll do anything if you will only let me come home!* But fresh tears erupt when I think my daddy will never find me here, far away at Lady Eden's school. A plan emerges as I turn on the screeching bed. Tomorrow I will sneak past the paintings of lords and ladies wearing white ruffs, whose eyes follow me, out through the heavy,

wooden, double front doors, down long lawns bordered with blooming pink rhododendrons, past the wrought iron gates to the village train station, hop on board a train, and find my way back to London and maybe even New York. Comforted by my plans, I fall asleep, exhausted.

"Do you think the rich American has any biscuits?" A beam of light crosses my closed eyelids, startling me awake.

"Nah, she's just a crybaby. Look, I've got some toffee here and some jawbreakers . . . Andalusian, what have you got?"

"My grandmamma packed some *miguelitos,* although they got a bit smashed in the flight over. I put them under the floorboard."

"Yum, yum, delish. How about you, Pinto?"

"I've got licorice strings, gum balls, and a jar of Marmite. No spoon or anything. We'll have to use our fingers."

"Well get them all out. Wake the American. I'm sure she has Baked Alaska hidden away somewhere." They titter, and I hear tins opening and candy wrappers crinkling. A gentle hand presses my shoulder.

"Come join our midnight feast, little one." I peek out and see honey-brown eyes fringed with long lashes looking kindly at me. She points to the floor behind the row of beds where several girls in pajamas are munching on forbidden treats. The electric torches make their faces look ghoulish.

"Aren't you afraid Matron will be angry if she finds us? She told me I'd better stay asleep until morning like the child with her eyes closed in the painting over the fireplace. And what about Mrs. Clamp, the principal? Will I be expelled?" I clutch the covers firmly to my chin so as not to be implicated in this dangerous enterprise.

"The girl in the painting died of a hideous disease, you ninny. You'd better not look at it, or you'll catch what she's got," calls the ringleader.

"Hush, Mac, she's new and younger than we are. Child, Matron is not so stern as she seems, at least not to us little girls. Clampy is a good egg, really. Firm but fair. Do you have any

Toblerone? When I ache for home, chocolate always soothes my heart." This angel pats my shoulder, and I dare to sit up.

"I do have some, but it's down in my tuck box in the cloak room."

"Tomorrow sneak it up here, and we'll hide it under the floorboard. What's your name?"

"M-Mary," I whisper guiltily, knowing it for a lie. "Yours?"

"Blanca."

"But I heard her call you Anna-something?"

"Because I'm from Spain." I must look confused, because she laughs and shakes her head.

"Mac gives us horse names because we're all gaga for horses. Andalusian horses are from my homeland. Jane is a Pinto because she has freckles, and Mac's last name is Mackintosh because she's from Scotland. Don't worry, you'll get used to us. It's lovely here really, although never as nice as home." She smiles a little sadly.

"Look at the moonlight shining on the old forest that surrounds school." She walks to the many-paned window, her dark hair swirling around the shoulders of her white nightgown. "Wild ponies live there. They are together sleeping under the trees. The stallion is guarding the mares and the foals as they dream. Tomorrow, maybe you'll see them. If not, I'll make you a daisy chain for your hair. Everything will be all right. You'll see."

Just then, a scout positioned at the door whispers, "Hide, everyone, footsteps coming!" In a flash, the food disappears, and the girls leap into their beds. I lie still and don't breathe as I watch Matron's prodigious bosom appear at the door. Her flashlight beam probes the rows of beds, and seeing nothing amiss, she departs. I close my eyes, comforted by Blanca's nearness in the darkness. Maybe I won't run away after all.

The next morning a bell wakes me, and I follow close behind Blanca as we all rush to a row of sinks to wash our faces. I hop from foot to foot while waiting my turn for the "loo"—a series of water closets with pull-chain flushes. We quickly change into our gray uniforms and stampede downstairs to breakfast. Filing into a large dining room, we cram onto benches with our class-mates. After Clampy intones a brief *thank you* to the Lord, we fall on the food like ravenous creatures. The scraping of chairs, clatter of cutlery, and chatter swell to a roar. I seem to be the only one dismayed by the greasy bread and strips of glistening white fat with a few pink streaks. I cut it into little pieces and try to hide it under my plate. But the teacher sitting at our table turns her glittering glasses toward me and says I must eat every-thing. Normally food is a comfort, but I swallow the greasy mess with difficulty and am relieved when my plate is clean and we file out.

I follow Blanca down the long, creaking central hallway to our classroom and sit at a small wooden desk. It has a hole for an inkwell, although we use pencils. Anxiously, I start chewing the eraser end. The room has elegant wooden molded panels and a large painting of an Eden ancestor wearing a Lord Fauntleroy suit, who gazes at us with a bored expression. A gleaming chan-delier lights the room. Through the tall windows, grassy lawns invite me out to play. But our twelve desks face the teacher's larger table. We stand for a moment as each teacher comes in to instruct us in English, Latin, French, biology, history, and mathematics. I'm good enough with languages and history, but my most hated subject is math. I'm delighted when I learn we will have paint-ing, dancing, and embroidery lessons, at all of which I excel.

After lunch, we don raincoats and Wellington boots and walk two by two through the woods out to the old World War II aerodrome. Blanca unfurls a string that she loops around me. She is the rider holding the reins of the string "bridle" that hangs across my chest, and I'm the horse. We canter in unison, the shapes of the trees softened by fog, water droplets clinging to clumps of grass, until our laughter and heaving chests force us to stop and inhale lungfuls of fresh air. Teachers beckon us back.

In the afternoon, the headmistress, Mrs. Clamp, arrives to instruct us in scripture. As we stand up, I get a closer look at her. She has a long, raw-boned face with sandy-colored hair sawed off in a straight line at her angular jaw line, and she wears a tailored dress with a slim belt. I'm scared of her, but she gently motions us to sit down.

"Have you all met Kim? She comes from America, so we must show her a warm welcome. Which brings me to today's lesson about the Golden Rule." She smiles at me and then sorts some papers on the desk. I look around and see a surprised look on Blanca's face about the name switch, but then she grins as if we share a joke.

"Today I want to tell you about Jesus who suffered little children to come unto Him." Clampy holds up a picture of Jesus surrounded by children, people in rags, and sheep. "He taught us to 'do unto others as you would have them do unto you.' Does anyone want to explain this?"

I recall my Grandma Tishie taking me to her worn, wooden church in Kentucky on Sundays. The preacher's sermon lulled me to sleep as I sat on the hard bench beside her soft, slumped form, and I'd awaken to the notes of "Amazing Grace." The preacher droned out the words, and the congregation caught the line and floated it back in their plaintive voices. The hymn was about sinners saved by God's love, and it made me aware of a longing—for what I wasn't sure.

"Blanca was kind to me last night when I was homesick. That's the way I want to be as well." I surprise myself by raising my hand and speaking up.

"That's right, dear," Clampy says, and from that moment she is my favorite teacher.

My understanding of the Golden Rule is crystallized by an incident at school. I am eight and no longer the youngest child. Now there is six-year-old Juliana who, like me, has blue eyes and long brown braids. We have a new matron who is young and unseasoned. This woman has a soft lap and strong arms. She is besotted with Juliana, brushing her hair and kissing her pink cheeks while the rest of us watch with envy.

One afternoon, I walk into our dormitory and discover Mac

and a clot of girls giggling as they surround Juliana's bed. Peering through, I see she is on her stomach, her wrists tied to the metal bedposts. She is crying, and her nightgown is hiked up, exposing her bottom.

"What are you doing?" I ask.

"She's Matron's pet. We're teaching her a lesson," retorts Mac.

"We're pouring beetles on her bum," says another girl, grinning and holding up a jar.

Instantly I grow fiery hot. It is time to put the Golden Rule into action. I can feel fear and indecision welling inside me. Do I side with the tormenters because I'm envious of Juliana as well? Or do I comfort her and run the risk of being called a goody-goody and becoming a target of teasing myself?

I bend over and whisper in her ear, "They're only playing a game." As a few blue-black beetles skitter across her back, I brush them away. Then Blanca walks in and says, "Matron's coming, you'd better stop," and the girls run giggling to their beds. I untie her wrists and go to bed myself.

The next day, the headmistress wants to see me. I am frightened enough to gnaw on my cuticles as I wait outside Clampy's office. Has Juliana got it wrong? Was I now the culprit? Has she tattled on me? What could she have said?

By the time I am ushered in, Clampy had become Mrs. Clamp, from whom I keep my eyes averted, not seeing the smiles or feeling the pats on my shoulder. It takes a while before I hear praise for being Juliana's protector. After that, I don't envy Juliana anymore. Instead I practice being her friend. Still, she doesn't return to school the next year.

Later that year, I travel by plane to Rome where, to my immense joy, I'm greeted by my tall, white-haired father. It has been so long since I've seen his pale blue eyes and wide-mouthed smile. I fling my arms around his neck.

"Hammerhead, careful about my tricky back. Look how big you are!" He extricates himself from my hold and gives my hand a squeeze instead.

"I want to show my special girl around the Rome I love. You are looking at the *New York Daily Mirror's* new movie editor! I'm here on their dime covering *Roman Holiday* with Audrey Hepburn and Gregory Peck." He smiles broadly. Daddy is as handsome as the actor, and I feel like the princess in the movie. He takes me to the Colosseum and explains about the Roman emperor having the crowds entertained with fights between gladiators, Christians, and lions.

"If I was there fighting in the arena, I'd be so brave you'd give me the thumbs up, Daddy!" Our photo is professionally taken. I stand gazing up at him, my small hand tucked into his. My face shines with unabashed adoration. He looks down at me with deep affection and joy. We are both nattily dressed in navy suits. I am nine, and he is forty.

"You are my firstborn child," he tells me in his deep voice. He escorts me to an outdoor café, where he orders something called *pasta*. He shows me how to wrap the long strands around my fork with the help of a spoon. Red sauce sprays over my white blouse, but he just laughs. The portly waiter tells my father, in Italian, that I remind him of his own daughter, which Daddy translates for me. The waiter uses a sharp knife to skin one long strip of an orange and hands me a plate with the sections artistically arranged. I wonder how I can remain in this perfection for all time.

But then Daddy asks, "How is school? How are your riding and your piano lessons going?" And the moment abruptly shatters. Dropping my voice into a whisper, I make my confession.

"The pony wouldn't go where I wanted, and I was scared of him nipping me, so I don't take riding anymore. But the wild ponies did run around the school grounds once! We had to chase them out. That was so much fun. Um, I didn't practice the scales, so I don't take piano either." I check his face to see how upset he is.

Daddy's brow furrows. "Why did you buy those clothes if you aren't going to use them?" He combs his hair back with his fingers. "I get the bills for everything you buy, even the sixpences you put in the church plate on Sunday. Those riding togs were expensive. Your mother thinks I'm made out of money. Don't let her buy stuff you won't use. You know, Lady Eden wanted to adopt you, but I said no. If she had, you could be going to that school for free! Well, it's a good thing your mother didn't buy a piano." I hang my head. Somehow it is my fault. Then, to my relief, he smiles and pats my head, so I know he forgives me.

"Sir Timothy, Lady Eden's husband, painted a portrait of me. He lives near the school. I was very good and sat very still. But I don't want to be adopted. I want to live with you."

"Well, there's something you need to know. You've met my fiancée, Franca, and you know we married last year. Well, she is pregnant, so soon you will have a baby sister or brother! I'm sure you'll visit us next summer."

I'm ecstatic. I've always wanted a sister to share my wan-derings with, someone to be an ally in the strange world of grownups. Daddy had first introduced me to Franca, a small, lithe blonde, backstage when she was dancing in a Broadway revue. One of the other acts—a large woman with a deep voice—shook my hand firmly and asked if I knew what an impersonator was. I didn't. She ripped off her gold hair and revealed herself to be a man in a moment that shocked me to the core. I stumbled back several steps and gaped while the adults laughed. This opened up a huge question—how could I tell who someone really is? So I'm a little uneasy about Franca, but also very impressed because she has danced with the Rock-ettes at Radio City Music Hall and on the Ed Sullivan Show. Now she is married to my daddy and hopefully will give me a sister and maybe have enough love left over to mother me. I brush away any doubts about her.

My father returns me to boarding school, and I proudly show him off to my classmates. Late in the afternoon, a taxi crunches down the gravel drive, and before he gets in, he pulls a quarter from my ear, and we laugh. He is my beloved daddy and can do no wrong. But when the car drives away, I run after him screaming, "Daddy, don't leave me!" Those words will reverber-ate throughout our lives.

After the Technicolor of sunny Rome, I return to the damp gray of boarding school. I silently keen my anguish at his dis-appearance. There is nothing I can do except hold his place in my heart.

As Christmas holidays approach, all the girls become excited about going home. I haven't heard anything from Mother and am wondering what kind of welcome I will receive. Clampy calls me into her office. "Sorry, dear, I know this must be a let-down for you, but your mother is going on a trip to Paris. You will be spending Christmas with the piano teacher, Mrs. Brown, and her family." I feel as if I have been run over but smile and say, "That's fine."

Clampy gets up from behind her desk and pats me on the back. "There's a brave girl."

I go with Mrs. Brown to a pleasant, two-story home that smells of baking, and sleep in the pink room of her teenage daughter, Winifred. Her husband chucks me under the chin, the three children all play musical instruments, and everyone bursts into song at the drop of a pin. Instant family of my dreams! On Christmas Eve, the family gathers to decorate the tree. Mrs. Brown thumps out "Good King Wenceslaus" on the piano while the children sing merrily. I observe from the stairs as I do at home.

At my mother's house, Christmas is just another excuse to party. Revelers with drinks sloshing in their hands fill the rooms. Eartha Kitt's smoky voice sings "Santa Baby" from the record player. Wafting from the oven is the delicious smell of roasting turkey with cornbread stuffing, but it is ready way past my bedtime, so I snack on canapés. As I sleep, the grownups cover the tree with snow-like spun glass that I mustn't touch. Mother wakes me, and I sit on the stairs while the grownups sing a sloppy rendition of "Silent Night." I'm given gifts by Mother's beaux, most of which I pretend to like but don't. This is what I expect from the Browns.

Mrs. Brown refuses to let me sit on the stairs, and the youngest boy, Thomas, coaxes me down to join them warbling "Away in a Manger." We decorate the tree by stringing popcorn and placing homemade ornaments on it. The unwrapping of gifts ensues, which is a long process, as each child must guess what is inside before opening. I am given a knitted muffler and a bear that Winifred has outgrown—although she doesn't look pleased about giving it up.

We don paper hats and blow party streamers at one another as we sit down to dinner. Stuffing ourselves with prawns, goose, roasted potatoes, and vegetables, I eat until I fear my stomach will explode. A flaming plum pudding is thumped on the table. Even though I say I'm too full, Mrs. Brown hands me a large slice and—so that I will find the silver sixpence—several more. I love the rich brandied fruitcake and gobble it down. Thomas finds the sixpence. Late at night, my stomach heaves over Winifred's puce coverlet and woven rug. She hisses at me, "You spoiled brat, you'd better clean that up." I spend the rest of the night in the claw-foot tub trying to wash away the mess. Although the next morning, Mrs. Brown says it is perfectly understandable, I'm horribly embarrassed. I just want to slink back to Lady Eden's and die. I return Winifred's bear to her.

School's familiar rhythms resume. One cold morning, fluffy white flakes cover the green lawn. Snow is a rarity in southern England's mild climate. Donning our jackets and wrapping mufflers around our throats, we run out to throw snowballs. Mac points to the naked female statues flanking the drive. We fling wet snow at them and it sticks.

She yells, "Let's put snow bras on them!"

In a flash, we are standing on the pedestals, patting lacy white brassieres on their stone breasts. I begin patting knickers on a voluptuous lower torso when I hear rapping on the window. Clampy is gesturing a negative, and in short order, a senior girl is shouting out the door,

"Clampy says to stop this at once!" We run inside giggling.

As the days get warmer, we play house under the arcing rhododendrons and squabble about which of us will play baby. No one wants to play Father because all he does is go off to work. Mother is a little less mysterious. We are sure that she cooks and tends baby, although few of us know how she does this. Our play consists of a lot of crying babies with a few harried mothers.

One day, Clampy stops me as our class files into dining hall and tells me my mother will be picking me up at ten o'clock the next morning for the weekend. I can hardly believe my ears. Mommy is coming here to school! In an instant, I am filled with excitement and dread. This is the first time my friends will see my beautiful mother.

Next morning I am out of bed and getting ready before the rising bell. I dress in a clean uniform, topped off by my best gray blazer and hat. Matron brushes and braids my hair while I try not to squirm. Then she packs a small overnight bag while I follow her around, hopping impatiently from foot to foot. I file in to breakfast but can't stay put. I run out the door, not caring if I'm scolded for not eating my portion of fried bread and fatty bacon. Unable to stay inside, I go out the front doors and down the drive to the huge wrought-iron gate through which cars always enter.

It is early spring and still cold enough for me to see my breath. The leaves of the rhododendron bushes remain curled in the chill air. After a while, an upper form girl is sent to fetch me back inside. I sit alone on my tuck box in the large cloakroom off the front hall where rain slickers, woolen coats, and scarves hang from myriad hooks. The foul odor of wet Wellington boots is so strong that I breathe through my mouth. I start filching boiled sweets from my tuck box and reading *The Wind in the Willows*. My mind begins to wander. I wish I were Toad and could steal a motorcar to meet Mommy out on the road. She always loves an adventure. We could go off together.

Then I shake myself and mumble aloud, "I am more like quiet Mole." I fall back into silence and wish that she would just come. Mother had given me a small, black, five-year diary with a lock and a gold pencil. "To write your secret thoughts in," she instructed. I flip through the empty pages, wondering what I will write after this weekend.

In the great hall, the grandfather clock chimes eleven. Noon follows, and with it comes my friend Blanca, who escorts me to lunch, where I sit in silence, unable to eat. After lunch, I return to my post. I stay seated on my tuck box, even when my classmates invade the cloakroom to don their coats and Wellies before filing out for walks. A part of me wants to go, particularly when I see Blanca slip a long string into her pocket for playing horse. Now I doubly ache, because my skinny rival, Mac, will take my place, and my mother is nowhere to be found.

More time creeps by. I begin to cry. Even the last bit of broken chocolate in my tuck box offers no solace. Clampy joins me. "Go upstairs and wash your hands and face. Everything will be fine, don't you worry." Suddenly, there is a pounding on the front door. Mother is here! She is battering the portal as though she were being kept out against her will.

Clampy's rubber-soled brogues squelch across the wooden floor. She opens the door and informs Mother in a curt voice, "It is too late in the day; come back tomorrow." I can't believe what I am hearing. As I try to wipe away the chocolate and tears from my face, all I can see is Mother.

She looks adorable in a fur collared pink coat and hat. But her face is fierce as she demands, "Don't be ridiculous! I have driven all the way from London to introduce Kim to my fiancé." She flashes a ring set with a shilling-sized sapphire stone while she points to a waiting limousine. A dark-haired man wearing a black overcoat looms up out of the black car.

I run down the hall and beg, "Oh, please, let me go! I've been waiting all day." Clampy looks down into my aching eyes and grimly consents.

As I climb in the limousine, Mother smiles and says, "This is David Merrick. You remember him don't you? We have just become engaged." David forces a stiff smile and then looks away. I vaguely recall him from some party or other. But then, meeting people at Mother's parties was an endless round of blurry faces that I soon forgot. Never before has she suggested she was engaged to anyone. Suddenly I am on alert. I was always trying to hook her up with a man I might want as a father. If David is her choice, I'd better pay close attention. His bulging black eyes and dark mustache on a paper-white face scare me. He wears a dark suit and a stiff white shirt with a wine-colored silk erupting like blood from his breast pocket. I can't imagine him teaching me to ride a bike or fly a kite.

We drive to a nearby stone restaurant known as the Bell Inn. Due to local liquor laws, children are not allowed inside until dinnertime. It's still early, and Mother wants a drink. She sits me outside at a wrought iron table on the flagstone patio and orders a bowl of peanuts and a Coca-Cola to be sent out from the bar.

I've been waiting all day to be with Mommy, but I know from previous experience I'd better not irritate her. Tired and hungry, I start to mope. Then I pour some peanuts into my Coke, the same way I did when visiting Kentucky, and try to conjure how it feels to be at my grandfather's general store.

This doesn't work so well in England. Still, there is some measure of comfort until I peer in the window and see Mother and David sitting cozy in front of a fire. I feel as if I'm always watching Mother suck the sweetness out of life, while I'm forever on the outside looking in. She is talking up a storm, and David is clearly besotted with her. He keeps picking up her hand and playing with her fingers where the huge sapphire glows. I try to recall what I can of her new beau. He is an American who does something in the theater. He isn't an actor because he said nasty things about them. No, he traveled to London to bring plays back to New York. He had taken us to see a play based on *Oliver Twist*.

Finally, Mother brings me in from the cold. When I sit at their table, she shows me the sapphire and whispers, "David bought it to match my eyes." Then she giggles, which makes my stomach ache. She is losing control. I want to protect her, but she doesn't like that, so it is a dangerous task.

After dinner, David takes us to see *Jailhouse Rock*. That night I fall in love with Elvis Presley's pouty lips, swivel hips, and American rudeness. Though easy to forget, I'm American too, and I want to be as carefree as Elvis. I want to rock my jailhouse and sing and dance without worrying about how to fit in. Most of all, I want friends and family and somewhere to belong, even if it is jail.

Later, with my stomach filled and my heart and mind alive to what is possible, we drive to a new kind of hotel called a motel. Mother books me a room by myself. I try to be excited. After all, I'm having fun while my friends are cramming away back at school. How jealous they'll be when I tell them I slept alone instead of in a dormitory, that I wore my underclothes to bed and didn't brush my teeth, because I rushed out the door, forgetting my overnight bag. It all sounds so much fun, but the truth is I beg Mommy to let me sleep with her and David. I ache not to be left alone in this strange place. I weep in a soundless agony. Her response is an icy "piano," which means I'd better shut up. Another time, when I fussed because she was going out and leaving me alone, she had flung a glass of water in my face. So I swallow my pleas and sit on the bed listening to her high heels click down the hall.

Late into the night, I lie awake listening to water rush through the pipes and voices echo in the hall. When I awake to birdsong, I am relieved that the night is over. The limousine drops me at the familiar brick mansion, and I'm overjoyed. I always feel ashamed when I'm with Mother. Somehow, her inability to love me seems my fault. I don't know how else to explain it. There is obviously something wrong with me. I write a terse description in my five-year diary: "Saw Jailhouse Rock and met David."

Chapter 2

FINDING A FATHER
AMONG CELEBRITIES

⁓⁓⁓

Pity the beautiful,
the dolls, and the dishes,
the babes with big daddies
Granting their wishes.
—DANA GIOIA

Fenny, with her white curls and Mr. Magoo glasses, is waving to me from the platform at Victoria train station. I'm so happy and relieved to see her at the end of school term. She never leaves me sitting on my trunk for hours as Mother does. Although, at nine, I may seem too old for a nanny, Mrs. Fenwick—Fenny—is my safe harbor. Otherwise, I might be dropped off to ski down a snowy slope in Austria while Mother has cocktails with a lover, or left with the donkey in a damp castle in Scotland while she disappears with the kilted lord.

Evenings spent with Fenny and her husband, George, in their comfortable London flat are my idea of heaven. I pretend they are my parents, and I'm a normal child. Of course, I have to make allowances: Fenny is more my grandmother's age, and we don't look alike. She is tall and square-shouldered with a cap of messy curls. Mother thinks she looks comical, particularly when seen next to her short, plump, red-faced husband. I don't care. Fenny and George love me, and this is all that matters. In fact, I confide to Fenny, "Someday I'm going to marry George. Then I can live with you always."

Fun at Fenny's starts with the elevator, through whose open grills I can see the walls slide by. There is no motor to raise the elevator. Fenny and I do this together by pulling on a thick rope. It is scary to see the cracked plaster slowly glide past and know the ground is way below. But Fenny is with me, and I am proud that we can raise ourselves all the way to the fourth floor where they live.

When we come in, we find George sitting in a stuffed chair and reading the paper, his tired feet propped up on a stool. Fenny heads for the kitchen and prepares my favorite meal of roast beef with mint sauce, mashed potatoes, and peas. Fenny doesn't criticize me when I mash together my peas and potatoes. In fact, she says, "Good girl," as I eat everything. Mother says a lady leaves food on her dish. Fenny says, "Food was hard to come by during the Second World War, dear, so go ahead and join the clean plate club, just like they tell you at Lady Eden's."

After the table is cleared and the dishes washed, it is Fenny's turn to sit down and read the paper with her feet up. I play with Fenny's grown daughter's stuffed bear. When I first encountered it, one of the button eyes had been lost, and under its skirt, the legs were coming off. Fenny taught me to sew on a shiny new eye and attach its legs. I even sewed a smock for it. This is my favorite toy. I'm safe here as I sit on the carpet between George and Fenny and alternately cuddle my child bear and smack it across the room.

This playacting goes on for hours, until it is time for me to reluctantly kiss George and the bear good night. Then I go with Fenny out the door, down the elevator, and back across London to my mother's house tucked at the end of Minera Mews.

We arrive just as a party is getting into full swing. My heart aches when I survey the wreckage of dirty glasses and overflowing ashtrays in the living room. How can this be my home? Actor Danny Kaye is sitting on the stairs with a drink, gazing deeply into the eyes of an elfin young woman. Fenny shoos singer Eartha Kitt off the upstairs landing and waits for me to change into my nightgown and get into bed. She reads me a poem from *The Child's Garden of Verses* and listens to my prayers. I can include my father, stepmother, and their new baby, and she doesn't mind. I grab her arm for one more hug, but then she leaves. I take up my station at the top of the stairs, checking out men to see who has father potential.

Mother has themes for her parties. This one is Southern. She is playing a record by Tennessee Ernie Ford, who sings in a deep voice, "It's dark as a dungeon way down in the mine." It makes me shiver. The smell of fried chicken and biscuits wafts from the kitchen. Mother is wearing blue jeans and has tied a red-checkered blouse at her waist. A red kerchief trails from her back pocket. She flashes her dimples at me from the bottom of the stairs. It's a good party.

She and her friend Barbara Taylor are working the room, topping off drinks, giggling at jokes, and making the men feel utterly important. Barbara is a beauty like my mother, and she has a heart-shaped face with red hair. The room purrs like a contented cat. Mother loves being hostess. She gets to be the center of attention all the way to the end. Men linger at the door just to hear her say, "Y'all come back now, y'hear?"

A man with orange hair and cat's eyebrows climbs the stairs and sits beside me. He lolls his head on my shoulder and whines, "Your mommy's mean, she calls me 'Mr. Meow.'" His shining eyes show he's in love with her, and she is spurning him—a familiar situation. She has a knack for nicknaming people with hurtful barbs.

Although his breath smells sour, I pat him on the back and say, "Don't you pay her any mind." Inside me crystallizes a determination not to be like my mother in any way. I want to say kind words that make people feel good.

As I look out over the party from my perch, I feel the room expand. All of us, including Mr. Meow, are held in tender intimacy. My mother's blonde hair, blue eyes, even her cigarette and the man she chats with softly scintillate. The laughter and talk of the party fall away into stillness. This moment seems to last forever. Then I contract back to my small self that is falling asleep clinging to the banister and take myself off to bed. The cat man goes back downstairs.

The next morning, my mother has to show up for work as the Savoy Hotel's publicity director. Fenny isn't available, so I accompany her. She is slightly hungover when we walk to the end of the mews and hail a black London cab. By the time we arrive under the shiny brass letters spelling out THE SAVOY HOTEL, and the uniformed doorman opens the door, she is coming into her own. She borrows cash from the doorman to pay her taxi fare. She is forever cadging money for Players cigarettes or to pay Fenny's wages. Although the kids at school taunt me with names like "filthy rich American," I worry about money—especially since I might be the one having to explain things to my father later on.

By the time we push through the revolving door, she is glowing, and I am thrilled to be enveloped by the Savoy's plush interior. Our tread is cushioned by thick, woolen carpet blooming with flowers. Above us, chandeliers sprinkle fairy light over everything. Elegant women draped in furs sit in ornate chairs while silver-haired men pull well-stuffed billfolds to pay bellboys who follow them with brass carts piled high with matching valises. When I am in the Savoy, I feel like a member of a privileged family.

We walk through the lobby, past the French doors leading into the Thames Foyer Restaurant. There they serve high tea with scones, clotted cream, and mounds of strawberry jam that fill my cheeks with the taste of clouds. It is far too expensive unless a man invites us. A white-haired gentleman wearing a camel hair coat greets Mother.

"Let me introduce you to Charlie Chaplin," she says. We shake hands, and I curtsy. I haven't the foggiest idea who he is, which must show on my face. "*The Little Tramp?*" Mother prompts.

"She's too young to have seen my movies," Mr. Chaplin says graciously and departs.

We turn down a hallway where the carpet becomes plain green and come to the door marked PUBLICITY. Here we enter the dingy, clattering heart of Mother's world. Usually she is late. Usually a phone call is waiting for her. She unclips an earring, tosses it onto the desk, lifts the receiver, sinks into her chair, and starts talking. From that moment forward, it is my job not to bother her. There is no point in trying to get her attention. Her crystal blue eyes and dimples are directed at the ceiling, charming the unseen listener.

Her assistants—the two musketeers, Mary and Annie—are already pounding on their typewriters and working the phones. Mary is a wren-like woman full of nervous energy. The fastest typist in the office, she is devoted to my mother. She also likes me. To keep me entertained, she grabs red and blue pens and a stack of typing paper, and sets me up at a corner desk to draw and write. Annie has worked at the Savoy forever. She has recently divorced and cries easily. She is always talking about starting a bar in Sardinia. Annie considers me spoiled because one time she babysat me, and I told her I was cold and to light another bar on the electric fire.

Barbara Taylor is the third musketeer, even though she works for a newspaper and isn't always around. The office is busy, and I'm expected to amuse myself. I write poems about the dog I want and the sister I don't yet have. Over and over, I draw a small square house with a flower garden and a mother, a father, and two sisters. Surely if I draw this scene often enough, my prayers will be answered.

Mary stands over me stretching and yawning. "Nice drawing, Kimmie." I don't know whether to be embarrassed by the nakedness of my longing or hope that someone recognizes how I feel. But they never do. Oh, yes, I have Lady Eden, Fenny, and my grandparents in Kentucky, but they are so far apart. Meanwhile, I am a trapeze artist swinging between them, praying that I will not lose my grip and fall into the abyss below.

Since it's payday, and everyone has extra money, we walk up the hall to a vacant hotel room and order room service. A uniformed bellboy pushes in a tinkling trolley laden with chafing dishes. He extends the leaves of the trolley and gathers our chairs. Mother hands him a tip before we sit down to feast on ham sandwiches and cold vichyssoise. Mary fusses about demitasse coffee when Mother orders a drink. Self-controlled Barbara orders tea, and Annie has to be dissuaded from a pint of Guinness.

The four women chatter away, flitting from topic to topic. There are always events to be planned and titled names to be gossiped over. Mother suddenly notices me as she lights a fresh cigarette from the stub of the old. As though doing her duty, she reminds me to sit up and stop slouching.

One day, my mother, the three musketeers, and I go to lunch, but nobody has anything to say. I look at Barbara, Mary, and Annie, whose faces are unusually glum. Mother is smoking with her back turned to us. She lifts a glass of vodka to her lips and drains it, saying, "Order me another. I feel like celebrating."

"Has something happened?" I whisper to Annie.

"Your mother is leaving us," she replies morosely and sits down before the bellboy has finished his preparations.

"Leaving?" I ask. "Why?"

"I've quit," Mother says, grinding her cigarette into an ashtray.

"Smoking?" I ask hopefully. I hate the smell.

"No, the Savoy. We're going back to New York."

"New York?" I wail. "How can we live if you stop working?"

"That's for me to know and you to find out," she says and turns to the bellboy. "Have the drink sent to my office." Mother leaves the room.

I search the faces of the three women. They look mystified.

"When are we leaving?" I ask Barbara.

"In a month or so, it seems," she says, pushing her plate away. "She's already made the reservations."

"She has?" I croak.

"Your mother has a suite of rooms on an ocean liner reserved."

We troop out, our meal forgotten.

The next weeks are a blur of cocktail parties, dinners in, and nights out, all intermixed with haphazard packing. During this extended spree, I spend most of my time at Fenny's flat. There the mood is different. We don't talk much about the upcoming departure. I don't understand this kind of leave-taking. Before, there was always a return. Now there will not be. I retreat into my play fantasies where my bear gets thorough bashings.

When we do go home to Minera Mews, Fenny and I stay busy sorting my belongings into "New York" and "'Needy Children" boxes. Most of my clothes are too small and dowdy to make the journey. I don't mind donating toys to needy children, because most are stupid gifts from Mother's boyfriends. They give me things like orchids, perfume, or a heavy set of marionettes whose strings tangle. Their gifts are given to impress Mother. Of course, if one of them gives me a box of chocolates, I devour it.

My tuck box holds treasures like Fenny's daughter's bear and my Red Riding Hood and Wolf doll that share a body. I keep the skirt hiding the Wolf. My five-year diary stays with my hand luggage. I want to record every moment of this ocean voyage. That way I can tell my school chums about my adventures—although I try not to think that I might never see them again. As we grow closer to departure, I become more excited. Soon I will live in the same city as my daddy, stepmother, and new baby sister.

Invitations for a final farewell bash, with a cartoon caricature of Mother on the phone, are sent far and wide. Among the luminaries invited are Gary Cooper, Satchmo, Chevalier, Sinatra, Ingrid Bergman, Marilyn Monroe, Truman Capote—the list goes

Best Wishes for a Happy Christmas

from *Jeanne Gilbert*   --- and the Savoy Press Offi‹

on and on. All of them have come, by the looks of it, when Fenny and I arrive. It is wall-to-wall people drinking, smoking, and bab-bling. Fenny clears a path up the stairs and into my room. She tells me to wait and returns with marmite on toast for me and a cup of tea for her. We eat quietly, although we can hear the party ram-paging outside. After we do last-minute packing, my room looks strangely empty. I crawl into bed and Fenny sits heavily beside me. At last, she bends down and kisses me good night.

"I'll see you off at the train station tomorrow morning when you leave for Southampton," she promises, and leaves, closing the door behind her.

I fall asleep, and when I awaken the house is quiet. I sit on the stairs gazing down at the living room. Everything is a jumble of half-packed boxes, dirty glasses, and overflowing ashtrays. I feel sad at the thought of deserting our house to the critical eye of the charwoman who has to clean it up.

Voices sound from Mother's bedroom, and I peer in. Slumped on her bed, she is propped up by pillows, blonde hair pulled back in a ponytail. She gazes into a vodka tonic as if it were a crystal ball. Her three musketeers stand around the room in a tableau of grief. Suddenly, I do not want to spend my last hours alone. I pick my way through myriad open trunks, boxes, suitcases, and piles of clothing before reaching the bed, and I lie beside her.

"Hello, Kim," Mary says. "I hope you're all packed, because we're just getting started on your mother." She lays an armful of dresses on top of some jackets and flings a mink stole over the back of a chair before looking into a cavernous trunk that stands open before her.

"Good morning, darling girl," Barbara calls out from the bathroom, where she wraps the contents of the medicine cabinet in newspaper while wearing nail-protecting pink rubber gloves.

Annie has collapsed in the corner where she silently weeps, unable to continue packing lingerie and scarves that flow out of open bureau drawers.

"I love your fur, Mommy," I say, brushing my forehead and

cheeks on the soft pelt. I reach out to touch the contents of her jewelry-filled biscuit tin that lies open beside her. "Can I pack your jewelry?"

"Shhure," Mother replies, slurring her words. "I don't have the heart for it. Put each piece in a pocket of this bag." She tosses a satin case in my direction as she takes a swig of her drink.

In the jumble of jewelry, I find David Merrick's sapphire ring. "Are you going to wear this?" I try it on, but it is much too large. I fit my hand against hers. Ours are shaped alike, square palms with tapered fingers.

Mother removes her hand, flips open a lighter, and ignites another cigarette. "I'll wear it when I get a plain gold band to go with it."

I dump the gleaming tangle of jewelry on the sheet. A brooch in the shape of a honeybee with diamond antennae and an amethyst body fascinates me. When I start to make buzzing sounds, Mother snaps, "Just pack it, Kim. You're here to help, not play."

Mary sits back on her haunches, resting from her labors. She takes a sip of scotch and says, "David Merrick is already married. He's not about to upset that apple cart." Mother just looks at her. In the frosty silence, Mary continues, "I know we've been over this before, but it's not too late."

"The Savoy would take you back," Annie pipes in. Mother glares at her, forcing Annie to get back to work, stuffing undergarments into the suitcase. "I just don't see what the attraction is . . . I mean, why did you have to pick him? You could have had any man you wanted. Like, for instance, that sweet fellow who gave you the bee brooch. Wasn't he landed, didn't he have a title?"

"He's an ass," Mother retorts, and Annie titters.

I pretend a loud yawn and slide down in the bed as though falling asleep. I've discovered that I learn more about what is really going on if people forget I am here.

There is a silence. Mother exhales a long sigh of smoke and says, "David's the only man who has interested me in ages. And so far as English aristocrats, they have about as much sex appeal as my kid brothers. Doing the down and dirty was like, oh, he's riding in a fox hunt." She mimes a galloping motion and laughs.

"What about HRH?" Annie asks.

"What about him? Annie, don't you get it? The prince has had everyone, and everyone's had him."

"Tally ho!" Barbara yodels from the bathroom.

"Is that why you didn't make it to the audience with the Queen?" Mary asks with a glint in her eye.

I crack an eye open to look at my mother. I'd been home the day she got dressed up for her audience with the Queen. By the time she left, she was so wobbly that she fell down walking out the door. After that, wherever she went, it was not to see the Queen. She didn't return home for the longest time.

Mother looks right at me. I shut my eyes and roll over. After a moment she says, "David's not like other men. He knows what he wants, and he gets it. He's the bull elephant, and I'm going to bag him."

Barbara pokes her head out of the bathroom. "I agree with you, darling. David Merrick is magnetizing, and you're doing the right thing. There's no future here. Not in London or at the Savoy. It's all happening in New York. In fact, I plan to get over there myself soon, so we won't be apart very long." Barbara weaves through the boxes and gives her a hug, then looks at the top of her head. "Darling, your roots are showing, and there's no time to get your hair done." She reaches into the suitcase that Annie is trying to close and pulls out a buttercup, black, and white scarf. "You'd better wear this Hermes for your big day tomorrow."

Annie looks up. "What *are* you going to wear tomorrow?"

Mother says, "I really have no idea."

Annie giggles. "I'd better pull out a pair of knickers from this lot then." She laughs even louder as she reaches for a pair of black silk panties and a matching garter belt. "You'll be needing these before you've completed your week at sea."

Mary lifts out several traveling outfits and asks, "Who's going to take care of you when we're not around?"

"David," Mother says.

"That man can't take care of a flea."

"He glowers all the time. Actually, I'm terrified of him," Annie agrees.

David Merrick, a bull who can't take care of a flea. That seems apt. It takes nothing to conjure him, looming tall with wide padded shoulders, sleek head jutting forward, and menacing onyx eyes framed beneath thick black brows. As usual, Mother is right on the mark, although why she finds him attractive, I can't fathom.

Annie pulls out a double-strand pearl choker and admires its heavy, gold clasp. "Who gave you these?" she asks.

"David did. See, he can be tender. Those are rare baroque pearls from Japan. Real pearls need to be worn next to your skin, otherwise they dry out." She rests her cigarette on the nightstand, takes the pearls, and fastens them around her neck. "He needs me to care for him."

She pours a dollop of vodka into her glass. "I'm the one who taught him where to get his suits made, how to wear cuff links and a black tie. Do you realize when I first met him, he put so much grease on his hair he left a smear on my pillow. Hell, I even had to tell him to change his underwear." Mother exhales cigarette smoke toward the ceiling. "We'll get married, you can bet on it. David and me and baby make three."

A tremor runs through me. What does she mean by that remark? I am no baby; where do I fit into the picture?

Barbara leans out the door of the bathroom. "A cat has more maternal instincts than you. Besides, you know David is already married. When you get to New York, concentrate on the job at hand. Have you lined up any prospects?"

Annie chortles from her corner. "I know you'll have some fairytale ending. You won't be made to slog into your old age." She thinks for a moment and then adds, "And neither will I. Not once I own my bar in Sardinia." She takes a swallow from her bottle of Guinness and looks gloomily around the room. There is still so much left to pack.

"I've talked to Max Eisen, who does David's publicity," Mother says. "He promises to get me a job once I'm there. But right now, God, I'm tired. I need a break."

I must have truly fallen asleep, because when I awaken, the house is silent. Then I hear Mother's teeth squeaking and grinding in her sleep. She mutters, "When will I get? . . . but I don't want. . . ." I put my arm around her, but she tosses it away. Pulling to the far corner of the bed, I fall back into my own troubled dreams.

Glimpses of Mother appear and disappear as I stand on tiptoes, looking through the crowd on the wharf. An Hermes scarf covers her hair and is knotted at her throat like a movie star's. Black sunglasses cover her eyes, and her crimson mouth is laughing. Photographers are popping bulbs while she shows too much leg, enjoying every inch of exposure. A tall man wearing a hat grips her hand as she steps up a pyramid of trunks and suitcases. She sways near the top, and he steadies her. Raising a flute of champagne to the crowd, she cries out, "I'll miss you, now. Love y'all."

Her fans roar in response, "We love you, Jeanne! Bon voyage." As newspapers, umbrellas, and bouquets lift in a toast, and bodies press toward her, I step away. I wonder if anyone knows I'm her daughter. There doesn't seem an obvious connection. One newspaper clipping called her "the American divorcee who is the toast of London." And here I am, a plump nine-year-old with a British accent, wearing pink-rimmed glasses and knee socks that wrinkle around my ankles.

I sit down near the band and find myself eye-to-eye with the horn player. We look at one another, and I ask, "Do your cheeks get tired of blowing?"

He wipes the mouthpiece and nods toward Jeanne. "She your mother?"

I smile—someone sees we are connected.

"Well, this is for her." He and the band play a soft, soulful rendition of "I Dream of Jeanne with the Light Brown Hair." The music squeezes my heart and speaks what I can't say: *Mother, how lovely and unattainable you are. I feel so unworthy and filled with longing as my love for you slowly turns to bitterness.*

I sigh. This parting celebration has been going on for days. Many of her fans have come with her on the train to Southampton. Fenny arrived at the station as the train was pulling away. I watched her wave good-bye with a sick feeling in my stomach. I'll never see her again. That's how it is. On Mother's whim, people appear and disappear. Now some of her dear friends are slipping away to their clubs or another afternoon entertainment. The photographers are packing up. She climbs down the tier of luggage to allow it be carried aboard ship.

I walk toward the gangway when a man wearing a hat strolls toward me. "So, you're Jeanne's daughter, Kimberly, right?"

Someone knows about me!

"Name's Rupert, I'm a reporter with the *London Times*, and I've just interviewed your mother. She's quite the lady." He pulls a legal pad with a pencil clipped to it from inside his raincoat and reads from his notes: "Grew up in the hillbilly state of Kentucky, US of A. There was no electricity and no indoor plumbing."

"The farm has a two-seat outhouse," I add eagerly.

"That sounds even better." He makes a note to himself before going on. "She's one of nine children." He looks up and smiles a lopsided grin. "And now she sails back to America, having conquered London as director of publicity at the world-famous Savoy Hotel."

I wonder if he will add any more details to the story that I don't understand myself. How did she get to London from the farm in Kentucky? Rupert cuts across my thoughts, "So tell me about you."

I look at him in surprise. People don't usually ask about me. "You travel a lot?" he asks.

I shade my eyes to get a better look at him. "There's been a bit of to-ing and fro-ing."

"How many times across the pond would you say?"

"Mother and I came to England in 1952. I was four. It is now 1958." I pause to count on my fingers. "I've made the journey ten times by air and ship."

He writes down the number and underlines it. "That's impressive," he says. "I mean it; most adults have never been on a plane, let alone an ocean liner. So what are some of the highlights of all this travel?"

I think a moment. "The stewardess pins a wings brooch on me, and I'm introduced to the pilots and shown through the cockpit. That's fun. But the ocean liner has a library and swimming pool. They have any dessert I want, although once I asked for watermelon and they didn't have any."

"You are one lucky little girl. What I wouldn't give to spend a week on that beauty."

I note the envy in his tone. Adults never understand that all the luxury means nothing to me. I would trade it all for a normal family.

"Right-oh," he says cheerfully. "You'll be seeing this in the paper. Or we'll mail it to you."

A blast from the ship vibrates the dock. Mother is hugging everyone in sight. She is walking along the pier now; I can sense this because of the surge of bodies.

"You'd better go," Rupert says. "Don't want to be left behind." He re-clips his pencil and tucks the pad inside his raincoat. I position myself near the gangway where I can be swept up by her entourage.

Chapter 3

MINING KENTUCKY

❦

Home! That was what they meant, those caressing appeals,
those soft touches wafted through the air,
those invisible hands pulling and tugging, all one way.
—KENNETH GRAHAME

We dock in New York, and Mother disappears looking for a Manhattan apartment. Apparently, it's decided I should be sent to my grandparents in Kentucky. I'm whisked by plane with my daddy down to a small airfield. The pilot draws back the door, and I'm breathing in the green humidity of hot summer air. My father points out Grandpa, dressed in his blue overalls and Panama straw hat. He is standing beside his red truck far across the tarmac. Two of my mother's teenage sisters are with him. Sixteen-year-old, cross-eyed Clara Belle leans against the truck's fender, while blonde, pig-tailed Sue Ellen, age fourteen, sits on a hay bale in the bed of the truck. All three of them shade their eyes as they gaze toward the plane. My father is going someplace else to cover a movie, so he helps me down, kisses my cheek, hands me my suitcase, and climbs back aboard.

I step away from the plane and wave hello to my mother's people, even as I wave good-bye to my father. *Why am I always being dropped off in strange places while the people I love disappear?* I wail inside as I put on a smile and trudge over to the truck.

Grandpa lays heavy palms on my hot shoulders, and his turquoise eyes bore into mine with concern. This is so unlike my usually merry Grandpa that I have to check his nose for the big black pore that proves he can be no one but himself.

"Sister," he says, "we've been looking our eyeballs out for you. I feared never to see you again, flying in one of them machines." He jerks his thumb toward the taxiing plane where my father is flying away.

For a moment, I'm disoriented by his accent and have to mull over the sounds until something shifts in my ear.

"You know I fly in airplanes all the time, Grandpa."

"Young 'un, the one time I was in New York, I hiked six flights of stairs just to not ride the elevator. You'll never see me in one of them contraptions. Fact is, these days I don't travel no farther than I can go in one day on a mule."

"When were you in the city, Grandpa?" I ask. "I don't remember you visiting."

"Sugar, you was just a baby. Your mother asked me to bring these two up to mind you, which they did for the better part of a year."

My aunts are picking at my suit jacket and giggling. They look cool and nonchalant in T-shirts and cut-off Levis. I'm already sweating and feel like an overdressed old lady. As I pull off my jacket, Sue Ellen notices the suspenders holding up my skirt and starts sliding one down my arm.

"Hey, Kiyum, good to see you, honey," she says, elongating my name as if it were bubble gum being pulled out of her mouth.

"Hey, Sue Ellen, hey, Clara Belle, how you doin'?" The

chameleon in me is already at work. My mouth slows down and draws my words out. Soon my English accent will evaporate like the morning mist.

"You comin' to stay with us for a while?" Clara Belle asks, her spectacles unable to conceal the fact that her crossed eye looks at her nose while her good one peers at me. "Don't you look a picture in them clothes? You gonna let me try that jacket on?" She jams her arm into the sleeve, and there is a ripping sound.

"Sister, cut it out," Grandpa orders. "Get up in the truck. Child, you ride with me in the cab." Sadly, I realize my presence means my aunts must spend the long, hot ride sitting on the hay bales in the truck bed. Sure enough, they sit back there, laughing and talking while I ride in the coveted spot beside Grandpa and feel nothing but misery.

At first Grandpa is silent, leaving me to doze to the drone of the engine. Once we pass the coal-mining town of Hazard, near the mountains in which he has spent his life, he begins telling its history. He points to a lake and says, "Under that water lies the one-room schoolhouse where I began courting your grandma." Or "On top of that mountain lies the cemetery where your people are buried." Of a field: "Used to grow the best sorghum there, but now I own the land and rent out the shack, get my molasses from over yonder."

By the time we enter the lush, green swath of our valley, I no longer feel like a stranger. I belong here. My spirits soar when I see the ancient swing on the familiar sagging porch of the house, nestled at the junction of a creek and a dusty road. Grandpa's general store is across the way. Tucked behind the house are rows of sweet corn, beans, tomatoes, and watermelons thriving in the summer sun. Dirt paths wind through every field and up into the green mountains. All of it is waiting for my bare feet to explore.

My aunts climb from the truck looking sunburned and windblown. We troop into the house with the screen door banging behind us. I smell fried chicken and run into the kitchen, where platters of crisp, succulent bird are already on the Formica table. My mother's mother, Grandma Tishie, stands in front of her tractor-sized stove looking as I remember her: salt-and-pepper wisps of hair curled up into a little bun on top of her head, soft jowls sagging. She wears a faded housedress and eyeglasses perched on her lumpy nose. She is feeding coal into the stove and doesn't turn to me, just wipes her hands on a rag hanging from her apron and gives me a pat on the head.

"I'm so glad to see you, Grandma." I hug her soft middle as she smiles absently.

"It's pleased to see old Granny, ain't that sweet?" She lifts a jelly glass and turns to cutting biscuit rounds out of a pad of white dough. I watch her hands shake.

"Can I help, Grandma?"

"No, honey, your Aunt Lonnie will be coming by. Your Grandma's feeling poorly today, that's all. I think I'll sit a spell." She walks into the parlor and sinks into her rocker with a sigh. "It's the anniversary of little Judy's death. You and her was the same age, remember, honey? In fact, having you come reminds me of her." She glances at me under hooded, sad eyes, her mouth quivering with the apologetic wisp of a smile. Without looking up, she nods across the room. "That's her picture on the wall," she says, and begins to rock back and forth in a soothing rhythm.

I study the ornately framed photograph of Judy: her blonde hair curled in ringlets, her lips and cheeks tinted so she looks like an angel. I have vivid memories of my Aunt Judy because we were almost the same age. The youngest of Grandma's nine children, she delighted in sleeping in her parents' bed. I wanted to sleep with them also, but got stuck in the crib. She used to crow at me, "They are *my* mommy and daddy, not yours." I had forgotten who my real parents were. Now she is dead, while I'm so happy to be here, alive.

"Could she be with Jesus down by the river?" I blurt, trying to hook my grandmother back from the sad, distant place where she always seems to be.

"Whatever do you mean, child?"

"I remember watching the minister walk into the river in his suit. He dunked people dressed in white in the muddy water. They came up throwing their arms around and shouting, 'Jesus is with me!'" I press on because her pale eyes see me, intent.

"Judy and I were hanging on your hands. We wanted to get dunked, but you held us back, said we were too young."

"You remember that? My father's spirit runs in you. He was a minister and died when I was three. My mother couldn't afford to keep us after . . . my twin sister and me was raised by relatives. I miss my mother." She lapses into despondence.

"But that's a long time ago. Child, those people was being baptized. Judy has gone to the shining city on the hill."

I can't stay sad in Kentucky. The sound of the squeaking pump catches my attention, and I go to investigate. Pastel washrags festoon the screened walls of the side porch. Toothbrushes and paste, hairbrushes and gap-toothed combs, shaving brushes and soap cups are heaped on the water-eroded table beside the pump. Clara is pushing and pulling the long, heavy handle, drawing cold mountain water into Sue's cupped hands. She splashes her face and then runs a comb through her bangs, peering into a shard of mirror propped against the pump. She nods to me. I stick my face into the icy flow and open my mouth to lap at the iron-tasting water. I shudder and shake my wet hair. Both aunts laugh. My blouse is soaked to the waist, but I don't care. For the first time in forever, I know I am home.

I dart through the bedrooms that have no doors until I find my suitcase. Shucking off my traveling clothes, I quickly pull on a blouse and shorts. My aunts' dresses hang off nails jutting from the walls. I stuff my despised city clothes into my suitcase and shove it under the iron bed. I want no reminders of that world.

Without thinking, I know where to head next: Grandpa's general store across the dirt road. There, peanuts, Coke, and some Double Bubble Gum are waiting for me. There is no sign on the weathered gray shed, yet all the locals know this place. The mail is delivered here by a woman riding a mule with bulging saddle-bags. She calls me "sugar tit," which makes me giggle. Sometimes a family with a swarm of kids pulls up in a wagon or old truck. The children jump down and go inside to examine the candy display. The father digs around in his pockets to see if he can afford something for each of them. Being the storeowner's grandchild puts me in a position of privilege. I try not to take advantage of it, but the sweet smell of bubble gum, tobacco, and rotting fruit is intoxicating.

I open the screen door and peer into the cavernous, dark interior. Washboards, bridles, rakes, and hoes compete for wall space. Sacks of seed, salt, and flour slump side by side on the floor. By the door are heaped half a dozen watermelons alongside a basket of bruised peaches and several churns. I make my way to the glass-fronted display case, my eyes searching through the jumble of licorice, jawbreakers, tootsie rolls, and tobacco plugs. Spying my prize, I ask, "Grandpa, can I get me some pop, peanuts, and gum?"

"You sure can," he replies, and I reach for the gum and a packet of peanuts.

For a moment I just stand here, inhaling the sweet air. Then, I make my way over to the wooden crates of Coca-Cola stacked beside the familiar red and white refrigerator.

I lift a chilled bottle out and flip off its cap in the opener. I rip open the small bag of peanuts and slide a few into the mouth of the Coke. Tipping my head back, I funnel some into my mouth and swirl the bubbly sweet over my tongue while I crunch the salty-sweet morsels. This is the taste that I relish every bite and swallow of.

I walk over to stand beside Grandpa, who sits on an over-turned crate, concentrating on a checkerboard set on a barrel. Across from him sits Uncle Elwood, whose coal miner's helmet lies on the floor beside him. Elwood glances up at me. His face is a smeared mask of black. Only around his eyes is the skin pink where it has been protected by goggles.

"Look what the cat drug in," he rumbles. He hacks up a

wad of tobacco and spits into a can at his feet. "Don't you know, I used to feed her sips of beer when she was knee-high to a grasshopper. Why that child would grab at the can and guzzle it like a trooper." He laughs a throaty chuckle.

I remember more than he is telling. When I was a toddler, Elwood would send me to Grandma to beg for money. She must have known who it was for, but after grumbling a bit, she'd go into her tin and hand me a quarter to give him.

Grandpa is different. There are certain things he is strict about. "Now, Elwood," he cautions, "you know I won't abide drinking or the talk of it on my property. There are two things you can't make nastier than they already are: tobacco and moonshine whiskey." He looks at the younger man to be sure he understands then returns to the board. "It's your move."

Elwood winks at me as if we have a secret and turns his attention to the game. I move closer to Grandpa. I hope Elwood lives somewhere else now, so I won't see too much of him.

"Why don't you go down to the barn and see if you can't help those girls milk the cow," Grandpa says, nodding toward the door. "Leave that bottle when you're through with it."

Gulping down the Coke, I deposit it in the crate. I walk barefoot down the path, carefully avoiding the stones under my tender city feet. In the yard is Grandma's wringer-washer, alongside a metal tub filled with white gluey bubbles. She has batch of lye soap going. A stink tells me the outhouse is close.

I set down my bag of peanuts on a stump and cautiously open the door. It is as full of buzzing yellow jackets as I remembered. I quickly settle my boarding-school-educated derriere over the hole. In no time I am leafing through the Sears Roebuck catalogue that serves dual duty as reading matter and toilet paper. I flip to the women's underwear section and study the painful-looking corsets and brassieres. I have seen my mother squeezing herself inch by inch into a rubber girdle. I never want to grow up, if it means wearing one of those torture devices. I use the page as my paper and throw it down the hole.

Glad to be done, I pick up my peanuts and head across the swaying, two-foot-wide bridge. I walk carefully at first and try not to look at the creek bed below. Then I remember plucking feathers off chickens and throwing them into the water with my cousins Gwen and Sonny, and begin skipping to the barn.

Sweet-smelling honeysuckle hangs in thick tendrils from the fence. I stop to pick a tiny yellow trumpet and lick the drop of nectar from its center. When I enter the barn, shafts of sunlight show Clara working under the cow as Sue holds the halter and the tail.

"You got peanuts from Pa? He won't give us any," Sue says accusingly.

"I also got bubble gum for the two of you. Here, take them," I say, handing over two pieces. "Can I milk the cow?"

Clara gets up from the stool, and I take her place. I breathe in the aroma of cow and warm milk. I look down at the frothing bubbles in the pail and wrap my hands around the rubbery teats, trying to recall the squeezing motion. Nothing happens. After a few more tries my efforts are rewarded with a stream of milk. My aunts laugh, and I top off the pail.

Clara blows a bubble that catches in her hair and yanks the gum right out of her mouth. She pulls it off quick before it hardens. Sue giggles. "Watch out, four eyes." They laugh even more when the gum ends up in the manure-wet straw. "That's all we're gonna get."

"Kim can get us more," Clara says.

"Yeah, Kim can, but not us. Dang, Pap don't even call us by our rightful names. Maybe he don't even know them." Clara shrugs. They pick up the milk pail and the three of us walk out of the barn.

"How can he not know your names?" I ask. "He's your father."

Sue answers, "There's nine of us, remember? He just calls us sister."

"And with a clown name like Clara Belle, ain't no way he's gonna say that," Sue says and then ducks, as her sister reaches across to slap her. I grimace, remembering *The Howdy Doody Show* and the clown named Clarabell. I'm glad they don't have TV down here. Being cross-eyed is hard enough on Clara. Yet I envy the sisters' give-and-take.

A question occurs to me. "If you have double names, what is my mother's?"

My aunts put down the pail and think for a minute. After a time, Clara says, "I'm not sure. We were kids when she left for New York."

"Maybe you should ask Lonnie," Sue replies. "She's the oldest. She was closest to Jeanne. Jeanne still sends her and Mama newspaper clippings about things she's been doing, but Mama won't let us mess with them."

"Lonnie let one of her kids carry a clipping to school one day for show and tell," Clara says, allowing a rare smile to illuminate her features. Then she shyly steps near me. "Can you keep a secret?" When I nod yes, she continues. "The last time Jeanne wrote Mama, she said she knows a doctor in New York who can fix my eye. She's going to bring me up there for an operation."

Clara swings her arms around herself at the wonder of the news. Sue nods as if to verify the truth of the statement and rubs her toe in the dirt.

"Clara," I say, "That's wonderful. You can live with us and be my sister."

When we return to the house, Aunt Lonnie is sitting on the porch swing with her three youngest kids. The eldest, ten-year-old Gwen and nine-year-old Sonny, sit on the steps. I rush to hug them but, except for Lonnie who manages an awkward squeeze, they stand smiling bashfully with their hands hanging at their sides. Hugging isn't what folks do down here.

Cousin Gwen, Aunt Judy, and I were playmates when we were small. We had all been born close to the same time. Aunt Lonnie with her gentle voice and slow movements watched over us. She lives nearby and is married to a coal miner. They rent a house without running water or electricity from Grandpa. I wonder why I'm not Lonnie's child when Gwen and I look like sisters. We share the same round-faced smile and glossy, brown hair. All my features tell the world that I belong here. *These are my people, why aren't I always with them?*

A pickup truck full of end-of-shift miners rolls to a stop. Lonnie's husband, Glen, gets out. He carries his helmet under his arm. His half-blackened face shows he has come from the mines.

Glen sees me and smiles. "Well, if it ain't little Kim," he says. "Good to see you, sugar." He gives his wife a pat and drops his helmet on Sonny's head, then disappears into the house. The screech and suction sounds coming from the pump tell me he is washing up.

Sue Ellen yells, "Dinner's ready!"

We troop into the kitchen, some wearing work boots and others sporting bare feet. Grandpa, Elwood, Glen, Sonny, and the three younger kids scrape their chairs around the table. Grandma goes into the parlor to sit in her rocker. Lonnie, Sue, and Clara pour sweet tea and pass around plates of chicken, biscuits and gravy, beans in bacon drippings, and stewed apples to the men and children. Sounds of slurping, crunching, and the smack of fingers being licked fill the air. I stand off to the side with my eyes wide open, taking in the scene.

Sue makes up a plate of food for Grandma that I carry to her. She sends it back saying, "I tasted everything while it was cooking. I ain't hungry for more." I sit on the sofa with the plate on my lap. My eyes are riveted on my three aunties. They never stop serving, helping the little ones to cut up their chicken, adding another portion to the men's plates. In London, when I went to a restaurant with Mother, the male waiters pulled out our chairs before we sat down. The men helped women with their coats, lit their cigarettes, opened doors, and paid for their meals. Here in Appalachia, the women served the men. Right then, I have a glimmer of understanding why Mother left.

After the men go outside to smoke, the women sit down to eat. Elwood returns carrying a watermelon, which he heaves with a thump onto the table. Grandpa follows him into the room and picks up a knife to slash the melon open. Wedges are handed out that require both hands to hold. We children slip out into the gathering dusk and run for the bridge, where we plop down. The sweet flesh drips pink juice down our chins. We spit seeds as far as we can into the creek. This Kentucky farm is a wonderful place to be young.

Strains of "Froggy Went A-Courtin'" ride the night air as we return to the porch. Grandpa sits on the swing, playing his banjo and singing in his mellow voice. We gather round to listen, enchanted by the whimsical lyrics about a frog who wears a sword and pistol as he courts Miss Mouse. The cicadas drone, and fireflies spark their tiny lights while the scent of honeysuckle wafts by on a stream of air. Out by the truck come the rumble of Elwood's and Glen's voices and the occasional scratch and flare as they light cigarettes. From inside come the lilt of women's voices and the rattle of dishes as cleanup continues.

After a while, Lonnie beckons to me through the screen door. I follow her into Grandma's bedroom where Sue and Clara sit on the big, quilt-covered bed looking into an open dress box. Grandma sits on a stool in front of her dressing table. Lonnie stands behind her, gently brushing her mother's fine hair.

Sue whispers as I climb on the bed, "It might cheer up Grandma if we look through Jeanne's photos and maybe talk about her for a bit." I make myself comfortable on a pillow and sift through letters, newspaper clippings, and photographs searching for pictures of my mother and her sisters when they were young. There aren't any.

Lonnie explains in her slow drawl, "When me and Jeanne were growing up, nobody had money, not even Pap. In fact, I didn't see a dollar bill until I was your age, Kim. Back then, people lived off what they grew in big gardens and were considered real fortunate if they had a cow and some chickens.

"At your Grandpa's store, folks bartered for everything: peaches for flour, eggs for sugar, bacon for gingham. Even the mining companies didn't pay cash money. They used their own printed tokens that had to be used at the company store whose prices were always jacked high."

Grandma interrupts and says, "It wasn't so bad because nobody had nothing back then. We was all in it together. That brought a kind of comfort."

I ask, "Did the kids have shoes for school?"

Grandma answers, "Sometimes we had hand-me-downs and sometimes not. But that wasn't the problem. It was the roads and the bridges. If one of them got washed out, it wasn't going to get fixed, and nobody went to school or anywhere."

Lonnie says, "Me and Jeanne got educated by boarding at the Hindman Settlement School. This was staffed by women from up North. They came from good families and were graduates of Ivy League colleges. The women weren't paid beyond room and board. They and the students cooked, cleaned, and sewed their own clothes. I loved book learning but gave it up after ninth grade because I was needed at home to help with the babies. But Jeanne, Jeanne was the smart one. She was accelerated and entered Alice Lloyd College when she was only sixteen."

Grandma interjects with a grimace, "Then she got kicked out."

Lonnie stops brushing her hair and gives her a calming pat on the back and continues. "It was a two-year college and only for girls. Alice Lloyd was a good Baptist who forbade dancing or listening to music, and when Jeanne climbed out the dormitory window to meet a boy and go dancing one night, she got expelled."

It is Grandma's story now. "I didn't know about that until I took a bus to check on her. I discovered she'd gone to South Carolina to work in the Wright Brothers' factory making airplane parts for the war. When she came home, she returned with a suitcase filled with pretty clothes, though."

"How did she get to New York?" I ask. Lonnie glances at Grandma, receiving permission to tell the story when Grandma gives a slight nod.

"Jeanne eloped with a local older man when she was seventeen. They were married a short while, and then Jeanne went off to New York and found a modeling job."

"And he still brings her a bouquet of flowers whenever she's down here," Sue Ellen sighs. "Isn't that romantic?" She rolls back on the bed and might have crushed the box of photos, had Clara not pushed her off.

"I heard he shot up the bar Jeanne and your Daddy was drinking at when they came down," Clara says. That got my attention. I guess this man wasn't happy about Mother leaving him. But Lonnie waves the information away. We start looking at a composite photo of Mother in five different outfits. It has "Vogue Modeling Company" and a New York address printed on the back. To my eye, Mother's head is tilted at an odd angle. She looks nervous, as if trying to be someone she isn't.

Questions pile up in my head:

Why marry the first husband just to turn around and leave him? Where did she get money for the bus and the hotel in New York? Did he give it to her or did she run away? What was it like to see New York's jagged skyline for the first time—the crowds walking down Fifth Avenue— and to hear the roar of traffic?

Most of all, I wonder at her courage.

I rummage through the box looking for clues and find newspaper clippings with notes attached in Mother's hand. Clara passes around an article from the *New York Daily Mirror* with a photo showing Mother in tiny shorts and a blouse knotted under her breasts, displaying her bare midriff. She sits in a wheelbarrow while a brunette dressed in a swimsuit pushes her. The article gushes about the two farm beauties newly arrived in town. Clipped to it is a note saying, "I think I met the man of my dreams during this shoot. He's a reporter for the paper. Love, J."

I am embarrassed by Mother's showing so much skin, but Sue looks at it with reverence, even lifting her blouse to compare the look of her own stomach before passing it on to Clara, who sighs dreamily. Lonnie and Grandma push it aside.

Then Sue finds a photo that I beg to keep. It is of my mother and father together. They are seated behind a table with a flower vase printed with the Stork Club logo. My father is looking at Mother as if he wants to take a bite of her, and she beams as if she has won the lottery. I feel sad, knowing how short their marriage will be.

Next is a letter wrapped around a photo, showing my mother dressed in a halter-top and sarong, and holding a macaw. Grabbing onto her leg is an enormously fat toddler with a suspiciously full diaper. Mother's stiff smile says it all.

"You were so fat that I could sink my finger up to my second knuckle in the folds of your knees." Lonnie chuckles as Sue reads the letter.

"Dear Mother,
"Justin, Kim and I drove out to Hollywood to see if I
can break into the movies. Kim slept most of the way.
We are staying with Justin's brother and his family that
includes this macaw. Don't you love my outfit? I'm
supposed to look like Ava Gardner.
"Love, Jeanne."

I glance at Lonnie and Grandma for more explanation, but they don't comment. I sense they don't exactly approve of Mother's behavior. Everywhere I go, certain subjects are secret. I have learned when to ask and when to keep silent.

Grandma says, "The first time you stayed with us was when your daddy's brother drove you and your mother back across the country."

"How long was I here?"

"I can't rightly recall, but I do remember teaching you to use the potty chair, and then you got chicken pox, so maybe three or four."

Sue unearths some photos of me. In one, Gwen, Sonny, and I, all wearing underpants, are making mud pies on the bank of the creek. I have a big grin on my face. In another picture, Grandma and I sit side by side at a churn, our hands on the dasher, making buttermilk.

This session of show-and-tell is winding down when I pull out a clipping from a newspaper announcing, EAT, DRINK AND MAKE MONEY, THAT'S KENTUCKIAN'S JOB ABROAD. It describes Mother as a lovely blonde from Hazard, KY, who eats three or four big meals a day at different British restaurants. She was sent by an American dining club to rate eating establishments.

"How'd she get that job?" I ask.

"I don't rightly know," Lonnie answers, shaking her head at the mystery of Mother.

"By the way, your mommy's name was Wilma Jean. Me and her was the best playmates when we were kids. She loved to climb that big sweet gum tree down in the meadow." She smiles at me and, not for the last time, I wish she was my mother. What fate had sent me to England with my own wild parent?

Grandma wants to lie down. Sue Ellen packs away the box, storing it in Grandma's wardrobe with her precious handmade quilts. Seeing them, I ask, "Grandma can I have a quilt for my own?" Grandma glances at me for a moment. "Well, make sure you don't lose it. Me and my quilt group make them with our own fingers." She holds up her hands that shake a little.

Lonnie pulls out a few smaller quilts and spreads them on the bed. There are butterflies, tulips, and girls with bonnets in bright pink, blue, and yellow. Holding my breath, I reverently choose the flowered patchwork and hold it to my chest. I kiss my grandma on her cheek, and she nods. Clara and Sue and I tiptoe into the other bedroom to sort out who will sleep where.

As I brush my teeth, Lonnie is outside gathering up her family. Elwood is leaving too. The noise settles down as I climb into bed with the quilt pulled around my neck and tug the string attached to the ceiling bulb. I lie in the darkness and listen to Grandpa's heavy tread on the other side of the house. I even recognize the sound of his boots dropping one at a time to the floor. Then he sighs with contentment, and so do I. Here I am surrounded by family, separate but together in the warm and friendly darkness.

Chapter 4

GRANDMA'S PULLOUT COUCH

~❦~

What scent lingers unrecognizably
Between that of popcorn, grilled cheese sandwiches,
Malted milkballs, and parakeets?

—MARK IRWIN

Daddy and I have been standing in the stuffy hallway smelling of cooked cabbage for way too long. He lets out an exasperated sigh and jabs his thumb into the doorbell several more times. Grandma Blanche's enlarged watery blue eye appears in the peephole.

"For God's sake, Ma, open up. You know who we are."

"Hold your horses there, Mr. Grumpy." She clicks back the multiple locks on her door and finally opens it. We follow her in. I usually stay with New York Grandma during the summer, so I'm

resigned to her irritating habits, but after the sun-drenched freedom of Kentucky, I really don't want to be here. She must have
been lying on the couch with a mint-scented cloth over her eyes,
because it still trails from her hand. Her short, salt-and-pepper
hair sticks out at odd angles. It had once fallen out by the handful when she had typhoid fever. Now it grows thick because she
massages her scalp every day. An electric fan flutters her dress as
she raises the blinds. The dark, hot living room brightens with a
beam of light.

"How are you, dear?" She pats my shoulder. "Is your grandma in Kentucky all right? I'm sorry I couldn't go with you, but that bus trip. . . ." She pinches the bridge of her nose at the thought of it.

Staying with Grandma means tugging out the living room couch into a bed each evening. We struggle to do this, even though on television the girl in her nightgown does it with ease. It means using a windowless bathroom with a shower rod dripping pink old lady underwear. It means eating hamburger and string beans on a tray in front of the television set. Staying with Grandma is about trying to be patient as I wait for my father to take me somewhere fun.

"Can I pour you some iced tea or a glass of milk to soothe your stomach? How about some Social Tea biscuits, Kim? It's much too hot for coffee, though." She putters around a kitchenette that is no bigger than a closet.

"I'm okay, sit down and stop fussing, Ma." Daddy puts down my suitcase and sits with his knees sticking up on the low, pullout couch. It is the one modern piece in a room of dark Victorian furniture.

"So . . . did you pay the rent this month, Son?"

"Quit worrying, Ma. Of course I did."

"How long will Kim be staying here?" Grandma asks. This question makes me hold my breath. I lean forward to hear Daddy's answer. "I don't know, Ma. We are waiting on Jeanne to find a place. You know how she is. When she's good and ready, she'll let us know. But I don't think it will be long."

Grandma Blanche whispers the words that I dread. "I'm too old to care for a child. I really can't do it anymore." I've heard her quaver this before into the spittle-caked, black telephone. Although Grandma is the person who takes me to Dr. Beckerman, the dentist, every summer and who took me to the optometrist for glasses when school discovered I was near-sighted and was there with ice cream when my tonsils and adenoids were removed—she always complains about my being too much for her. Where will I live if she isn't willing?

Daddy gives me a hug and promises to come by tomorrow and take me to the Automat and the carousel. I love putting coins in a tiny window that swings open so I can remove a sandwich and crave the joyous freedom of swinging around and around on the back of a golden horse that swoops up and down. He leaves to get back to the paper to finish his column. Grandma Blanche and I look at each other as if we are marooned together on a desert island.

Time passes more quickly when we browse her scrapbook. I ask her to get it from the top of the armoire, and she does so with soft groans. A tinted photo of her in a bonnet adorned with a cloth rose is pasted to the black paper with little triangles.

"Is that really you, Grandma?" I'm amazed that the luminous young woman is the same wrinkled grandparent with drooping eyelids and cracks around her mouth.

"Yes, dear," she sighs. "That's when I sang operetta. I was in costume as the Little Quaker Maid. Your Grandpa Henry said I was the most beautiful girl in the world. He brought me a bouquet of flowers to the stage door every night for three whole weeks! He insisted I go out with him. He was a medical doctor, a great catch. I couldn't believe it when he asked me to marry him." Her faded eyes brighten at the memory.

A photo of Grandpa shows a stout man with frog-like eyes wearing a stiff, white collar and dark suit. He doesn't look handsome to me. Daddy told me his father never played with him. Grandma Blanche was the parent who knelt on the kitchen linoleum to demonstrate the game of marbles.

In another photo, she leans her chin on a finger while her hair drifts in soft tendrils over her bare shoulders. She looks innocent, but those naked shoulders suggest something else. "What about these? When were these taken?"

"Oh well, I gave up all that nonsense after we married. He wouldn't stand for that theater foolishness."

Then I turn over a sepia portrait of my father as a baby. On the back is written "Justin Goldberg," but the surname is crossed out and our family name, "Gilbert," is written above it.

"Why is the name crossed out?" I ask.

"Your grandfather Henry was . . . Jewish, and he wanted a more . . . American-sounding name." Grandma Blanche fumbles for an answer. "So he changed it. But then his family . . . well, we never got to know that side of the family. We had a good life. But then. . . " Her voice falters.

"He gave a rattling sigh over a book one night and died right before the Great Depression. We were suddenly very poor and moved to Hell's Kitchen." I know these lines by heart.

"And your poor father had to be sent to South Carolina because of his asthma. That was the worst . . . being separated from my boy. He started in the newspaper business when he was only fifteen." She dabs at tears forming at the corners of her eyes.

Listening to her makes me feel so sad that I flop on the couch and cover my eyes with my hands.

"Enough of that. Stop being such an actress." Grandma puts the photo album away. "Let's go down to the health food store. Now that you're here, I need more whole wheat bread and honey." She puts on a wide-brimmed navy hat, stabs a long hatpin through it, and gathers her voluminous purse and white gloves. I'm not keen on the dusty health food store, where they sell carrot juice and cookies with no sugar. Grandma has told me many times about malnourished children dying from eating white bread while the pigs fattened on wheat germ. There is no getting out of this.

"It's so desperately hot on the sidewalk. Maybe we can stop at Woolworth's where it's air-conditioned and buy a malted milk. Would you like that?" I perk up at the thought.

After a week, the black phone rings, and Grandma picks it up. "Your father and Franca are inviting us over for a party. Could it be someone's tenth birthday and the baby's first year? We'll pack your suitcase, because afterwards you are going to your mother's new place." My stomach clenches in a knot. She smiles, but when she sees my face, she looks away. Grandma is annoying but familiar. I'm afraid of what staying with my mother will be like.

I ring Daddy's doorbell while Grandma stands behind me and sucks a mint. He throws open the door as he and Franca call out, "Surprise, happy birthday, Kim and Justine!" I set my suitcase by the door and run through the living room to the table. On it is a pink and white birthday cake surrounded by gaily wrapped presents and a large cardboard box.

"I knew you wouldn't forget! Happy birthday to us both!" I sing, giving Justine a smooch on her plump cheek. Our birthdays are three days apart, and she is one year old. Her pink head is covered with blonde hair—gone is last year's peach fuzz.

"She's so sturdy now," I say. "Can I hold her?" I sit on a chair by the table while Granny folds herself onto another. Franca places Justine in my lap after wiping her chin with a bib.

The baby is warm and smells of talcum powder. I can feel her moist breath on my neck as she squirms around and grabs my braid. Here is the sister I yearned for. No more will I be one small person in a confusing world of adults. With a sister, I have an ally.

"I'm going to be the best big sister to you," I promise her. She reaches up and grabs my glasses.

Franca explains picking up Justine and handing me my spectacles, "Glasses fascinate the baby. I don't wear mine around her because of that. I'm as blind as a bat, my dear," she says in her British accent, acquired from English nuns who taught at Catholic school in Italy. She was born and raised in Florence, Italy, although her parents are Americans. Her mother, sister, and she had moved here, and she had become a working ballet dancer when she was just fifteen. I had forgotten about Franca's accent and glasses and feel the links connecting us. I am thrilled with Franca for giving me a longed-for sister. I want to call her "Mommy" and write, "Mommy and Daddy are giving me a birthday party" in my five-year diary. In my secret heart, I hope she might have enough love left over from the baby to spill onto me.

A raucous cry pierces the air. I have forgotten about Mackie, the blue and gold macaw who lives in a large cage in a corner of the living room. Daddy opens the wire door and lifts him out.

"Don't take that bird out now, Justin. It will frighten your mother," says Franca.

"Mackie needs to be handled, otherwise he gets lonely," Daddy fondly ruffles the bird's pinfeathers on top of his head.

"Can I hold him? I haven't held Mackie since last year." I hold out my arm, and after giving me a canny look from his beady eye, the large bird clambers on, gripping me with his sharp claws. He sidles onto my shoulder and nibbles tenderly at the roots of my braid, making me giggle.

"See, Dunder, he hasn't forgotten you."

Justine pulls herself to a standing position and yells, "Bird!" as I sit on the couch near her playpen, stroking the bird's long feathers.

"This place is much too small for the three of us and that great bird." Franca's voice rises as she comes out of the kitchen carrying plates and forks. "It was fine for you as a bachelor's pad with a fancy Sutton Place address, but we have no storage space. We stuff crates of Justine's baby food under the bed."

With a grimace, my father picks Mackie off my shoulder and carries him back to his cage. "Will you stop? He's in. He's not bothering anyone. The kids were enjoying him."

But Franca swivels toward him, her words erupting with machine-gun rapidity that ends with a shriek. "We have a baby now. She has to come first over that creature. His cage takes up half the living room, he spills sunflower seed on the carpet, and the baby gets into it when she crawls. His screams are awful. The neighbors complain. I can't stand this anymore!"

"Will you calm down? I hand-raised Mackie and won't part with him. So forget it, let's get on with Knucklehead's party." He lowers himself onto a chair and taps his fingers.

Mackie lets out an ear-splitting shriek that bounces off the walls, crashing into my eardrums. I clap my hands to my ears but feel the fierce joy in the jungle sound. I am scared of his powerful beak, but he is a wild being who likes me.

Hearing the noise, Justine plumps down on her diapered bottom, adding her cries to the commotion. Franca thrusts her in a high chair while muttering in Italian. She disappears into the kitchenette for a tense few minutes while I count the squares in the tablecloth, and nobody speaks.

Daddy glances at me. "She gets these brainstorms, but they pass."

Sure enough, Franca comes out singing "Happy Birthday" and carrying a carton of ice cream. Everyone joins in. I look at her high cheekbones, penciled eyebrows, and red lips and can't detect any signs of craziness. But I better stay on her good side.

Father sticks ten candles on the cake and one extra for Justine. He lights them, and I take in a big breath and blow them all out, wishing from the deepest bottom of my heart for us to live together as a family. Franca cuts the cake and spoons out three flavors of ice cream. We are all quiet as we let the cold velvet melt on our tongues. Franca places a bowl of cake crumbs in front of Justine, who mashes them into and around her mouth. She looks like she is wearing pink and white clown makeup; this makes us laugh. I love that she distracts the adults without even trying. Usually, this is my job.

It is time to open my presents. I am not surprised when Father pulls a volume out of a carton and hands it to me. We are both big readers, and he always gives me books.

"This is volume A-B in a set of encyclopedias. I never had anything like this when I was a kid." I prefer a good novel but think this might be handy.

Father takes the book back and reads hungrily through a page. "These encyclopedias are expensive, so I'm letting you take one at a time, like a library. The rest I'm keeping here, because gifts vanish when you take them to your mother's."

"Oh, not something else to store under the bed," Franca mutters. She hands me a tissue-covered package and says it is a new nightgown from her and Justine. I rip it open and hold the long flowered gown up to my shoulders. Attached to the bodice is a pink satin rose. It looks like something a princess would wear.

"It's lovely." I stand and twirl around, holding it against me. Then I lean over and plant a kiss on Franca's cheek. "Thank you so much. I'll wear it the next time I stay with you." Her penciled eyebrows rise anxiously behind her glasses.

I hold out a package of bibs, inscribed with the days of the week, to Justine. "We figured she could use at least one every day," I explain, and tie Thursday's bib around the baby's neck. She obligingly lets down a ribbon of drool, and we all laugh.

My gifts are nice, but the happiness I feel bubbling inside me comes from being part of a family. A shadow hovers over my joy. Soon I will leave and move to Mother's apartment.

"Couldn't I stay here tonight? As a special treat for my birthday?" I burst out.

"Whatever for, Kim? You know we're awfully tight here," Daddy says as he packs up my presents in a shopping bag. He slaps his hat on his head. Franca throws me a look while she slides leftover cake back into the box.

"C'mon, get your coat on," my father said. "You too, Ma. I'll drop you both off in a cab and go back to the paper to finish my column." I let the subject drop, but when I pick up my suitcase, its weight pulls me down.

⟨≋⟩

"Mrs. Gibson has gone out for the evening," the doorman says as he unlocks the door. We enter a messy living room where drink glasses sweat rings on the marble coffee table. Lipstick-stained cigarette butts fill the ashtrays, and one is still burning, smoke streaming into the air. High heels are lying in front of an arm-chair, and a nightgown is squished into the seat pillow. Card-board boxes are open everywhere, their contents exploded around them. She hasn't done much unpacking since she moved here two months ago.

Father says, "Goddamn it!" right in front of me, and puts down my suitcase and bag of gifts. He lifts his hat and runs his fingers through his white hair as he looks around. His gray eyes, surrounded by worry lines, are level with mine as he crouches in front of me. He cups my two elbows. I am still carrying my tenth birthday cake box.

"The meter is running on the taxi downstairs with Grandma waiting in it, Hammerhead. You understand the problem?" he asks, and I nod. I know what is coming. This has happened before.

"Your mother has squirrels for brains, but I need you to be a big girl so I can go to the office." He pulls his business card out of his pocket and hands it to me.

"Call me at the paper if anything comes up, anything."

I want to scream, "Daddy don't leave me!" and throw myself

on the carpet, kicking and beating my fists. I don't. Something in me isn't surprised, just very sad. I nudge aside the ashtrays and put down the cake box.

Father gives me a hug and walks into the hall. "Don't forget to lock up after me," he says, as he pauses by the elevator. I stand at the door and wait for him to disappear.

When he does, I look at the doors in the hallway, some with mats that say WELCOME. This is similar to Grandma's hall, except here it is quiet as a tomb and doesn't smell of cabbage. I have the urge to ring all the bells and find someone loving to take me in. But who knows who lives behind these doors? I'm not going to run away until I know where to go. I close my door and click the lock. It's similar to Grandma's, who has a million locks on her door. She even has a gold chain across the top. I wish I were back at her place.

I pick up the cake box and search for the kitchen. The first room is Mother's bedroom. I can tell, because clothes cover the bed, chair, and bedside tables. In one corner, her trunk spews dresses onto the floor. High-heeled shoes surround her bed—she prefers going barefoot.

I find the bright, clean kitchen. Mother hasn't been here yet. There is a wooden table and chairs with woven seats like Hansel and Gretel should be sitting on them. Red-and-yellow-flowered curtains frill the windows. A cuckoo clock with a balcony waits for the bird to pop out. Fifteen minutes past five, time for dinner.

I open the refrigerator and say, "Goddamn it!" A tiny bulb blinks on and reveals bottles of vodka, soda water, a bowl of lemon wedges and green olives with red centers, and a jar of milk. That must be for me because Mother never drinks the stuff and . . . what's this? Witch Hazel. I unscrew the cap and look in—no eye of newt or toads' legs, but it does smell awful enough to be a magic potion. I close the door and lean against it, just to feel its hum, and slide the birthday cake box onto the counter.

Grandma Blanche must be cozy in her apartment by now. She is probably unlacing her tight shoes, sliding into her slippers, and then standing up with a sigh to put the kettle on for tea. She is not missing me or our struggle to open the pullout couch. She is reaching into a cupboard for the Social Tea biscuits and a jar of applesauce. That is our favorite treat. I wish I were there, snug and bored. I hate being alone in this strange place.

I find a glass and pour myself some milk. It's important for a growing child's bones, Grandma told me. I open the cake box. There is still a lot left. I want to hang on to the happiness I felt at my party. I dig my forefinger into the A in Happy, pinch off a chunk and drop it into my mouth. That is for Granny enjoying herself without me. I scoop the P out and lick it from my palm. That is for Franca's screaming fit. The other P is for Daddy leaving me here alone. And the rest I stuff into my mouth until my cheeks bulge. That is for Mother, who says a lady always leaves something on her plate—and for her going out on my first night in our new place. I savor the creamy sweetness, pick up crumbs out of the box, and lick my lips and fingers, postponing the moment when it is gone. Finally, the cake box looks back at me with its round empty eye.

Silence is pressing against me, squeezing the air out of my chest. I feel like a punctured red balloon with air hissing out until I will be a rag on the floor.

I run through the rooms, searching for a book to carry me far away. This is what I have always done. Books are my best friends. They are always there when I need them, ready to take me into another world. But the book I really want has not been written: what to do about a mother who is never here.

I find a room that looks like it belongs to a boy. Someone has sewn curtains and a matching bedspread with sailboats floating on them. Watercolors of boats hang over the bed. I imagine the boy's mother sewing, her needle flashing as it weaves through the cloth. Cardboard boxes are stacked in a corner with Fenny's neat handwriting labeling them "Kim's Clothes," "Kim's Toys." Fenny is far away in England, and this is my room now.

I go to his desk, spin the globe, and find the pink blob of England, then peek through the spyglass. Outside the window, there are rooftops where a few pigeons strut around, their irides-cent feathers shining in the fading light. I switch on a sailboat lamp, pull open the drawers, and find paper, pens, and colored pencils. A calm feeling drapes around me like a warm blanket as I start sketching the birds. Next to the desk are shelves whose books have boy's titles: *Treasure Island, White Fang, My Friend Flicka.* I pick up the last and fall on the bed, reading.

The next thing I know, my cheek is digging into the book on my pillow. It's morning, and a hush of sleep hums through the apartment. I jump up and run to Mother's bedroom. Yes, she is there in her bed, a large lump under clothes and wrinkled sheets. One naked arm is flung over the edge. I examine her fiery red nail polish. It looks good; she's had her nails done since I last saw her. I mustn't wake her. This is a strict rule. An adult who is woken early is always cross.

I find a box of corn flakes in the kitchen, pour it into a bowl with milk, and carry it back to my room. I spoon it up, sit at the desk, and look out the window. Some pink clouds fluff across the sky and reflect in puddles on rooftops. Someone has thrown corn out for the pigeons that crowd to gobble it up. One large bird is bossing the others around. This mama pigeon is pushing out her chest, strutting around, showing the other birds where she wants them to eat. They don't seem to mind. They are a flock, and she is their leader. I wish I had a clan to be part of.

The shrill call of the telephone rips through the quiet. I run to Mother's side as she murmurs, "Umm-hmm, umm-hmm" a few times into the receiver and hangs up. She swings her legs down to the carpet and sits up with a small moan. One cheek is crisscrossed by sheet wrinkles, and makeup puddles under her eyes, which are red and unfocused. She leans her head against me. She smells bad, but I don't move away. Her bedside clock ticks—it is ten minutes after nine. I wonder if she has fallen back to sleep, but she raises her head and looks at me.

"David invited me out last night, and that's him again, ask-ing if we want to go to lunch. Isn't that wonderful? He keeps me waiting and wondering the whole goddamn month since I got here, and now he wants me quick on the double. Over here he's Mr. Big Britches." This explains why she wasn't here last night. She shakes her tousled head and stumbles into her bathroom, pouring a tumbler of water and gulping it down. She reaches into the shower and turns it on. I watch her shuck off her nightgown and step in.

Back in my room, I open the box marked "Kim's Clothes" and pull out my school uniform. It's always impressed adults. The waistband is tight, and the jacket is wrinkled, but I put it on anyway. When I return to Mother's room, she is wrapped in a towel, searching through her open closet, a cigarette burning between her fingers. I push aside some clothes and sit on her bed, watching. Her blonde hair is swept back by a wide, white band, and her unpainted face is like clean paper waiting for an artist's brush. Only her red toenails seem ready for dancing. I love to see her change from a small person I want to take care of to—presto!—Queen of the Universe.

She holds a blue silk dress and jacket up to her shoulders while looking at the mirror on the closet door. She nods and flings them beside me on the bed. She bites the cigarette between her teeth as she dives into the trunk for the supporting cast of black brassiere, girdle, slip, and stockings. I love to watch her shimmy this armor over her soft flesh. She is like a snake in reverse, sliding into her skin.

She sits in front of the mirrored dressing table and pours vodka into her water glass. She stubs out the end of the first cigarette and lights another. I wish she wouldn't smoke or drink, but if I say something, she gets mad. She picks up a sponge and starts applying pancake makeup in even strokes across her face. This is followed by rouge, eyelash curler, mascara and brush, eyebrow pencil, powder, and lipstick. She places a tissue between her lips, prints her lips on it, and tosses it aside. She stands up, bringing her nose an inch away from the glass, and glares at the right and left sides of her face. She brushes away something I can't see, then smiles at her reflection.

She sits down again, pulls off the headband, combs her fine blond hair around her forehead, and pins it back into a chignon. She dabs Jean Naté perfume on her neck and wrists. The lemony scent wakes me up and makes me want to skip. She picks up the dress and steps into it. She turns her back to me, and here I perform my one duty of sliding the long zipper all the way up. Shrugging on the jacket, she searches for patent leather heels, steps into them, and—ta da!—twirls around to show herself off.

"How do I look?"

That's easy. "You look ab-so-lutely beautiful." But I have to say it several times, otherwise she gets doubtful.

"Your eye shadow perfectly matches the dress. You are totally gorgeous!" We smile at each other for the first time that morning. My shoulders soften, and relief rushes through me.

We walk to Fifth Avenue and hail a yellow taxi. Mother tells the cabbie to take us to Schubert Alley and Broadway. We sit silently side by side. The blat and blare of traffic falls away. I'm aware of our breathing, mine is slow and hers rapid. She is looking out the window, alert and nervous as a young filly. I feel protective of her. A silent presence envelops us, thick and loving like gelatin.

Mother points out David's name—DAVID MERRICK PRO-DUCES—on three theaters in the same block. We enter through a small door to the side of the St. James Theater and climb up dingy stairs. Mother knocks on the door with his name printed on it. A voice calls, "Come in," and we are in a dark, file-filled vestibule. A secretary with frog eyes sits behind a messy desk. Mother says who we are, and the woman introduces herself as Helen Nickerson, Mr. Merrick's secretary. She beams at us and shakes both our hands. I curtsy. We are getting special treatment.

We enter David's office. Everything is the color of red roses: drapes, carpet, couch, wall paper, framed theater posters, even the cloth draped over the piano and the carnations in the vase. Mother and I turn around in circles, taking in the many shades of scarlet. She acts like it is her first time seeing his office. I stroke the velvet wallpaper and sit back on the wine-colored couch. This is what an empress must feel like.

"Hello, ladies," David says. Mother jumps. I hadn't noticed him sitting behind his red desk piled with papers.

"Why, David." Mother walks around to him, laying her gloved hand on his dark sleeve, and says in a voice as smooth as silk, "I feel like I'm entering the lion's den."

His black eyes peer at her from his white face. "You and I know we have to show the rabble who's boss, otherwise they step all over you. Actors are the worst, they're like children."

I ponder this as I investigate the contents of a purple candy dish and discover that, under the red cellophane wrappers, the candies are white. I decide to confiscate the evidence by sliding it into my mouth. I'm hungry for lunch.

"You don't want to be an actress, do you?" he growls at me. I cough on my mint but notice the corners of his mouth turning up.

"You remember David, don't you?" Of course, I remember his visit to my boarding school.

"Do you live here?" I ask him.

"No, I live in a hotel."

"Why in a hotel?"

"You spent a lot of time at the Savoy. Don't you know why?"

I remember the delicious tinkle of covered dishes and cutlery as the uniformed busboy pushed the linen-covered trolley into Mother's office.

"You can order room service," I crow in a moment of understanding.

"Yes. Maids clean up every day. The benefits are endless in my opinion."

"But there's no garden to play in or oven to bake cornbread. If I could live anywhere I wanted, I'd live in the country with my family and a dog."

"I don't like the country. It makes me sneeze," he says. I look at him carefully. No wonder his skin is so pale. My mind forms a snapshot of him sleeping in his pinstriped suit.

"Why don't you go to Sardi's, and I'll follow after I've made some phone calls," he suggests, picking up the phone.

Mother's fingers dig into my shoulder as we walk to the restaurant next door. She must be worried about David. At parties in London, I watched men fawn over her. She made fun of them to their faces, but they adored her. I don't think it will be so easy with David.

When we stand in front of the maître d', Mother says in a firm voice, "We are dining with Mr. Merrick, who will be joining us shortly. I am Mrs. Jeanne Gibson, and this is my daughter."

The bored face of the man changes immediately and he whispers reverently, "Sir David." He leads us, smiling, to a round table covered with linen and many sets of silverware. We slide into the half-moon banquet. A waiter appears and clears away extra settings. Mother orders a double vodka on the rocks and tells him to be quick about it.

I feel as if someone is pinching the back of my neck. When Mother drinks, bad things happen. To distract myself, I look around and notice drawings lining the walls. I turn in the booth, kneeling to have a clearer view of the pictures behind us. One cartoon clearly shows David disguised as a mean Santa setting fire to a Christmas tree and presents. He wears a devilish grin on his mustachioed face.

"Look, Mother, here's a picture of David." I pull her sleeve.

She jerks it away. "Yes, this is his table. He sent that as a Christmas card to the critics." She is busy with her drink.

"It's a caricature. I'm more handsome than that, don't you think?" David says, walking up and sliding in beside Mother.

I'm wary of him after seeing the pictures. "Why would you want to ruin their Christmas?"

"I don't like critics who write bad reviews of my plays. They deserve that and worse."

"One time, when David didn't like the critics' reviews, he found five people with identical names and published their rave comments. Isn't that a hoot?" Mother leans her head on David's shoulder. He pulls away a little.

"Can you recognize anyone else?"

I think I see Frank Sinatra and Elvis Presley, but most of them are unfamiliar. Then I identify the star of the movie, *The Robe*.

"I slept with him once," I say pointing to the drawing.

Mother looks at me sharply. "That's Victor Mature, a friend of ours. I had to go out of town and he offered to put Kim up. He has a tiny *pied a terre* in London, so they slept in the same bed. End of story." She mashes out her cigarette in an ashtray and pulls another from her purse that the waiter lights. He takes our drink orders. Mother gets another vodka for herself, a Shirley Temple for me, and David orders seltzer water.

I watch him frown as Mother's drink is placed in front of her. He doesn't seem to smoke or drink. He might be a good influence on Mother.

"How did you two meet?" I ask.

Mother smiles and they look at each other.

"Your mother and I met at the Savoy Hotel. I stay there when I go to London to find plays I want to bring to the States. She was the prettiest press agent and threw the most exciting parties in London."

"You know I had to greet every important person staying at the hotel," Mother says. "Well, as soon as I clapped eyes on David"—her eyes shyly seek out his—"chemistry happened. And, David, you must have felt something behind that indomitable exterior of yours, otherwise you wouldn't have bought me this." She flashes the robin's-egg-sized sapphire ring at him. "But a wedding ring would sure look sweet alongside it."

David's voice cuts like a cold knife. "Jeanne, I've told you I'm already married. Changing that status would cost too much. Be satisfied with your ring." His brows form a black V. He walks his fingers around his glass as if he'd strangle it.

My hands ball into fists that press into my thighs. My breath is locked inside my chest. I cautiously let air out as I notice smoke streaming out of Mother's nose. She is looking around as if she might know someone on the other side of the room.

"I'm hungry. Can I have a hamburger, Mother?" My voice sounds high, as if it belongs to a younger child.

The waiter appears, David and Mother order, and quickly the food is set in front of us. I take a big bite out of my burger. It is really juicy and good, but David and Mother are just picking at their food. If this were boarding school, they would be made to finish what is on their plates. Mother stubs out her cigarette in her shrimp salad and pushes away her plate. She takes a big gulp from her glass.

"Jeanne, you're drinking too much, and I don't like that," David snaps into the silence.

"You can't make me kowtow to you," she retorts coolly, blowing smoke in his direction. "You don't pay my salary, like your damn Miss Nickerson with her hatchet face. 'Miss Nicked Hatchet,' you should call her. I swear she's in love with you, the way she sighs over your every word. 'May I kiss the hem of your Savile Row suit, Mr. Merrick?'" Mother widens her turquoise eyes and lowers her voice in imitation. "Which, you remember, I helped you get made in London. Not bad for a little hillbilly who never wore shoes until she was eight."

David laughs, but it looks as if it hurts his face. His eyes lick Mother like she is ice cream. She is so pretty with her peach skin and cornflower eyes.

"How do you do it, Jeanne?" He shakes his head as if she is a mysterious being who just arrived from the moon. She doesn't answer, but they look at each other as if they have made up.

I forgot I was holding my burger up to my mouth and now finish it off in several big bites. I was hoping for dessert, but no, now they want to be alone together without a kid bothering them. I am the Jack-in-the-box who was amusing for a while, but I am put in a taxi and sent home alone.

Chapter 5

FAIREST IN THE LAND

﹏﹏

Before you know kindness as the deepest thing inside
You must know sorrow as the other deepest thing.
—NAOMI SHIHAB NYE

Gray morning is behind the window when my eyes open. I run through the hushed apartment to Mother's room. She is inside the mound of rumpled sheets. My breath enters my lungs, and I want to let out a shout of joy. But it comes out as a rush of air because I know I mustn't wake her. I slide down to sit on the carpet, noticing the clock as I make myself comfortable. Eight twenty. How long will I have to wait before she gets up? After a long five minutes, I go to the kitchen for breakfast. I pour the cereal into the bowl, but only a few drops come out of the milk bottle. This isn't right. A mother is supposed to feed her child. Now I have cause for action. I march boldly into her bedroom.

"Mommy, there's no more milk," I whisper. No movement comes from her inert body. "I'm hungry, there's no food." I say more insistently. "You're supposed to feed me, Mommy." I feel a rising panic as my own urgency scares me. I push her heavy arm that hangs naked outside the sheet.

"What do you want?" she mumbles.

"Food. I need food."

"Get money from my purse," she rasps and burrows her face in her pillow.

I sit on the carpet and snap open her black patent leather pocketbook, knowing I am entering a private, grownup world. I have a purse, but it only holds a lacy handkerchief, a tiny bottle of perfume, and a chocolate wrapper. The zingy scent of Jean Naté steals out of her bag. I push aside a gold lipstick and powder compact and a folded tissue with red lipstick blots, and pull out a fat leather change purse stuffed with unfamiliar, crumpled, American bills and change. I slide out some paper money and smooth it on my knee. They are dull green and unimpressive compared to bright English bills with the Queen's pink face. What should I do now? I don't know where the grocery store is. I don't know how to make correct change. Hoping to find more clues, I empty the contents onto the carpet, reading through the business cards— one is David Merrick's and another is my father's. The last object to fall out with a small sigh is a tiny bottle of vodka.

The click of the front door unlocking catches my attention. I look around the bedroom door to see a dark woman wearing a squashed hat and drab coat walk in the living room. She stops when she sees the mess and sighs, then disappears into the kitchen.

I follow her in. "Are you the charlady?" I ask. "There's no food in the house, and Mother said I could take her money and buy some, but I don't know where to go," I mumble with embarrassment.

"Honey, I don't know about *char*, but I am the cleaning lady. My name is Minnie. Your mama hired me last week, and she did mention something about you. You're Kim, right?" Her strong hand grips my shoulder as she looks me over. "You know you're a sight. How long you been wearing that night gown? Don't you never comb your hair? Just let me put my things down, and I'll fix you up." She removes her hat and coat and laces up her worn work shoes. Finally, she ties a green-spotted apron around her generous middle. She checks the empty state of the refrigerator and the dirty dishes in the sink and turns around to me.

"Let me see if I got this right. Nobody's been cookin' or cleanin' since I last was here. No clothes or linens been washed, and there's no food anywhere?" I nod, relieved that at last someone understands.

As she leads me into my bedroom, she mutters under her breath, "There isn't enough time in one day to do all the tendin' that needs being done here. If I didn't need the money, I wouldn't be puttin' up with such aggravation." She gathers my dirty clothes from the hamper, tells me to wash my hair, and she will help me dry and comb it.

When I come out of my room drying my hair, I hear laughter in the kitchen. Minnie, who is washing dishes, and Mother, looking like the Good Witch from *The Wizard of Oz* in her shimmering negligee, are chatting about batters their mamas used to turn out crisp fried chicken. "Your mother can charm the birds out of the trees," Daddy once said, and I see it's true.

I hand my comb to Minnie, who begins braiding my hair.

"Minnie has agreed to go to Gristides and fry us up a batch of chicken," Mother says. "Why don't you go with her and walk some of that lard off your ass? You know, if your father would cough up his child support, we could have Minnie come more than one day a week." Then she sweeps back to her bedroom.

As Minnie and I walk to the grocery store, she says, "I have four children who live with me in the projects. My youngest, Delia, is a year younger than you and can wash and braid her own hair, and do the laundry and cooking."

"I know I should learn to do these things, but how can I, if there is no one around to teach me?" Minnie sighs and trudges inside to make her purchases.

I stop outside, halted by the sight of an immensely tall,

bearded man costumed as a Viking with leather leggings, voluminous cloak, and leather helmet complete with horns. He
stands still as a statue, gripping a long spear in one hand. Beside
him is a full satchel, and attached to some railings above it is the
sign, "MOONDOG—POET AND MUSICIAN. PLEASE MAKE A CONTRI-
BUTION AND TAKE A POEM."

I hover around this strange being, fascinated and afraid.
Finally I call out, "I write poems, too." He doesn't respond so I
say more loudly, "I've written poems about living in the country
with my family and illustrated them." He sits suddenly and beckons to me. I inch closer until I can see his seamed face beneath
his long, shaggy hair and beard. His eyes are scarred and blind.
He hands me a card with a poem on it.

"Why do you stand out here? Where do you live?" I burst
out, unable to contain my curiosity.

"I always stand here. Fifty-fourth and sixth is my spot. I'm
a beat poet and musician, neither for nor against anyone. I make
a little money and meet interesting people like you."

"Can I give you money for a poem?" I fish out a bill and
hand it to him. The poem reads:

> Machines were mice and men were lions
> Once upon a time.
> Now it's just the opposite,
> Once upon a time.

I consider it. "Can girls be lions, do you think?"

"Be anyway you want. Don't let people chip away at you."

Minnie walks out of the grocery store carrying two bulging
paper bags. I say good-bye and rush to take a bag. We carry the
groceries into the kitchen. I let her put them away and wander
into Mother's bedroom. She is standing in front of the mirror in
her black lace underwear, eyeing her reflection critically, tapping
a bare foot and smoking. She holds in front of her a black dress
with a full skirt topped by a bolero jacket with red piping.

"You're going out?"

"Of course," she says with an irritated exhalation of smoke. "How do I look?"

"Beautiful." What she wants to hear is "fairest in all the land," like the Magic Mirror said to Snow White's wicked stepmother. But she doesn't look so well. I notice a yellow sheen to her skin. She bends unsteadily to pull a pair of black-and-red heels from the closet. She reaches, misses, and reaches again for a matching belt.

"Good but not good enough. David is in the public eye. I need new clothes. Did your father say anything about my alimony check?"

Whenever either parent mentions money or the trouble it takes to maintain me, I feel as if my insides are being squeezed. Grandma Blanche called my father, complaining she was too old to take care of me. Franca said their apartment was too small to include me. The message is clear—there isn't room for me. I should be a good girl, make no demands, and be invisible. I can't win a game with these rules.

"I'm going to set that man straight. I'll wear this for now. David's seen all the rest. I have an interview for a job at Max Eisen's office before I meet David. Max does all of his publicity." She sits wearily on the bed and begins the delicate maneuver of scrunching a stocking into an oval and gliding it over her foot. Her fingers are stained with nicotine, and her hands are shaking so she can't direct the stocking over her foot.

"Are you all right, Mommy?" I step closer to grab her arm. She reeks of sweat and something else.

"Oh, it's no use. I've got a ripsnorter of a headache." She sighs and sinks onto the bed fully dressed. "Get me a couple of aspirin and a glass of water, will you?"

I do. As I pulled the door quietly closed behind me, I can hear her canceling her job appointment on the phone.

Minnie is not in the apartment. She is in the basement doing laundry. I go back to my room and look at Moondog's poem. It doesn't rhyme.

The telephone's ring rips through the silence. I run into the living room to pick it up.

"Knucklehead, this is Daddy. I'm coming by in a taxi. Be downstairs in a few minutes. I need to talk to you." I get my coat as Minnie walks in carrying a basket of clean laundry. I tell her Mommy is resting and my father is picking me up. She makes sure I have the apartment key in my purse in case no one is there to open the door when I get back.

Father's hat is perched on the back of his white hair, and his breath smells sour when he gives me a kiss on the cheek. In the taxi speeding toward Grandma's apartment, he silently leans forward with his elbows jammed into his knees as he raps the knuckles of one fist with the fingers of the other. He seems tense, and I hope I haven't done anything wrong.

The bare hall resounds with clicks and pops as Grandma fumbles with multiple locks before she opens the door.

"Hello, Son, whatever is the matter? You sounded upset on the phone. Hello, Kim."

"I am upset, Ma. I just got a call from Jeanne's new boyfriend, threatening to sue me if I didn't send her alimony and child support. He's a lawyer as well as a producer, a nasty son of a bitch. I want to show Kim something." He draws me into Grandma's dark bedroom crowded with a dark mahogany bedstead and dresser. He pulls a slew of receipts, checks, and notes out of a drawer, throws his hat on the bedpost, and we sit on the bed.

"Hammerhead, your mother and David are telling lies about me. These are bills from Lady Eden's school. I've saved every one of them. That was an expensive school but all these bills are marked paid." He spreads them out. Even my report cards are included, and the receipt from a man who accompanied me on a flight to England. "See? Paid. All marked paid. They may tell you that your daddy doesn't send his alimony, that he's a liar and a cheat. This is not true. I may be a little late now and then. I have a wife and another child, but I pay for my daughter." His voice chokes as he gives me an earnest look, tears welling up in his gray eyes.

"I laminated *The New York Times* announcement the day you were born and carry it with me always." He pulls out his wallet and displays the shiny card. "See. You are my firstborn, and I'm your daddy. Don't believe anything that bastard says about me. He's telling lies." His head falls into his hands, and he breaks into hoarse, choking sobs.

The image of my strong father cracks and crumbles. *He is just another man my mother has fooled. I must be the adult and comfort him.*

"I would never think you were a liar and a cheat, Daddy. Don't worry. I never wanted to go to that school. They thought I was a rich American. Don't cry. Let me live with you and go to a cheap school. There, there, don't worry, everything's going to be okay." I pat his shoulder, repeating the empty words.

"Sweetie, I think I'll stretch out for a while. You go to your granny."

I find her hovering outside the door.

"Son, what can I do for you? You want a cold cloth on your forehead?"

"That would be nice, Ma. I'll just rest a bit."

Grandma bustles about and comes into the living room, where I am seated on the couch. She sinks into her easy chair with a sigh.

"Your father's a good man. He's always given me part of what he earned, even when he was a boy and starting out at the newspaper. Now he pays my rent, pays your mother, supports his new family. What a shame they torment him like this. If only your grandfather hadn't died . . ." She lets out a quavering sigh.

The silence between us lengthens as shadows filled the room. A blanket of guilt smothers us for being dependent on my father. For me, there is the added guilt of my disgust at seeing him cry. *If only life weren't so hard, if only it didn't tear at your tender parts like a ravenous wolf with sharp teeth. Why did Mother marry Daddy if she just turned around and left him, leaving me caught in the middle?*

We hear feet hitting the floor, and the bedroom door opens as Daddy stumbles out, rubbing his eyes.

"I must have fallen asleep. Why are you two sitting in the dark? Grandma reaches over and turns on the wrought iron floor lamp. I shield my eyes from the glare.

"What can I do for you, my poor boy? Don't bother about the rent check. I have a little savings put by. I can use that this month."

"No, no, Ma. I know you're saving that for your funeral. But could you make me some strong coffee? I had a couple of beers after talking with David. You know I can't drink, it always knocks me out. Forget what I said in there, Kim. I need to take you back to your mother's and get home. Francesca will be wondering where the hell I got to."

Just like that, he wants me to forget his performance while I am still drowning in it?

Grandma goes to the tiny stove.

"Can I warm up a little soup to sooth your stomach as well, or would you like some Social Tea biscuits? What about you, Kim?"

"No, Ma. Francesca has probably cooked, so we should go soon. Just some coffee."

"It's okay, Granny, I'm not hungry," I lie. I know Minnie will have left a plate of fried chicken in the kitchen for me.

Father sits in one of the tiny chairs by the table for two, pulls out his checkbook, writes in it, and lays the check on the table. Granny measures coffee and water into the percolator and sits down in the opposite chair, tucks the check into her purse, and waits for the coffee to perk. They look completely comfortable murmuring together, not noticing me. Father munches on the tea biscuits, my favorite treats when I am with Grandma. They don't need me. I'm not in the picture at all.

I'm deposited at Mother's dark apartment. True to her word, Minnie's pile of chicken sits on the table covered with a cloth. I put a few pieces on a plate and check every room, turning on all the lights as I go. Once convinced I'm the only person there, I sit cross-legged on my bed, without taking off my coat or shoes, and eat. Then I change into the clean nightgown Minnie has washed. I pick *White Fang* off the shelf and begin to read. For a while, I see myself with the wild husky as my friend and protector. Some part of me listens for my mother's key in the door.

When I can distract myself no longer, I wander into Mother's bedroom and open her clothes closet, inhaling the lemony scent of her perfume. I go into her bathroom, stand on the edge of the bathtub, and peer into the jumble of creams, compacts, and curlers. I lift a tissue blotted with lipstick and smear it on my mouth. I feel closer to her as I look through her things. But she is still doggedly absent. In the living room, I turn on the TV. Shouting people run across the screen shooting at one other. There are no familiar BBC children's programs. I turn it off.

I return to my favorite place, the bedroom. I picture Daddy, Franca, and Justine eating dinner together, and then Daddy draping Mackie's cage so he can tuck his head under his wing and go to sleep. Then I see Daddy sitting in his easy chair reading while Franca knits. Justine is curled up asleep in her crib, wearing her footed pajamas. Picturing this makes me want to cry. Why should I be stuck here while my mother is off somewhere enjoying herself? Why do people always assume that mothers and daughters love one another and should be together? Why are all the mothers in books, TV, and movies so kind, when mine is not? Why has God put me here, if nobody wants me? Above all, why has He made me so alone?

I start to cry loud, violent sobs. These sounds rip my chest with pain so intense that something draws apart and observes from a safe distance. I can't stop the angry, helpless howls of grief that wrack me. Tiny bubbles dance along my veins as I gasp for air. I exhale each lungful in an animal wail that dies back to sobs, only to be overtaken by a fresh scream of anguish. The pain feels inexhaustible. Finally, I don't have any more strength and lie down on the bed and imagine I am in a little rowboat being drawn by a current that begins above my head and slides down through my body. The movement is comforting, and I relax as I flow downstream, slipping around the bends until I fall asleep.

Morning comes with its gray light and silence. I lift my head off the pillow, listening, but decide not to run into Mother's bedroom to see if she is there. I lie in bed drifting, daydreaming about White Fang and pigeons. I wonder what time it is, but I have not wound the clock on the bedside table, so it has stopped. I wait. If Mother is at home sleeping, a few more minutes won't change things. I'm afraid to think she might not be there.

I notice the pigeons are drinking from puddles on the rooftop. I wonder if they have been to Central Park. I wish Mother would take me there, but she has never done things like that with me. Only Grandma and Daddy take me there. It is time to check her bed. I walk into her bedroom and feel a sharp pang when I find it empty. Energy seeps out of my legs as I look at the neat hospital corners Minnie folded yesterday. The bed has not been slept in. I slowly collapse onto the carpet.

Time spreads around me like a fog. I can't think or move. I feel forgotten and invisible. Nothing matters. It doesn't matter whether I sit on the carpet until Mother returns. It doesn't matter if I get a book and read. It doesn't matter if I live or die. It doesn't matter. The world will go on perfectly without me. Mommy won't have me slowing her down. Daddy won't be worried by David and his lawyers. Grandma won't have me on her hands all the time.

I lie down beside Mother's bed and resolve to die. I lie there for what seems a very long time until I have to pee. I get up and use Mother's bathroom. Then I go back to my bed and fall asleep.

I awaken and lie there, listening, focusing first on my right ear and then my left. Maybe if I lie here long enough, I will slowly evaporate as clouds do. I wonder if I can will myself to die. I feel pale already, like a shadow on a partly cloudy day. My stomach rumbles loudly. Swinging my legs over the bed and putting my weight on them makes me dizzy for a moment. I drift into the kitchen, where the cuckoo clock shows it is nearing nine o'clock in the morning. I go through the routine of eating cereal and milk, then return to bed and sleep.

When I awaken, sunlight has entered the room, and I can see the sky is blue. But it is too late; even if my mother did come in now, I am disappearing. I have swum too far out and can't come back. My eyes wander over the books on the shelves. Now I won't read them.

Sadness washes over me. It seems a shame to die, when outside there are children riding ponies, throwing balls to their dogs, shopping with their mothers, milking cows, singing to their baby sisters, blowing out birthday candles, riding the carousel, jumping rope, riding their bicycles, flying kites, cleaning out bird cages, painting, and reading. If I die, I will never do any of these things.

Something speaks up deep inside of me. *It is true you are stuck here, but if you are patient, if you wait long enough, one day you will grow up and be free to live the life you want.* I listen in awe, knowing I'm receiving guidance.

Suddenly I know I can't stay another second in this apartment. I have to go live with my father. Otherwise, Mother will kill me before I grow up. She wouldn't mean to, she would just forget to water me like I had forgotten to water an orange pit I'd once planted in a can. Cracked soil with nothing growing is all I found when I remembered to check on it. That would be me if I stay here.

Father loves me. Of this I am sure. He will be sad if I die. I have to make him see this is a serious situation. I jump up, strip off my nightgown and put on the clothes that I had heaped at the foot of the bed. I wash my face, pick up his card, go to the telephone and dial the newspaper. A voice answers and I ask for Justin Gilbert.

"Justin Gilbert here."

"Daddy, this is Kim. I have to come live with you right away."

"What are you talking about, sweetie, what is the matter?"

"Mommy didn't sleep here last night. She's never here. The place is always dark. It makes me so sad. I can't stand it. Please, can't I live with you?"

I hear shuffling of papers and muttered curses. "Knucklehead, these things are decided by a judge whose decision was you should live with her. You can visit us all you want, but you live with her." A shock goes through me, as I realize a judge who has never seen me has this power.

"But she's never here, she doesn't feed me. I hate it." I begin to sob during another long pause.

"Sweetie, I hate to hear you cry, but my hands are tied."

"I'm going to die. I'm alone all the time. I can't stand it another minute, Daddy."

"Jesus, I don't know what to say here. A child is always put in the custody of its mother, especially a girl. That's how it's done. Even though she has left you before."

"Aw, Daddy, can you take me?" I whine impatiently. I need an answer now.

"You know, I'm going to have to talk to a lawyer about this. Can you give me an hour or two? Can you calm down and go read or something? I promise I'll pick you up, but I need to find out what's what first. Kim?"

"All right, Daddy, as long as you promise you'll pick me up today."

"I will, sweetie, I will."

"Don't forget about me."

"I love you, you are my firstborn, never forget that."

"I love you too, Daddy."

As soon as I put down the receiver, I get my purse with its key. I can't be in the apartment one second more. The click of the closing door is satisfying. I rejoice that this is a rehearsal for the real thing when I never will return. I'm not sure where I am going, but once I am on the street, I realize I want to tell someone—Moondog—about my new life. He is standing where he was, dressed in his Viking helmet, cloak, and leather leggings, holding his spear. He stands so tall, and I am intimidated, but I think of poems and walk up to him.

"Hello, Mr. Dog, remember me?" His ravaged face is distinct in the sunlight.

"Oh yeah, the little girl who writes poetry, isn't it? And please call me Moondog."

"I wanted to tell you that you won't be seeing me anymore. I'm going to live with my daddy."

"Well, that's nice, I guess. But don't forget to keep writing poems. And come say hello whenever you're in the area. Here, have a poem as a gift." He reaches into his satchel to find a slip of paper and hands it to me.

"I'm so happy. I'm getting what I've always wanted, to live with a real family—my daddy, stepmother, and baby sister. And Mackie the Macaw."

"So you're going to live with your father's wife and child? What does your mother say about that?"

"Oh, she doesn't even know yet, but I don't think she'll care. She's never home anyway."

"Hmm. And your stepmother, she okay with this?"

My excitement dampens for a moment. "Well I don't know, but I just can't live with Mother anymore. I can't. Franca will have to understand."

"Maybe she will, maybe she will. I'll play something for you before you go." He tucks a set of bongo drums under his arm and begins beating. He raps a happy rhythm as I walk away.

"Thank you, Mr. Moondog." I skip back to the apartment building.

Daddy calls and tells me to meet him on the corner in half an hour. I pull out a small suitcase and pack the encyclopedia and nightgown. I speak into the silence, "I'm never coming back."

My father opens his apartment door and we walk in. Justine sits in her high chair with her mouth open while Franca spoons in baby food. The baby reaches out when she sees me, knocking the spoon sideways and spilling orange mush on the blue carpet.

Franca yells something and dives to the floor with a sponge. I run to help clean up, but Franca fends me off, so instead I receive a messy kiss from the baby that thrills me. Father motions for me to sit down on the couch. He puts his hat on the coffee table. Franca pauses feeding the baby, and they both turn to listen.

"Hammerhead, I need to explain the situation. I contacted a lawyer who knows some dirt on David, so I think he can convince him and your mother to let you live with us. I paid a hefty sum for this guy by the way. We don't have a lot of room here, and at some point you have got to go to school. Everything is up in the air right now. I have to get back to work, so you and Franca get to know each other better, and I'll see you this evening."

I throw my arms around him—"Daddy, I'm so happy!" — and can't stop myself from dancing around. He places his hat back on his head and leaves.

Franca asks if I am hungry and makes me a tuna sandwich. She clears space in a bureau in the bedroom for me to put my things. I play peek-a-boo with Justine, feed Mackie a piece of carrot, and so my new life begins. I don't have to imagine what they are doing now. I know. I am part of their life. I have a family and a home.

A week later, Daddy's deep voice calls me on the phone, "Knucklehead, there's been a development. Your mother and I have been talking and she wants David to speak to you."

"Why does she want David to speak to me? Are you going to be there?"

"I don't know, Kim, this is what she wants. And no, I will drop you off at the apartment so you and David can talk, but I'm not going to be part of it." The thought of going back to that apartment with David sends a ripple of fear through me.

"I don't want to. David scares me."

"He has a bad reputation, sweetie, he frightens grown people, but I'm afraid you don't have a choice. If you are to stay with me, you have got to talk with David. That's the arrangement." So I agree and we hang up.

The next day Franca braids my hair, I dress in clean clothes and go to Mother's apartment. I ring the bell. She opens the door with a cold look, pushes me toward David, and disappears into her bedroom. He is sitting on the living room couch. The drapes are drawn so everything is dark. A lit lamp silhouettes David's bulk. He motions me to sit in a chair opposite him. As I move closer, I see his thick eyebrows are drawn down into a V. I grip my pocketbook to keep myself from shaking.

"Kimberly, do you know why you're here?"

"Mother wants you to talk to me?" My voice quavers slightly.

"That's correct. It's about your wanting to live with your father. Your mother is very upset, unhappy about this."

I don't think this is true, but I can't tell David he is wrong, adults don't like that. I need to handle this carefully. Maybe I can be so meek as to be unnoticeable. I will act like Wile E. Coyote in the cartoons I've seen recently and let them steamroll over me so I look like a pancake flattened on the road. Then, while they aren't looking, I'll pop up and run away.

"But let me start at the beginning." David places his fingertips together thoughtfully. His face relaxes slightly. I do as well. "Why do you not want to live with your mother?"

"She is not here very much and when she is, the drapes are drawn, it's dark, and she's sleeping. It makes me very sad. There's no food in the refrigerator. I'm here all alone. . . ." My voice trails off. I don't understand why he is talking to me and not her. If David is the judge in this court of law, why isn't he smart enough to see what is going on? It's hard to explain what wasn't happening.

"So that's it? It's dark? You are willing to hurt your mother because she likes the drapes drawn? Think carefully about what you are saying. Do you want to cause your mother pain?" His dark eyes glitter dangerously. I clutch my purse like a shield. I can see now that he could never be a father to me. Mother might be in love with him, but she is making a bad mistake. He likes to hurt people. In his dark suit, his red silk tie, he looks civilized, but he isn't fooling me. My desperation makes me reckless.

I suck in a quick breath and my words come out in a rush. "I don't think I'm causing her pain. If she's not here to see it, how can she be upset I'm not living here?"

"You think you're clever, but I'm asking the questions." David's deep voice enunciates the next words slowly. "Do you know what a bad seed is?"

"No, sir."

"A bad seed is a child that breaks her mother's heart. That's what you are."

A shock goes through me as I take in what he is saying. He is calling me the worst name. She must really want to keep me here, or maybe she wants David to think that she is a caring parent. All I know is if I continue living with her I will die. It doesn't matter what he calls me, no law court or even God will punish me for saving my own life. I feel as if David is holding my head under water while saying, "Be a good girl and drown." I am clawing to free myself from the suffocating downward pressure. I have to have air, I have to breathe, and I have to get out of here. I take a deep breath and feel exhilaration sweep through me. I am going to speak my truth, no matter what it costs me.

"I'm sorry if this makes Mother unhappy, but I just want to live a normal life. I don't mean to be a bad seed. I can't live here by myself anymore. I'm too sad and lonely."

"All right, I wash my hands of you. There is nothing I can do to change your mind? This is your last chance."

"I'm sorry to upset anyone, but I need to live with my daddy." David nods and looks toward Mommy's bedroom door that is open several inches. Only silence comes from there. I wonder if she has also washed her hands of me. Perhaps she will never speak to me again. If so, this is the price I am willing to pay.

"Don't let the door slam you in the rear," David says, pointing to the door, and I understand the interview is over. I feel a delicious draft of freedom brushing my face. Within minutes, I am in a taxi headed toward my father's Sutton Place address.

❧

I'm in heaven the first few days, but as the weeks wear on, I hear Franca and Daddy arguing. They keep their louder fights in the bedroom, but I can hear them from my bed on the pullout couch. Once I hear my name mentioned, and I cover my ears with the pillow. The baby often cries, which gets on everyone's nerves. But I know she is teething, so I find a toy for her to bite on or dance around to distract her. Mackie's raucous screams sometimes awaken her from her nap. I go food shopping with Franca and try to help out in the kitchen, but she says it is easier for her to do it alone.

"There is not enough room for two people," she says, giving me a look. I discover the best way to keep out of Franca's hair is to read Daddy's books. They are very grownup, but I plow through *Anna Karenina* and a book with the baby's name, *Justine.*

Daddy starts taking me with him to review kid's movies. He gets bored sitting through so many films and wants my help. We develop a pattern that begins with us eating at Schrafft's Restaurant. He orders cheesecake that tastes weird, although I eat a forkful to make Daddy happy. He finishes it. Then we see the movie, and I give him my impressions on the way home. We discover, however, it is a mistake for me to see horror films. After I view *The Fly,* I have nightmares where my head is stuck on a tiny insect body screaming, "Help me!" but no one can hear. I wake everyone up at night.

I start attending Riverside School, where I meet my best friend, Ruth, from whom I'm inseparable. What more could I want? I tell Daddy about my drawings of a house in the country with a family and a dog. One evening he comes in with a box and sets it down on the floor.

"Guess what's in here?" he asks. "Some books?" I answer, going for the obvious, afraid to spook the surprise, but I hear scratching and whimpering. Daddy lifts out the tiniest, daintiest creature—fawn colored with bulging eyes and elephant ears. It is a Chihuahua. The puppy lets loose an arc of pee as Daddy lifts him up. He laughs and names him Wee Willie. I am ecstatic beyond measure and want the puppy in my arms at all times, even on my pullout bed that he promptly wets.

When Franca spots Willie, she immediately calls Daddy into the bedroom. I hear her say, "Who do you think is going to take care of this puppy while you're at work and Kim's at school? I am! I already have enough to do taking care of the baby and that macaw. Why didn't you talk to me about this beforehand?"

Daddy bats away her objections. "It's easy, all you do is put the little guy on a newspaper after he drinks—that's why I got a small dog. You don't have to walk him. If he makes a mistake you swat him with a rolled newspaper."

We all pitch in to train Willie, but Franca is right about his care falling to her. Willie is incorrigible, however, and leaves puddles on the living room carpet that the baby crawls through. Franca's tirades about the dog, accompanied by Mackie's shrieks, Justine's cries, and Willie's yapping, become a nightly concert. We are all squeezed into a one-bedroom apartment, and the cacophony ricochets off the walls. Our home may have an exclusive Sutton Place address, but we are more like the old woman who lived in a shoe. Eventually, Willie is given to Grandma Blanche, who adores him and murmurs baby talk in his ear in a way she never did with me.

Chapter 6

A NORMAL FAMILY

For everything flowers, from within, of self-blessing:
Though sometimes it is necessary
To reteach a thing its loveliness.
—GALWAY KINNELL

As my breasts and hips swell, boys start brushing against me in the halls of the public junior high of Huntington, Long Island, where we live. Although before I'd spent hours hiding in the public library reading and writing papers, now any thought of schoolwork is out the window. My new friend, Susan, is a farmer's daughter from whom I carefully withhold my multisyllabic words and bookishness. I gain maternal advice about menstrual cramps and tampons through her mother. She drives us to the store where Susan and I buy bras, garter belts, stockings, and Tangee natural lipstick.

When I get home to our suburban split-level house, I strap the dangly belt around my belly. There seem too many straps, and I can't figure out how to slide the filmy nylons on my legs, let alone hook them up. Desperate and embarrassed, I call Franca to show me. She crowds into the powder room while she blows cigarette smoke in my face.

"What a half-assed mess you make of everything!" she scolds. Her body still has a lithe dancer's physique. I feel fat and humiliated standing next to her, my round belly dangling with garters. With irritation, she demonstrates the maneuver of folding stockings over your fingers, rolling them over your toe, up your legs, and snapping those dangling garters on the tops. When I try it, something is wrong. The hair on my legs sticks through the stockings. Franca becomes angry when I point this out.

"Your mother should be showing you these things." She grabs a razor out of the cupboard, mimes the sweeping motions, and stalks out. I don't know to soap my legs first, so when I shave, bloody ribbons run down. I staunch the blood with bits of toilet paper that are visible when I finally slide on the stockings. I'm never going to get to school on time.

I hide my legs during morning classes, but I don't have to worry, because nobody notices me, a nonentity without any clique. At lunch break, I dash to the girls' bathroom, roll down the stockings, peel off little wads of bloody paper, and flush them down the toilet. Susan and I meet here to primp before we dance to 45 rpm records on the school patio. She shoves open the door, and we quickly tease our hair, decorate it with little bows, sweep on mascara, and finish with a dab of lipstick. We emerge onto the patio as if it were a ballroom. Holding hands, we step together, step back, swinging our hips gracefully as the boys watch. We dance to "He's a Rebel":

> *But just because he doesn't do what everybody else does*
> *That's no reason why I can't give him all my love*
>
> *He's always good to me, always treats me tenderly*
> *'Cause he's not a rebel, oh, no, no, no*
> *He's not a rebel, oh, no, no, no, to me*

At the end of recess, a blond boy, whose hair is slicked back in a duck's ass, crowds me against a wall. "What's your name? I really like the way you move. You're very pretty." He reaches forward and smoothes a stray lock of my hair. I can feel his breath on my face and notice his impossibly curly eyelashes. My heart dances wildly. He is older than I am and looks dangerous in his black leather jacket. This only makes him more exciting.

He asks if I want to meet after school and ride on his motorcycle. I tell him my name and fling out "Yes!" as I run to class. Apparently, every girl in school, who never before knew I existed, has witnessed our encounter. In class and the hallway they slide me notes naming him as Bill Lutz, leader of the JDs or Juvenile Delinquents. He's seventeen and was held back a year in school. I'd better stay away from him, or my reputation is going straight to hell.

I meet him in a side street where he revs up a good-sized motorcycle. Boys with duck's ass haircuts smoking cigarettes and girls with teased hair wearing white go-go boots cluster around him. They scatter when he motions me up behind him. He draws my arms close around him, and I smell his salty sweat. Being this close, I have no choice but to lay my head against his warm back. I have never been this close to a male other than my father. He drives away to a tree-lined street, parks the motorcycle, and we get off. I stand there as if my legs have grown roots. He puts his fingers on the nape of my neck and draws me close so we are facing each other. He is taller than I am.

"I can tell you're really smart, not like those other jerks I hang around with. I been watching you. What would you say if I kiss you?" I stand on tiptoe. His face comes toward mine until I'm seeing double. I close my eyes and feel his lips on mine, dry and smooth, with a wet space in between. They press hard for a long moment and are gone. My lips and breasts tingle, and I can't breathe. The world around me sings, *First kiss! This is your first kiss!*

"See, that wasn't so bad, was it? What do you say to bein' my girlfriend? Want a cigarette?" He pulls out a pack of Camels and politely taps one out for me.

This breaks the spell. I've always hated the smell of cigarettes. Also, this guy, although incredibly cute, is not very bright. But I've received my first kiss, and I hold that close like a flower.

I tell Bill, "I'd better go back now, my mother is expecting me home," which is a complete lie, since Franca and I avoid each other. He drives me around to where his gang waits, the girls giving me poisonous looks.

"I'll think about being your girlfriend, B Full of Lust," I say making a play on his name, Bill Lutz. He looks at me blankly. I float off to catch the last school bus home. I whip out my five-year diary and fill page after page about the kiss.

"Franca, will you drive me to Bible Study?" I slam my books down on the dining room table. A month earlier, I'd decided to give God a chance to clear up the mess He had made of my life. An angry stepmother, an absent mother, and ostracism at school was just too much for a girl to deal with. I started attending Congregational Church classes with the goal of being baptized. The river baptism I'd witnessed as a child in Kentucky gave me hope that a major transformation would occur, as it had so long ago to the other congregants.

"Oh all *right*," Franca fumes, "but I'm *not* your private limo service. Justine, get in the car while I drop your sister off." My six-year-old sister fiddles with the blonde hair of her look-alike doll as she sits in the back seat.

"Why do you have to go to church, Kim?" Justine asks.

I think about this for a moment. "Because I want to learn how to be good."

"You are good, Kim." I just shake my head. Franca drops me at the back of the church and disappears. I slide into a chair late. At fourteen, I'm the oldest kid in class, but I'm desperate. The minister has dark, liquid eyes like Perry Mason on my favorite TV show. As his earnest voice drones on, I notice I've scribbled Bill Lutz's name in the margins surrounded with flowers and curlicues. I wonder if it's okay to pile onto my bargain with God that I acquire a boyfriend.

The minister carefully goes over the Ten Commandments, but when we come to "Honor thy Father and Mother," I balk. I raise my hand, and he nods.

"What if she doesn't honor me? I mean, if she's sarcastic and mean to me all the time. I'm talking about my stepmother here."

"She feeds and clothes you. You sleep under her roof. You owe her civility for that." But I'm not happy with that answer. Franca drives me home, and neither of us says a word.

I meet with Bill the next afternoon. His gang is always slouching around him, looking bored and smoking. I notice how sleazy the girls look with their ratted hair and black eye makeup. This doesn't stop me from kissing Bill right in front of them. Bill drapes his arm across my shoulders and brushes his hand across my breast. Pleasure thrills up and down my body, but I move away.

"What's the matta? Don't you wanna be my girlfriend?" asks Bill. I shake my head to give myself time to settle down.

One of the boys says, "C'mon Bill, who cares about her? What are we doin' tonight?"

Casually, the gang groups around him, and I overhear them making plans to steal some beer from a convenience store. So I tell him, "Bye" and go off to my school bus.

That Sunday, I'm to be baptized. Daddy and Franca protest about getting dressed in workday clothes on their one leisurely morning.

"What has gotten into you?" Daddy teases. "Have you been bitten by the religion bug? Maybe you should study with a Zen master who hits you over the head with a stick!"

I don't let him dissuade me. We sit through the long service while Daddy looks bored, and Franca nods into a doze. When everyone is gone, the dark-haired minister beckons us over. He wears a suit with a black shawl over it. I kneel in front of him while Daddy and Franca stand to one side. The minister's warm voice pours over me. At first I keep my eyes closed, waiting for something to happen. When his fingers drip water on my forehead, my eyes pop open. He is praying so hard that sweat beads his forehead. I glance at Daddy and Franca, who look embarrassed.

"I congratulate you on having a fine daughter." He says at the end, shaking their hands. But I am *not* her daughter. During the next few days, I watch Franca for signs she has started liking me. When this doesn't happen, I give up on God and throw myself into my flirtation.

Each day Bill and I kiss for longer, and his insistence that I be his girlfriend gets stronger. I hold him off. One day he presents me with a hand-written poem on lined paper about how mysterious and removed I am. This is an adorable gesture from a guy who can barely write. I am very tempted to give in, skirting the edge of the pit, looking but not ready to jump.

This new life of flirting with boys demands pretty clothes. I want to go shopping and need Franca's help. She is resentful of having to drive me and shell out hard-earned dollars on frivolous party dresses. We wrangle bitterly at every shopping expedition. I hear her complaining to Daddy at night. He says, "Let the kid have her clothes. You're only young once." But Franca's mouth is set in a thin line against me.

I get back at her by not hearing anything she asks. She doesn't exist for me. I come and go directly to my room. If she asks me to take out the garbage, I forget. If she yells dinner is ready, I don't hear. I sneak down in the middle of the night and bring food back to my room where the dishes pile up. I don't clean my room, or the parrot's cage that is my job. Franca's fury takes the form of slammed drawers with occasional shrieks in my direction as I vanish up the stairs.

Daddy sits me down at the dining table after another missed dinner and says, "Your sins are those of omission not commission." This doesn't help at all.

I begin visiting my mother in New York. No mention is made of my leaving her dark apartment four years earlier. She seems to want to make up with me. We go shopping at Bonwit Teller and Saks Fifth Avenue. She helps me pick out a velour, wrap-around skirt, matching Nehru jacket, and a low-cut, pink sweater. I feel beautiful and sexy in it, and best of all, my mother doesn't mind.

Mother and I travel by limousine to a doctor's office in which I am fitted with something I have never heard about before: contact lenses. I quickly get used to sticking the hard contacts directly on my eyeballs when I realize how much better I look without glasses. They flick out of my eyes when I look sideways, so at almost every party there is a moment when I yell, "Don't move, I've lost my contact!" and everyone drops to their hands and knees and gingerly crawls around until someone spies the tiny disk.

David Merrick takes us out for Sunday brunch at the Plaza Hotel. I love the Palm Court with its stained glass ceiling, columns, and graceful greenery. I love the serene deference accorded us by the dignified waiters. I love the elegant older women who sip tea and eat scones with children wearing party dresses. While I am there, I can believe that David, Mother, and I are a family. The "bad seed" scene is never mentioned. It's as if it never happened.

I experience David mostly through opening nights of his many productions. My mother gets dolled up in a pink satin suit with rhinestone buttons and a pillbox hat, and we troop down to the theater with Aunt Clara and Barbara Taylor. Clara has been an *au pair* in France and now lives in New York, reinvented as glamorous Claire. Barbara is on her way to becoming a world-famous novelist, Barbara Taylor Bradford.

My favorite musical is *Oliver!* It's about little Oliver Twist who grows up in an orphanage, has the temerity to ask for more food, is taken in by Fagin and his raffish gang of thieves, and eventually finds a loving home. I can belt out Lionel Bart's lyrics to "Food, Glorious Food" and imagine the streets of New York ringing as the flower vendors, merchants, and urchins sing "Who Will Buy This Wonderful Morning?"

But the words to "Where is Love?" become engraved on my heart.

Where is love?
Does it fall from skies above?
Is it underneath the willow tree
That I've been dreaming of?

We emerge from the theater caught up in the joy of the production. But David doesn't sit with us—I glimpse him in his black suit and black mustache, looking like an old-time villain, pacing the lobby and listening for audience reaction. He seems anxious. *How can such a grim man create such enchantment?* If things go well, later he might take us out to eat. He never attends the cast party.

One night, my father picks me up at my mother's apartment to take me back to Huntington. I am surprised when Mother invites him up. He sits on the couch drinking club soda while she drinks something stronger. She wears a blue lacy peignoir, and I can see her oval nipples through the shimmering fabric. Daddy doesn't seem to notice. They discuss child-rearing practices, on which suddenly my mother is an expert. She says, "If a child is whining, toss a glass of water in her face." He nods as if this is right out of Dr. Spock's *Baby and Child Care*.

Later, I overhear Daddy telling Franca about Mother's ideas. Franca explodes: "Why don't you remarry her, if she knows so much?" She runs from the room, slamming the door.

Daddy is bewildered. "I was only trying to help."

One day I hang out too late with Bill and his gang and miss the last school bus. I have to call Franca from the pay phone to drive me home. Bill and I are kissing when she arrives, and my lips feel bruised. I worry she has seen us. When I get in the car, her blonde hair sticks out at odd angles, and her hands are clenching and unclenching the steering wheel. She doesn't say anything, and neither do I. We ride along in tense silence.

Suddenly she shrieks, "When I was your age, I was already dancing and supporting my mother, sending my paycheck back to her while I was on tour! You and your clothes and your fat ass! What are you doing with that disgusting gang?"

Suddenly, there is a squeal of tires. Franca's arms make rapid turns on the wheel, and a dirt embankment hurtles toward us. The car smashes into it with a loud metallic crunch. Our heads whip forward and back. Her face snaps against the steering wheel, mine against the dashboard. Then all is quiet, just a ticking as the car settles.

Franca turns the key in the ignition. Thankfully, the engine starts up as if nothing happened. She backs up with a few roars of the accelerator, and we swerve down the road. The thunderous clamor of the motor is accompanied by a scraping noise.

We walk into the house in silence, and I go to my room. I sit on my bed and touch my sore forehead and cheeks. When I look at my hands, they are smeared with blood. *What do you do after a car crash?* My stepmother marches in and stands in front of me breathing hard. *This is odd, she never comes into my room.* Her teeth look jagged, and one side of her glasses is shattered. *Will she ask me if I'm hurt? I wish she'd tell me what to do.*

"You're destroying my marriage, you bitch!" she shrieks.

I look at her with incomprehension.

"You know what I'm talking about. You go to Jeanne's, he spends time with her. If he leaves me for her, it's all your fault. You are a home-wrecker. You are destroying our marriage!" She rants endlessly.

I gasp for breath. I feel like I did when a crazy boy at school punched me in my stomach. I can't get enough air; bubbles are dancing along my arms. Then some part of me moves to the side and watches her mouth moving. Sunlight is streaming through the window on this April afternoon. *I'd better listen to what she's saying; make sense of it. Maybe she was trying to kill me with that car crash. I've got to get out of here, got to get help.*

Finally Franca stands silent as if she has no more words left. Then she leaves. I stumble into the bathroom and peek through half-closed eyes in the mirror. My right cheek is oozing blood, both eyes are puffing out, and my nose is a little off-kilter. I go to the phone and dial my mother's number.

Surprisingly, she answers after a few rings with her breathy, "Hallow?"

"Come and get me, Mommy, there's been an accident."

I throw a few things into a bag, including Grandma's quilt, and lie on my bed as blood oozes onto my blouse. My face and head ache. I can't think of what to do.

After several hours, a large black limousine pulls into the driveway at Cove Road. The vehicle looks ominous against the tidy lawns of our suburban neighborhood. My father drives in behind it, having endured the long commute from the city. He knows nothing about our car crash.

He sees me emerging from the house, bag in hand. "What's going on, Knucklehead?"

"I'm moving back with my mother," I mumble. I hadn't thought of facing him when I made my call.

"Don't leave." When he sees me unwavering, he says, "Don't forget, *you* are leaving me. This time, *you* are leaving me."

The weight of his blame falls on me, and I accept it. I stiffly walk past my six-year-old sister, Justine, peeking around the front door.

I climb into the protective armor of the limousine, see that David is with my mother, and drive away from Huntington forever. Mother looks at my bruised, swollen eyes and bleeding face and insists I be driven to a doctor. He meets us in his quiet office, dressed in a shirt and pants—by this time it is night—sews up the cut, and pushes a bone in my nose back in place.

"The facial bruising will take time to heal," he says. The same could be said for my psyche.

⸙

Overnight, my father, stepmother, and sister vanish, and I'm living alone in a dreary furnished apartment beneath my mother's in midtown Manhattan. All I do is sleep, but I have dreams that a gleaming knife has killed my family, and I'm in solitary confinement. Mother won't let me see or speak with my father. I write letters saying how much I miss his deep voice and Justine's blonde cuteness, but he seldom replies. *Do you forgive me for leaving you?* That's what I want to ask, but never do. President Kennedy is shot, and as the national tragedy unfolds on grainy black-and-white television, I weep inconsolably for my and our country's shattered hopes.

Meanwhile, Mother is placed in hospital for bed rest for an at-risk pregnancy—a little freeloader, she calls it—where her friends sneak her bottles in brown bags. She delivers a premature girl, and then my mother, tiny Cecelia, formidable Nanny Weeks, I, and, presumably, David Merrick all move into a luxurious high-rise apartment with a doorman on the corner of 79th and Madison. Everyone has spacious bedrooms with airy views, except that I have been relegated to the tiny maid's room. Mother ignores me with icy disdain. Now that she has won her battle to become Mrs. David Merrick, I'm the most expendable part of the household.

One day she calls me into the living room. "It's your father," she says, and holds the phone far away from her as if it were the rotting carcass of a dead animal. I take it and turn my back toward her, shielding our conversation. I haven't spoken with him for a year.

Daddy's words spill out rapidly, as if he is fearful mother will cut him off. "I've been trying to reach you, but neither your school nor your mother would let me speak to you. I think you may have heard about the strike my paper, the *New York Daily Mirror*, has been on for the last few months? Well, it's folding, going out of business, kaput. Honey, I've lost my job, and the whole news business is going down the toilet. Or over to TV—which is worse. Anyway, the only job I can find is with Paramount Pictures in London. So we are all moving there, including your grandmother. So now you will be over here in New York, while I'm over there in England. Isn't that crazy? Such is life."

My heart plummets down a dark canyon. I can't think of anything to say except, "Daddy, I will miss you so much." God is playing a cruel joke on me, that is clear. I tuck this latest loss deep inside for a time when I can tend to it.

❧

"Lili, c'mon, tell me!" I race up the wide, white steps of the Metropolitan Museum of Art, around clumps of school kids and seated tourists studying maps. Pausing by the massive Greek columns at the entryway to let the guard search my book bag, I see her dash through the vaulted central hall and up the stairs. I follow at a more sedate pace, glancing into the large galleries hung with glorious paintings where I often sketch, tiptoe meekly past the grouchy guard with pocked skin who had once threatened to evict us for inappropriate giggling, and finally burst into the smoking room, laughing and flinging myself beside her on a Naugahyde-covered couch.

"Are you going to tell me, or what?" But she shakes her head, drawing out the moment, pulls up her navy knee socks, crosses her legs, and smoothes her school uniform skirt over her Twiggy-slender hips. She taps a Camel out of its package, lights it, and takes a long drag. Normally I hate smoking, but on Lili it looks elegant and cool.

Lili is my best friend at the private girls' school we attend. Lili lives with her recently divorced, depressed mother and avoids going home, as do I—so we make Manhattan our playground, and the Met is one of our favorite haunts.

"All right, I'll tell you, but don't be upset." Lili purses her rosebud mouth and blows a smoke ring. "I've lost my virginity!" Her green-flecked orange eyes gaze at me, gauging my reaction.

I'm stunned into silence. I haven't dated or even been interested in boys since junior high in Huntington. Actually, I'm relieved to wear a uniform and not compete for boys' attention.

"I didn't know you had a boyfriend. It's not like males are climbing out of the oak paneling at Miss Hewitt's Classes for Young Ladies. How on earth did you meet him?"

"He's a friend of my brother's. His name is Ross, he goes to Temple University, he's Jewish and circumcised. His penis stays cleaner that way."

I blink at her stupidly—university, circumcised, penis?— I'm scrambling to keep up.

"Don't look at me like a lost puppy. We're probably going to college next year, and it's really important to lose your virginity before college, or else you're stuck with it."

"Well, that would be a national tragedy," I say slowly. "Does Ross have a friend?"

"Atta girl. I'm sure he does. So where should we go on our double date?"

"On the double-decker bus, obviously—up Fifth Avenue to the Cloisters. But most important, what are we going to wear? We look like kids in these uniforms."

"Let's check out the gorgeous outfits in the thrift shops on Third Avenue." With Lili's lead once more firmly established, we companionably stride out.

"Kim meet Larry. Larry, Kim. This is Ross. 'Nuff said." We follow Lili's narrow hips up the stairs to the top of the red double-decker bus, and they sit in the back where she and her boyfriend light up.

Larry and I eye each other nervously and slide into seats in the front. He's a nice-looking Jewish boy with curly brown hair, shy chocolate eyes, and a sweet smile. He is still in high school.

"My mother died when I was little, so I was partially raised by my older sister. When she married the previous summer, I fainted at the wedding. I have Freudian issues," he jokes.

I never know what to say in exchanges like this, so I cast about for the most normal thing in my life I can share. "I have a two-year-old baby sister we nicknamed Little Tear. . . ."

I relax a little as the bus lumbers up Fifth Avenue past Central Park, Harlem, Washington Heights, Grant's Tomb, and the rolling Hudson River. This is a favorite trip that I've made many times with Lili. I'm dressed in a short velvet skirt and a wine-red cloak—clothes a medieval lady might wear. They looked great in the thrift store, but now I worry what Larry must think.

We enter the peaceful Cloisters through heavy wooden doors, echoing vaulted passageways and quiet monastic gardens with plashing fountains. I love it here and head for The Unicorn Tapestries while Lili and Ross hang back, necking. I spread my arms before the seven enormous hangings that depict, in elaborate detail, the hunt by a medieval court for a unicorn that succumbs to the charms of a virgin. He is lanced by spears and bitten by dogs, but in the final tapestry is shown alive and happy, chained to a pomegranate tree.

"What doest thou think of this beauteous work?" I ask, speaking in tones sweet enough to induce a unicorn to surrender to me. I look at Lili because we have always spoken in old English when we are at the Cloisters.

"Thou art being silly, drop it for now." Lili shrugs her shoulders while the boys exchange looks as if we were from another planet. She laughs. "It's only silly gibberish we used to play." She leads Ross to an antique bench in a shadowy corner and plasters her lips to his.

Larry looks at me uncertainly, so we wander outside into the herb gardens where I pinch fragrant lavender from the bushes while we listen to the fountains. But I can't pretend to be a medieval nun safe inside a shared fantasy anymore. That is shattered and gone.

We have a second double date wandering into Greenwich Village, through the marble arch in Washington Square, around the large fountain where Lili and I like to sing and play our guitars, and finally settle into a café. Lili and Ross sit at a separate table away from Larry and me. They watch us while whispering and giggling.

"You'd think we were their pet hamsters, for goodness sakes," I say, irritably rolling a pellet of paper napkin and pitching it at Lili.

"You're being childish," she mouths to me. I know I am, but I can't help the feelings of anger and loss that are rolling through me.

"Ross is a good friend," Larry says loyally, and I like him for it, although I'm not feeling that way about Lili. "Look, my sister and her husband are going away in a couple of weekends, and I have keys to their apartment. Lili and Ross are going to spend the night. You want to come?"

"Okay," I whisper, inhaling an unsteady breath. I don't really feel ready, but this is my opportunity. Larry's hand reaches out and covers my own.

We take the subway to Morningside Heights, making awkward conversation. I'm perspiring with anxiety. The apartment is decorated in gold and white with every pillow in place. After we stand for a few minutes in the immaculate kitchen sipping beers while Larry wipes away the condensation rings, we head directly to the bedrooms. Lili and Ross appropriate the sister's bedroom, while Larry and I go into the guest room where he frequently stays.

Larry and I kiss for a while until I can't stand the suspense and say, "Let's just do it." We take off our clothes and get into bed. I glimpse an erect penis for the first time. I could never figure out how a boy's organ, seen beneath a Speedo swimsuit, was straight up while it hung limply in baggy shorts. When I slide between the sheets, Larry is so close to me that I smell his warm breath. I open my legs and feel him pushing into me. I'm surprised by the sharp pain, his thrusting, moaning, and collapse against me. We check for blood on the sheets and find stains, so we know the deed is done.

"How do you feel?" Larry asks, trying to slide his arm around me but poking me in the eye instead. Frankly, I'm disappointed. After all the sexy novels, romantic songs, and movies, this is a huge letdown. I thought once I had sex, I'd understand the stupid way men behaved around women, particularly my mother. I feel duped by adults as usual. But I can't say this.

"I've never seen a naked man before except statues of Michelangelo's David. You're smaller than I expected." Larry makes a sound and clutches his groin. Maybe I haven't said the right thing and try again.

"You're only small in comparison to a huge statue, you understand." But Larry is getting dressed. We pull off the sheets and re-make the bed. I don't see much more of him after that.

Lili seems to have crossed over to another world and left me behind. Graduation is coming toward me with the momentum of a speeding train. Everything is changing so fast.

We have a beautiful graduation ceremony at Hewitt's, where we all wear white dresses. David and Mother both attend, and the event is reported in *The New York Times*. On the surface, all looks glamorous, but inside I'm a roiling sea of uncertainty. Where am I going to college? And where is David?—for after graduation, he disappears.

Mother starts giving parties, and Frank shows up, a fool for my mother, like all men. Although he has acne-scarred cheeks and bottle-bottom glasses, I like Frank a lot. But I can't see what attracts him to my mother. I have the urge to clap him on the

shoulder as he lights her cigarettes and pays court and say, "Sure she has those azure eyes, large breasts, and tells funny jokes, but get a hold of yourself, you're a lawyer and supposed to see what's in front of you. This woman is a falling-down drunk, and her life is a complicated mess with two children from two marriages and an angry, powerful husband." Were Mother and David still together? I couldn't tell, but he wasn't around anymore, that was for sure. I sense the inevitable downward slide as our roller coaster trajectory gathers momentum.

There isn't enough money coming in. Any pretense of paying me an allowance has stopped. George, the cook, has long since vanished. No more lamb chops or Sarah Lee cake topped with raspberries and whipped cream left in the kitchen. Bouquets of yellow spider mums no longer grace the dining table. Nobody eats together anyway. Nanny Weeks makes something for herself and Cecelia, and they dine in the nursery. Mother doesn't touch food anymore. She has completely stopped dressing and stays in her bedroom, although she puts on a dress when Frank comes. He is our one hope. He is a fool stepping in where angels fear to tread. Then Frank vanishes. No need to guess what happened. Mother, with her talent for self-destruction, scared him away—lucky man to be cut loose from this ship of fools.

Finally, David's secretary calls and says I will attend Brandeis University, where David endows a scholarship. I'm desperate to escape. Wanting to borrow Mother's Russian lynx coat or coveted beaded moccasins, I sneak into her bedroom and open the folding mirrored closet doors. Her long shoe bags are reflected in multiple mirrors. Six bottles of Absolut vodka nestle among high heel shoes that she never wears anymore. My eyes fix on those clear bottles. Here is proof of my mother's obsession. Here is the smoking gun that explains her dearth of maternal feeling.

In all my growing up, no one had used the word "alcoholic" about my mother—the word was only for winos lying in the gutter in the Bowery. No one even admitted she drank to excess, perhaps because all her friends did. They said she needed rest or she needed a hair of the dog. This hidden stash makes it perfectly clear, as clear as the vodka: her rages, her unpredictable behavior, her inability to eat, and most of all, why she can't love me.

She pads into the bedroom on bare feet in the stained peignoir that is all she wears these days. I point to the bottles. "Why do you need these?"

"You leave those alone!" she screams and reaches forward to slap my face. She has done this before, but this time I'm ready and grab her fragile wrist.

"Don't you dare do that!" I bellow back. We glare at each other, breathing heavily like combative bulls, eager to strike the next blow.

"Get out," she moans, collapsing on her bed. "You came from my body and will do as I say, get out."

I stand trembling, energy coursing through my body. Evidently, I'm the victor—this time.

Chapter 7

NO DIRECTION HOME

And the time came when the risk to remain tight in a bud
Was more painful than the risk it took to blossom.
—ANAIS NIN

"Daddy! Daddy!" I yell in excitement as I see his tall, stoop-shouldered frame in the welcoming crowd of London's Heathrow Airport. Earlier in the summer, Mother finally had given me permission to visit my father. He had to pay for the ticket, of course. I'd had four years of growing up since I had last seen him.

"Hammerhead," his familiar voice rumbles as he draws me in for a hug. "Although perhaps you're too grownup for that now." I see his shoulders are more rounded, his stomach broader, and his gait shambling. He wheezes as he carries my suitcase, and his new, white beard flakes dandruff onto his dark suit. A polished old Rolls Royce with a driver named Wheatley is waiting for us at the curb. He has a neat mustache, wears a crisply ironed uniform, and has impeccable bearing. Instead of bolstering my father's image, as I suspect he is supposed to do, Wheatley makes Father look bad in comparison.

At their apartment, Franca's blonde hair is neatly coiffed and her eyebrows perfectly penciled as she leans in to give me an air kiss. "How are you, dear? I'm working at the Royal Humane Society, and I love it. How could anyone be mean to animals? Although we couldn't bring Willie the Chihuahua with us—we gave him to a neighbor back in New York." She keeps up a clipped pace around the apartment as she prepares dinner and seems determinedly cheerful. I watch her in puzzlement. I haven't seen her since the day of our car crash and have been anxious about a confrontation. Now I realize the subject isn't going to be broached.

"Justine, how old are you now? You're so tall!" I say in amazement at seeing my little sister's long legs and longer blonde hair.

"Ten—isn't that wizard?" She speaks with a British accent and has left the American child I knew far behind. Trying to keep up our relationship, I had sewn a doll and sent it to her. Now I realize she is too old for such playthings.

"And Grandma, how is she?" I inquire of my father as he lounges, reading a newspaper in a wingback chair—it seems that Franca does all the housework as well as maintaining a job.

"She's in a nursing home; I really can't stand to visit her." He winces. *Her greatest fear of being warehoused has come to pass*, I think sadly. Over the dinner table, all Daddy talks about is how much he misses the *New York Daily Mirror*. The car crash and my painful departure to my mother's aren't mentioned. I want to scream, "Daddy do you miss *me* and forgive *me* for leaving you?" But words freeze in my throat.

I decide to visit Lady Eden's school and take the train down to Lyndhurst as I had done so many times as a child. Clampy herself picks me up at the station, because it's the holidays, and the school is on skeleton crew. She is much as I remember her, the same raw-boned face with her hair cut straight at the jaw line—

except her hair is completely gray, and she continually rubs the base of her throat so that the skin is speckled red. I remember her surreptitious cigarette breaks. But she has the same steady eyes and the same firm stance.

"Aren't you a young lady now? It must be seven years since you were here," she says in her smoker's voice as we shake hands. I tug down my Mary Quant miniskirt and wish I were wearing a uniform again. As we drive through the high, wrought iron gates, memories hit me with an almost physical force.

"I sat by these gates for hours one day wanting to run back to my mother—until I realized she wouldn't be happy to see me, and I was better off where I was! Being here was lovely, the best place for me, really."

"You were so young—only six was it? We don't take them quite so small anymore. Around age ten is the limit now."

The generous brick mansion comes into view. The wide lawns surrounded by rhododendrons and flanked by tall cedars bring back visions of myself making daisy chains with Blanca.

"I'm putting you in sick bay—it's a smaller room and has just two beds." Clampy ushers me in, and I open the latch on a mullioned window and look at the soft sky with misty light that seems to cocoon me.

"I was so often stuck in here with colds. I hated the wobbly gray mush they brought in on a tray." I shudder. "Do you remember when the whole school came down with German measles, and you hung giant yellow onions on our beds to combat it?"

"We were pretty desperate to turn to an old wives' treatment," Clampy chuckles ruefully.

"But, you know, I had an experience one night of moonlight flooding the room, and I thought I saw Mother Mary reaching out to comfort me."

"I'm not surprised; you always were a lively member of scripture class."

"I really did love it here, although I longed for a mother—not my mother particularly—just a mother who smelled like baking bread and knew when I was cold before I did. Maybe those mothers don't exist except in my imagination. Or maybe if the Edens had adopted me . . . did you know they wanted to?"

"Yes, of course. That's why Sir Timothy asked to paint you—to know you better."

"Sitting still for all those hours was hard. Do you still have the painting? I'd love to see it."

Clampy shows me to the drawing room where she had read *Jane Eyre* and *The Hobbit* to us in front of a peat fire. Students' portraits line the paneled walls. There I am with my hopeful blue eyes and long brown braids.

"This is proof that I really was here. Although now I feel, speak, and act like an American; no part of me is English anymore. . ." I sigh dejectedly. I don't say what I'm thinking—the Edens hadn't adopted me, and I must face the future for which I feel so ill prepared. All I know is that I don't want to be like my mother—and that isn't nearly enough to go on.

"I don't know who I am," I wail to my father when I'm back in London.

"You're Kimberly is who," he answers firmly, but that is no help at all.

❧

Wrapped in Grandma Gibson's worn quilt, I'm lying on my bed in a white cinderblock dorm room in Brandeis University, alone. Pulling the faded colors over my head, I try to block out the lively commotion in the hall created by girls and parents carrying lamps, posters, and rugs to decorate rooms. It's isolation-cell-quiet in here and reeks of paint. I'd never heard of Brandeis University until a few months ago. Some of the angular modern buildings aren't even finished, it's so new. No trees soften the bare quadrangles or cement walks, and already a chilly north wind is sweeping through the window. I'm lying here because David endows the school with a scholarship. He does this because he is Jewish, and so, evidently, is Brandeis. The news that David has a religious affiliation is a big surprise, and I wonder where he is, since he has disappeared from home. Every day of my high school years, I burned for emancipation from my mother and the painful baggage of my childhood. Now I'm in this strange place, cramped in a fetal ball, facing the unknown alone.

The door opens, and a girl with chopped-up hair trudges in carrying a suitcase. She drops it and sits heavily on the other bed.

"Oh, I'm so relieved to see you," I say, uncurling slowly and sitting up. "You must be my new roommate. I don't know anyone here, do you?"

She just stares at her trembling hands and says nothing. The silence lengthens.

"I—is everything all right?"

Finally her gray eyes glance at me, and I see they are frozen with fear. She bolts from the room before I can say anything else.

"Wow, where's she going so fast?" a voice says from the doorway. The wild curls and thick frame of a familiar looking boy emerge.

"I heard through the grape vine you were coming here. How's the rich, spoiled daughter of David Merrick?"

"Josh Mostel, is that you?" I scream in delight. His father is the famed comedian, Zero Mostel. When we met back in New York, we shared an immediate empathy for the weird assumptions people make if you have a famous parent. Josh encloses me a big bear hug. He can't know how good it feels to have his arms around me. Tears wet my eyes.

"I wouldn't know about rich, since as of this moment I have about one dollar in my pocket. Spoiled . . . well, maybe. I don't have a clue how to operate the coin laundry. I don't know how to type my school papers, so I'll probably flunk out. What are you doing here?"

"I am—big drum roll, please—a theater arts major. I've a leading role in an upcoming play. You have to see it and tell me how wonderful I am." He grins at me impishly.

"I feel so out of place. Summer on a kibbutz in Israel and the awful things going on in Vietnam is all I hear people talk about. I didn't even know they had theater arts." I want to cry with relief that I've found someone who speaks a familiar language.

"Honey, every male I know is hoping the war will be over by the time he graduates." He scratches his curls, tugs his T-shirt over his belly, and makes a shy face. "Wouldja wanna come over to my place and meet some of my friends?"

"Would I ever! Honey—I'm glue."

Josh takes me to his off-campus apartment that he shares with two handsome, leading-role-type men who are hanging out with some equally gorgeous girls. One has the straight black hair and curving cheekbones of a Cher. She wears a bright print frock that stops an inch below her crotch. Her eyes give me a cool appraising glance before dismissing me as no competitive threat. Then Josh introduces me as David Merrick's daughter. I don't correct him when they crowd around me.

"So when's your dad coming up, and can you introduce me?" inquires the Cher lookalike.

"Me, too," adds a blonde. "I'm wearing an angora sweater that lifts my role as Curley's wife in *Of Mice and Men* into sheer genius. When he sees that—instant stardom."

I'm tongue-tied trying to say something about David, who I know hates actors.

"The Abominable Showman will appear when he sees fit." I shrug, hoping to appear casual and mysterious. It seems to be enough. Pushing aside old pizza crusts and empty beer bottles, someone brings out a baggie of marijuana, rolls a joint, and passes it around. I've never smoked it before, although I've wanted to, because I've read how it expands and relaxes your mind. But the smoke burns my eyes, and I fumble the joint as it's passed to me. When I manage to inhale, I cough furiously against the acrid taste. Embarrassed, I'm aware that everyone is waiting their turn, and I'm holding them up. Finally someone shows me how to inhale and hold it in. I take a short puff and like how the muscle tension in my shoulders melts away. A few puffs later, I find myself leaning back against someone's warm chest.

"Who are you?" I ask dreamily, and Michael with hazel eyes and dirty blond hair introduces himself. Afterwards, we all eat dinner at the cafeteria and hang out at Cholmondeley's coffee house listening to Richie Havens. Michael asks me if I want to come back to his place. I don't want to return to my lonely cell of a dorm room, and I don't want to play the seduction game with men, teasing and refusing them, like Mother. So I simply say, "Okay."

The pot has worn off, leaving me with a headache, and I don't want to be in his room with clothes and plates of food piled all over it. But I don't know how to say this, so I take off my clothes and curl next to him. Really, all I want is to be held. My body feels removed and untouched as he goes about his exertions. The next morning, I find him looking at me as if he can't figure me—or his good luck—out. I can't figure me out as well. I grab my clothes and run to the dorm in the cold light of early morning.

As I walk by, Rachel, my stout neighbor with a large head calls to me. "Your roomie was found wandering in her undies around the campus. She had a nervous breakdown or something. She was sent home—so you have the room to yourself, you lucky girl. I would kill for that. My roommate snores like a freight train."

But I don't feel lucky at all. I'd been hoping for a friendly roommate who could show me the ropes, or at least we could find our way together. Now my bare room feels even lonelier.

I've got to get help, I realize. I won't be able to walk away from my childhood without some kind of reckoning, so I check in with university counseling services. They are still unpacking boxes, getting settled in their new offices.

"We're not up to speed just yet," says the head psychologist, a dark-haired woman with a sympathetic air. "Why don't you tell your life story to this psych major for now?" The nervous girl grabs a notepad and pen, and we drag a couple of chairs into a vacant room.

"I don't know where to begin," I confess. "There's last night's sexual fiasco and my mother's drinking . . . my baby sister. . . ." The psych major chews on her pen with a frown.

"Just start with your birth," yells Mrs. Schultz from the other room. I hope I'll be through by the time I graduate.

My first class is in basic philosophy, where the white-haired instructor tells us about Martin Buber. As he strides back and forth across the stage of the huge amphitheater classroom he intones, "Human life finds its meaningfulness in relationships. Usually we view discrete objects in the world in an 'I-it' mode—but with God we have an 'I and Thou' relationship."

I reflect on my relationship with my mother, from whom I always want love that she won't or can't give. This is definitely an "I-it" relationship. An image of her, swathed in a creamy lynx fur dripping with pearls, shimmers before me—but she is behind a metal grill like a bank teller. I slip forward my plea for a withdrawal of love, her forehead wrinkles and her freezing blue eyes bear down on me. Her cerise mouth snarls, "No!" as she snaps the metal partition closed. I cringe, refusing to make a deposit of love, as if there is a rule of "You give me this much love, I will give you that much in return." This love seems small and petty.

But with God it is different. A yearning for intimacy with God unfurls inside me like a fern reaching for the sun. This call for union feels familiar and true, as if it has always been there. I want a love so big I can give my entire self to it. I drift out of class into the sunshine. Someone pins a button proclaiming "Nirvana now!" to my turtleneck, and I dream about going to Nepal to work in a new thing called the Peace Corps.

Michael, his friends, and I smoke pot frequently. Pot distracts me from my worries about my mother, whom I never hear from. If she and David divorce, will Brandeis take my scholarship away? How is my youngest sister, Cecelia, faring? She was so elfin and strange with her one eye covered with a patch to strengthen the muscles of a wandering eye. She cried when I pushed her on the swings and the wind blew in her face. I mourn my leaving yet another sister behind. I reassure myself that she is protected by that pillar of strength, Nanny Weeks.

Michael becomes possessive and grabs my breasts in front of other people. I break with him and go to bed with the next boy who invites me—no teasing, just doing my duty. The university health center is handing out dials of birth control pills, so I don't worry about pregnancy.

Rachel draws me into her room and sits me on her bed. "You know you are getting a terrible reputation, don't you? What are you getting out of these brief transactions of the flesh?"

"Although it's none of your business, that's a good question. What's the point, if I'm not enjoying it? Okay, I'm going back to my room now; you've done your good deed." To the next boy who wants to have sex, I insist on a platonic relationship. Suddenly I have a coterie of lovelorn swains hanging around. My favorite is a young man with flowing mustachios and long hair who wears a white suit and writes me poetry in frustrated desire. This is so much better—but still not satisfying.

I get a job slopping paint on plywood sets in the vast twilight of backstage. The work is relaxing and is a godsend, since I have zero money. Over the semester, I manage to save up $600. I have a nice singing voice and am cast as one of the chorus in *The Pirates of Penzance,* an important fund-raising event for the university.

"I'm freezing here all the time!" I exclaim to an oboe player after one of the rehearsals as we pause to button our pea jackets and curl scarves around our necks before hurling ourselves outside into the sideways-sweeping snow.

"Allow me to escort you to the hottest spot in Waltham." He's a compact teddy bear of a boy with coppery hair and beard and eyes as bright as a new penny. He twinkles and extends his arm courteously. How can I resist an invitation like this? I find myself in the YMCA's coed steam room, sitting cheek-by-jowl on wood benches with twenty other refugees from the brutal winter. No one is uttering a word—we are gratefully thawing out our fingers and toes.

Suddenly, my new friend, Rudy, intones, "'Real isn't how you are made,' said the Skin Horse. 'It's a thing that happens to you. When a child loves you for a long, long time, not just to play with, but REALLY loves you, then you become Real.'"

"That's beautiful," I whisper, "It sounds familiar. Where's it from?"

"*The Velveteen Rabbit*," whispers Rudy and then waggles his eyebrows at me suggestively. "Want to get real with me? Or I could just teach you to play the recorder."

"Maybe after I've absorbed more of this glorious heat," I giggle. "But I'm not promising anything."

We take the bus back to his apartment, and Rudy introduces me to his roommate, Ratner.

"Oh my God, Rudy's brought a girl home!" Ratner shouts, raising his arms. "It's a miracle!"

"Don't listen to him; I bring a different woman home every night." Rudy says, opening the refrigerator and looking inside. "I don't have much else to offer you besides a PB and J." I look at him blankly—I've never heard of this.

"Uh . . . we had a cook . . . and that wasn't on the menu," I explain tentatively.

"Then this you have to try." He proceeds to carefully spread peanut butter and jelly to the very edges of the bread with his sensitive musician's fingers. I'm almost salivating as I watch.

"Open your mouth, I'm gonna feed you this ambrosia."

"You've got to be kidding," I protest, but I acquiesce when I see he is intent.

Bite by bite, he watches me savor the creamy sweet morsels. I'm so moved by his tenderness I feel myself opening to him already.

We go into his room and kiss a little while he shows me how to play a recorder. Although I've warned myself about jumping into sex, I'm ready to spend the night. But Rudy says, "It's time for you to go home, young lady," and walks me all the way to my dorm. I lie on my bed, feeling happiness bubble inside me.

Soon I'm going over to his place several times a week to talk, eat, play the recorder, and cuddle. I'm enjoying the build-up but wondering about the slow timing.

"Maybe I should tell you I'm a virgin," Rudy says as we smooch. "I'm probably not going to be great at first, but give me time. I'll be the world's greatest lover with practice!"

As soon as he enters me, he comes immediately with a shudder. Apologizing, he wraps his arms around me, cupping my body with his own, and we fall asleep. I turn around to face him, kiss his sleeping eyelids, and touch his red-gold hair.

"You're the most adorable teddy bear," I whisper in his ear. "I love you—for your vulnerability."

Later, to allay fears of pregnancy, he takes me on a frigid winter morning to be tested because my pills have run out. We wait several anxious days and are relieved to find I'm not. With shaky steps, I am finding my way.

As opening night of *Pirates* approaches, excitement mounts. A rumor circulates that David will be attending opening night. I'm as eager as anyone else to see my famous stepfather. I wonder how I should greet him. In my room I practice saying a cool "Hi, David," but that doesn't seem enough, while giving him a hug is too demonstrative. Instead, what happens is that Mother calls days before the opening from a hotel in Boston.

"I'm throwing a party for your debut," she insists. Hearing her breathy voice is a shock, but the idea of a party is embarrassing. I'm only in the chorus, for Pete's sake. I curl the pay phone cord around my finger in indecision. I still crave her attention. But what will Rudy think? Although I've met his mother, I've never told him about mine. Maybe he should know what he's getting into.

"Well, okay, but nothing too fancy." Trembling with anxiety, I call Rudy and invite him and Ratner while warning him of Mother's unpredictability. I run over to the theater and invite a few of the top theater arts students as well. As I dress, I wonder what outfit suits this weird occasion. I'm just a college girl, so I decide on a miniskirt and turtleneck.

Mother's door is open, so Rudy and I and the others walk into a hotel suite that is absurdly opulent with antique French furniture, luxurious carpeting, and subdued lighting. I hang onto Rudy's hand as we whisper and look around. She emerges from the bedroom dressed in her most elegant opening night regalia: a tight turquoise sparkly gown with a slash up one leg.

"Darling, who have you brought to see me?" She eyes up and down a lanky young man who has recently grown a silky mustache, and she flirtatiously smoothes his long, dark hair.

"Aren't you a knight with an upraised sword . . . why don't you fix me a drink?" His cheeks flame red, and he seems rooted to the carpet. When she doesn't get her desired response, she launches into a tirade.

"Don't stand there with your chin scraping the floor. You," she says, pointing at me, "pour me a drink." When I won't do it, she screams, "You think you're so high and mighty, Miss College Freshman, well you can't hold a candle to me. I had New York by the tail when I was your age. I was modeling for *Vogue*. Newspaper reporters followed me around because I made such good copy. Hell, New York and London were at my feet. I slept with the Queen's husband, what's-his-name? An earl proposed to me, but I turned him down. I snagged my millionaire before I was thirty. And you've got this little twit, here." She points at Rudy, who is shorter than me. "What have you done with all your advantages? You're not going anywhere with that fat ass, my dear, better get the lard off, or you'll always be in the back row of the chorus."

Emotions surge through me. I want to say something but I'm awash in shame, ashamed of her, of myself. Everything she says is true. I can never be prettier or smarter than she is. I don't have the gumption to thrust myself forward and compete the way she did. At eighteen, I'm a failure. I, too, stand rooted to the spot. Finally, Rudy grabs my hand and pulls me out. He holds me against his chest as I sob, shake, and scream before we cram into a car and head home.

Someone yells through the door that I have a call on the pay phone. It's Nan Patterson, my sister Cecelia's new nanny. Evidently, solid Nanny Weeks has been fired. Nan P. is a slight Scotswoman, who speaks with a burr and giggles when she is nervous, which I find annoying.

"Are you planning to come down to New York for a wee spring holiday?" she titters.

"I guess so," I reply morosely. I don't want to see my mother but I worry about my sister, so I'm going anyway.

"Did you know we have moved; that is, your mother, Cecelia and I?" I notice no mention is made of David.

"No, I didn't know."

"Well, it occurred to me you might not," she says, and gives me the new address.

I assume my mother's marriage has finally self-destructed. I take the train from Boston to New York, find the new address, and ring the bell of the apartment. If Nan P. hadn't thought to call me, I would be wandering around the city without a clue.

"Hello, Kim." Mother lets me in and accepts my kiss on her cheek. She has bags under her eyes as she stands with her arms crossed over her chest, and her hair is pulled back into a greasy queue. I look the place over. It's much smaller than our old home.

"The satin striped couch and chairs look new." I say, trying to be positive.

"The old furniture was rented, and I returned it." She replies. I slowly take this in. We had lived in that apartment four years. To me it was home, but to her it was just a stage set to be discarded.

Nan P. comes out of her bedroom and pecks my cheek. "Cecelia will be so glad to see you when she gets up from her nap."

Mother's cracked-ice eyes confront mine as she shows me her bedroom.

"There are only three bedrooms, you can sleep on the couch in the living room."

I totter to the couch and collapse, as if I have received a body blow. "Where's all my stuff, my books, my records and clothes?" I whisper.

"I gave them away."

"What happened?"

"David and I have divorced—for the second time, you know. I put a notice in the *Times* that I will no longer be responsible for his bills!" She flashes me a triumphant smile. "I'm living on a small settlement."

I feel as if Mother has fed me poison that is slowly seeping through my body and turning it to stone. I always longed to escape her, but now that she is throwing me out, the pain is bottomless. I can't sleep on the couch, that's for certain. I call Lili and ask to spend the night at her apartment. She has decided against college and is taking a stab at acting. Her abrupt disappearance from my life has left an enormous chasm. Now I'm desperate to bridge the gap between us.

We sit on the wooden floor of her empty apartment and listen to the Beatles' new album, *Sergeant Pepper's Lonely Hearts Club Band*, while we pass a joint back and forth. Her black-and-white Great Dane puppy lies with its head on our feet. I'm gathered into a warm cloud by the Beatles' voices as the music weaves back and forth between the speakers. They whisper that only our generation can comprehend life's magic. Adults are oblivious and insane.

Lili tips her chestnut hair against the wall and blows smoke to the ceiling as she listens to the latest saga of my mother and me.

"I just came back from the Haight. You have to go there."

"Hate?" I ask.

"No," she corrects me, "the intersection of Haight and Ashbury in San Francisco, where a whole new way is happening. Your life will be wasted if you don't go. I went to this place on the ocean called Esalen where I dropped acid, had sex with a guide, and reached orgasm."

She rolls another joint and passes it to me. "But the most important thing is, I visited a commune where people are raising children in a whole new way. See, the kids are raised by everyone, not just their parents. Partners are free to couple with whoever. The old order is crumbling. You've got to go out and see this.

"I stayed with our Hewitt's classmate, Mimi, in San Francisco, and she'll let you crash there, too. Her father teaches at Esalen, so she knows it pretty well. And you must get a sleeping bag so you can sleep wherever you want."

Lili's orange eyes look like twin flames as I peer at her through the smoke. I know exactly what I have to do. Burning with urgency, I return to Brandeis and tell Mrs. Schultz at the counseling center, "I need to leave for San Francisco right away."

"Why can't you complete the term, why must this be done now?" She asks pointedly.

"All I know is I have to get as far away as I can." I shake my head. "Immediately."

I fold my college clothes and my grandmother's quilt in a trunk to be left behind. I will be traveling light and pack a few exotic outfits in a bag. These include a poppy red, satin, Chinese gown with a plunging neckline, a scarf and matching purse covered with pastel silk flowers, and a thick-soled pair of beaded moccasins—all borrowed from my mother. I empty my bank account of $600 and buy a sleeping bag and a one-way ticket to San Francisco. Rudy drives me to the airport.

"When will you be back?" He looks at me uncertainly.

"Perhaps a month," I say as we kiss, and I get out of the car. I smother a pang of guilt because I don't know if I'll ever return.

Chapter 8

CALIFORNIA SEEKER

As you strode deeper and deeper
Into the world
Determined to do
The only thing you could do—
Determined to save
The only life you could save
—MARY OLIVER

Wandering across the emerald lawns of Golden Gate Park, I gaze longingly at families lounging around open food hampers, picnicking. People wearing beads and feathers toss Frisbees while dogs bark in excitement. Everyone belongs here except me. The awareness that I have no home opens like a void before me. There is no welcoming bed or full larder waiting anywhere. Terror is nibbling at the edge of my consciousness, and I pray for fate, God, or *something* to show me the way.

Lili had called Mimi's pad and said, "Kimbiddy, honey, hate to spoil your scene, but your mom is on our case. She found out it was me who turned you on to the Haight. Her Maleficent Highness is livid and ready to strike me down! She threatened I'd never get an acting job in New York. But that's okay. Just warning you she's out for blood."

Mimi didn't want Mother tracking me to her place, so she got me a job as a live-in mother's helper for a pregnant actress. I was expected to put a cold cloth on Nancy's brow if she was nauseous, make her tea, and wax her legs. That was the worst. Slathering on hot goo and ripping it off while uttering consoling sounds was beyond me. I wasn't a harmonious addition to the household and was fired. Too ashamed to tell Mimi, fear ratchets my shoulders to my ears, which are, in turn, trying to climb to the top of my scalp.

The sounds of a group dancing in a circle waft toward me. I veer toward them and pause upon hearing a boy wearing a cowboy hat, strumming a guitar, and singing.

"What an awful racket you're making," I scold him.

"Bob Dylan has a worse voice."

"That's sacrilege. Dylan has the lyrics. 'Like a Rolling Stone?' It was written for me." I howl the words at him, knowing now I'm going to live them:

> *You've gone to the finest school all right, Miss Lonely*
> *But you know you only used to get juiced in it*
> *And nobody's ever taught you how to live out on the street*
> *And now you're going to have to get used to it . . .*
> *How does it feel?*
> *How does it feel*
> *To be on your own*
> *With no direction home*
> *A complete unknown*
> *Like a rolling stone?*

To sing those words while strumming my guitar, comfortably seated on my bed back in New York, or around the fountain in Washington Square, was one thing—but to be living it was terrifying. *What am I going to do?*

I stumble away and sit in the shade of a eucalyptus tree. Trying to calm myself, I pick sword-shaped leaves off the ground, crumple them in my palm, and sniff them. A kid with a blond pageboy plops down beside me.

"I heard you singing over there. I like Dylan too, especially that part about living out on the street. You been here long?"

Tearfully, I explain the mess I'm in.

"Well, I left home about eight months ago. I'm seventeen, but I been doing okay without a job or a place to stay. This place is groovy. People help each other out. I can show you. My name is Don, by the way."

Don's hair is cut in a blonde pageboy, and he looks like a child—no stubble on his pink cheeks. Can I trust him? My stomach rumbles, and I complain I'm hungry.

"I know just the place to get a free meal—the born-again Christians. Come with me." He grabs my hand and takes me to a rambling basement apartment filled with children and adults. The senior members nod to Don without enthusiasm, as if they have seen too much of him. We endure an hour-long Bible study taught by a tired-looking mother while the children crayon. I try to be respectful, but I dispensed with Christianity after God failed to hear my prayers at the Congregational Church in Huntington. Now my belly is rumbling, and I have to pee.

I wander into the kitchen looking for a bathroom. There I see a frail blonde girl spooning food into the mouth of an enormous baby with bulging cheeks. As soon as the child gulps, it makes grunting, squealing noises, demanding more. The young mother glares at the child and says irritably, "All right, all right, I'm feeding you as fast as I can," while shoveling more into the infant's gaping maw. I stumble to the toilet with the scene emblazoned in my mind.

Is that what happened between my mother and me? When I was that baby's age, I'd been called "the baby whale" because I was so fat. Had I wanted more from my teenage mother than she could possibly give? I wonder if we were locked in the same impossible wrestling match I just witnessed in the kitchen. I demanded love that she didn't have, while she craved freedom that I couldn't give her.

The group assembles around a long table laden with brown rice, Jell-O, lettuce, beans, and Rice Krispies treats. The children are served first. They gobble their food so fast that by the time the adults start to eat, they are ready for more. After we leave, I tell Don I feel guilty about eating under false pretenses. Don sulks a moment and then says, "That's how you get a free meal."

"Where can we sleep tonight?"

"If it's a nice night, I sleep on a park bench." He looks at me. I'm dressed in my mother's red satin gown with a plunging neckline.

"I guess you wouldn't like that. I know—there's this woman named Sara who's really generous. She lets people sleep in her spare room. Sometimes there's too many, but we can go see."

He leads me past gabled Victorian houses painted lavender with lime trim, pink with orange bric-a-brac, or sea-blue with sky-colored columns. Their bay windows glow in the mild spring evening. My shoulders soften as I watch a couple whisper and laugh under a lit streetlamp while sharing a joint. *Maybe I can become a flower child and just let things flow,* I think. We enter a run-down, unpainted house whose porch is radiant with red geraniums, climb three flights of stairs, and knock on the door. Don introduces me to Sara, who welcomes us in with a beaming smile. She is a small butterball of a person with a blonde toddler wrapped around one hip.

"You'll be comfy sleeping here." She shows us a mattress on the floor covered with a bright Indian bedspread. "There's only one other person here at the moment. Would you like some green tea with honey?" Relieved, I spread my sleeping bag on the mattress.

The bitter brew makes my mouth pucker, but I don't want to be ungracious when Sara is so hospitable. We sit around her kitchen table making small talk about the many concerts coming to the Haight.

"The Mamas and the Papas are my favorite, and I'm hoping to save up enough dough so I can go," chirps Sara as she hands around cookies. I feel odd acting as if I know her and this is a normal evening. I wish she were my friend instead of a generous stranger providing a place to crash for the night.

"Will you be my old lady?" Don whispers, laying his head on my shoulder as we lie together in the dark. At first I'm not sure what he means, because sometimes that's what I called my mother, but when he pulls up my shirt, I get the idea. I let Don make love to me; it seems only fair after all he's done. I'm on the pill again but worry about running out. Where will I get more?

So begins our life together as a homeless couple. He says he is seventeen and may be younger. I find him unthreatening and useful, although he can be whiney at times. Since I still have a few hundred dollars left from my set painting job at Brandeis, we explore the Haight, my treat. We dress in our wildest costumes: I in my crimson Chinese robe, and he in Sergeant Pepper's pageboy livery.

We look through the strange head shops in the Haight that sell hookahs and rolling papers up front, and mescaline, peyote, and LSD in the back. Marijuana joints are passed casually between strangers standing on street corners. Simply inhaling the air on the street is intoxicating. Tourists drive by and snap our picture. We feel sorry for them being left behind in dead America. Kids of all colors and both sexes dress alike in blue, red, and yellow tie-dyed T-shirts, beads looped around their necks, their hair in Afros, dreadlocks, or falling down their backs, their belongings carried in macramé bags, their feet wrapped in biblical style sandals. Girls strike tambourines and dance along wearing diaphanous gowns, flowers woven in their hair. A singer called Donovan, or someone who looks like him, wanders barefoot dressed as St. Francis in a hooded robe, handing flowers to those who are sad. Don whispers he can perform miracles. We eat at a café called The Drog Store that serves a new kind of cake with carrots in it and chocolate ice cream studded with nuts and marshmallows. They have a not-so-secret stash of hashish-filled brownies in the back. We are impressed by the free clinic run by hippies called "the Diggers," who are helping hundreds of kids who arrive every day in the Haight.

As we saunter down the street, a guy with an Afro says we look groovy and lays some free Avalon tickets on us. The ballroom is filled with gyrating hippies, and we dance to wailing electric guitars against a backdrop of jumping pink and green amoeba lights. A young god with shoulder-length blond hair, who wears a leather vest and pants, offers me a free tab of LSD, but I decline. I tell myself I want to feel safe when I drop the big one. I do another sensible thing and the next day deposit my money, now depleted to $300, in the bank. It will be my ticket home if things get bad. I don't dwell on the fact that I have no home to return to, but it's there like an all-consuming pit, if I let myself think about it.

To make money, Don and I stand on street corners and peddle *Berkeley Barbs*, the radical newspaper put out by university students. I sell them but seldom read them. When I was in New York, I had marched down Fifth Avenue to protest the war in Vietnam. Now that I'm homeless, my days are consumed with finding food and a place to sleep. A headline screaming that Robert F. Kennedy has been assassinated catches my attention, and I show it to Don. He looks at it disbelieving for a moment, then shrugs, and we go back to worrying about filling our bellies. It's too frightening to acknowledge my country is in the midst of a violent upheaval.

If the *Barbs* don't sell, and our funds are below the $1.50 needed for a portion of fish and chips, Don tries to convince me to panhandle, but I can't do it. I'm an able-bodied person who isn't working, and I know this isn't right. Yet I'm not ready to give up searching for a new way of life. When our bellies are rumbling without respite, we beg the fish joint manager wearing a stained apron for the fried batter that falls from the fish into the fryer. After soaking off the extra grease in a paper napkin, we savor the opaque crunchy slivers.

"We've slept too many nights at Sara's place, and I feel we're being exploitative," I complain to Don one evening after a hard day searching for food. "I want to explore some places like Esalen. We could hitchhike down—it's not too far away in Big Sur." I don't tell him—because I don't think he'll understand—that I hope, by being put in the hot seat in a support group led by psychologist Fritz Perls and screaming out my rage at my mother, I can shed my past like an old coat. I see myself soaking in the hot mineral baths and dropping acid with a guide like Timothy Leary. Or my mind might open to ancient wisdoms under the influence of a spiritual teacher like Ram Das.

"We're not going to find grub out here, and I'm already hungry," Don whines on a foggy morning as we hitch a ride with a psychedelically painted hippie van that drives down the Pacific Coast and delivers us in front of Carmel, a quaint village further south. The blue ocean ripples serenely behind us as we stand for a long morning with our thumbs out. As the sun rises in the sky and burns off the mist, we start to sweat. I notice when I am hot and thirsty that the town doesn't look so cute anymore. We trudge down the dusty road and find a gas station where we buy a coke and peanuts, and I go to use the bathroom. As I push the door open, I see a girl washing her hair in the iron-stained sink.

"What are you doing?" I ask.

"I live on the road and wash up in gas stations, living the free life." She laughs. I nod as if this is a fantastic idea but recoil at the thought of scrounging through life like a bum.

The last ride deposits us farther down the coast where the Big Sur wilderness begins and cars become few. Don and I stand in vain with our thumbs out until, over the cliffs, the sun begins its descent toward the ocean.

"I want to go back to the Haight where I can find free food," Don whines with more insistence.

"I'm tired and hungry too, but we're so close!" I can almost feel the mineral waters of the hot tub, but as it darkens, my own fears gain strength. Against my inclination, we cross Highway One and stick out our thumbs going back north.

A car pulls to a stop in front of us. I peer in and see two people whose heads are covered with a gray convict-like stubble and who wear shapeless black T-shirts and pants.

"Are you going to San Francisco?" I ask. They are and will take us all the way. Don and I crawl into the back seat with apprehension, but we need the ride. The men speak to each other with a strange intensity. Don and I look at each other in alarm and hunker down, trying to be invisible. One turns around to look at us and said, "Are we frightening you? This is our first time out of the Zendo after a three-month silent retreat. We work in the kitchen, and it gets pretty intense." They shriek with laughter.

My curiosity is piqued. I had heard of Zen many years ago when my father made fun of the mad teachers who hit their students on the head.

"What's a Zendo?" I ask.

"We're monks at Tassajara, a Zen monastery in the mountains of Big Sur," the driver answers. "We've been feeding a hundred people three meals a day. Our brains are a little fried." They both snicker.

Don murmurs, "I wish I had some of that food right now."

"Maybe you do and maybe you don't," says the other monk. "We're vegetarians, and we eat stuff like miso, brown rice, soy sauce, and seaweed."

"Yuk," said Don. "You're so right. I don't want any of that."

"How come you're vegetarians?" I ask.

"We don't believe in killing," says the driver.

"You're monks, like St. Francis or something? Do you pray a lot?"

"Well, yes we do, but in Zen you meditate. We focus on our breath to calm our mind."

"What's the point?"

"How to explain this? Zen teaches that thoughts clutter your mind. If you want to commune with something bigger, you need to quiet the monkey mind's constant chatter."

I sit quietly. A technique like meditation could help me become less tense. I like the idea of being a vegetarian and not killing animals. Living in a monastery appeals to me.

"Can I come to Tassajara and learn to meditate?" I ask. They laugh. Don looks at me as if I have gone insane.

"Maybe you'd better learn to meditate first before jumping into a retreat."

By the time they deposit us back on the streets of the Haight, I promise to meditate each morning and to cut down on eating meat. But I can't keep my commitment. My life is too chaotic. I have no control over where I'll wake up or what I'll eat. A dark current of anxiety is eroding my enchantment with the free hippie life.

I need to find someplace where I feel safe. A commune's big happy family sounds like the solution. But where were these places? I persuade Don again to stick out his thumb with me, this time toward New Mexico where I've heard about a great commune. After a morning of breathing truck fumes and being blown about like discarded newspaper, a car stops to pick us up. We are in the back seat when they lock the doors. Two men sit in front while one is in the back with us. Something about their plaid shirts and the set of their mouths makes my breath catch in my throat. We drive in silence for long minutes.

One with red pustules on his neck says, "We were going to have some fun with that girl" —he jerks his thumb toward me—"but changed our minds because hippie girls are dirty and diseased, and we'd get sores on our tools. Go on, filthy hippies, get out."

They open the door and we exit fast. I'm trembling, and my legs won't hold me up. My breath comes out in huge sobs, and I collapse to the ground as cars *whizz* past. Don sees an overpass up ahead, and we crawl under it as I heave and cry. I have just seen the face of evil. This is my first experience of being part of a hated minority. Ironically, that has spared me violence. We spend the night listening to the thuds of fists on flesh as drunks beat each other up. In the quiet dawn, we get a ride with a VW bus back to San Francisco. Don and I agree to split up. I will continue my search for a commune.

"I'm so frustrated at not finding my tribe with a new family structure like my friend Lili told me about," I complain as I drink tea at Sara's place. She is puttering around readying her toddler, Max, for bed.

"I know a beautiful man named Tony who is staying at a commune called Morningstar near Sebastopol. Maybe that's the place for you. I can borrow a car and drive us up there." The next morning I pack up my sleeping bag, a pillow I borrow from Sara, some apples, cheese, and bread. I have no experience camping. Aside from trips to Kentucky, I was raised in cities. I don't know how to drive a car for the same reason.

Sara chops vegetables, boils rice and beans, makes egg salad, and throws in bags of raisins and cookies. She prepares more food for this one day than I do for my longer stay. As she hefts a bag over one shoulder with Max balanced on her other hip, she looks over my meager provisions and suggests I take a few garbage bags in case it rains. I wonder how they can be useful.

Sara borrows a car, and after an hour of highway driving with the windows rolled down to catch breezes, we cut off into the green fields of rural Sonoma County and then drive up a dirt road into some woods. We park in a rutted clearing, get out of the car, and look around. There is a dilapidated farmhouse and, across from it, rather incongruously, a telephone booth. Sara and I both need to use the bathroom, so we peer inside the house. Through the open door we see an overflowing toilet and an excrement-littered wooden floor. I gasp and back into Sara. We agree to pee in the woods, which I haven't done since I was a small child in

Kentucky. I'm glad to find some tissues wadded in my jeans skirt pocket but don't want to think how few of them there are.

Sara spots Tony doing sun salutations on a blanket spread in the shade of some trees. I'm startled to see that he is naked. This is the first time I have heard of or seen yoga. We sit respectfully, Sara holding Max quietly in her lap, and watch. Tony has dreamy blue eyes, shoulder length blond hair, and a slender body. As I watch him perform the stretches, I'm half in love with him myself.

Tony slides on some shorts, and Sara introduces me. We unroll the blanket and spread out our food. A few hippies materialize out of the woods and stand looking hungrily at our picnic. Sara invites them to join us, and we all eat while she feeds the baby. After a while, Tony, in a soft voice made more indistinct by a stutter, explains about his guru. He pauses so frequently that Sara chimes in, evidently having heard the story before.

"Sri Chinmoy is a spiritual teacher from India. He lives in Queens, New York. He has reached God realization, and through him his followers can reach God as well. I am purifying myself through meditation, vegetarianism, and celibacy. I hope to be invited to live in the guru's ashram."

I glance at Sara when I hear the part about celibacy, but she is beaming encouragingly at him.

"I taught myself to meditate from Guru's books. Would you be interested in learning how?"

The hippies slip away. He shows us how to sit cross-legged with spine erect while breathing slowly through our noses. We are to think loving thoughts. I can imagine whom Sara is thinking about, but I'm puzzled by the crazy bits of conversation, images, and feelings that dance through my mind. I don't have much control over my thoughts. They do what they want. Still, it's a restful experience, and I need relief from tension.

"Good-bye, come and visit me." I wave and watch Sara packing her bag, preparing to leave. I don't understand why I feel as if I'm being abandoned when this was where I wanted to be. "Go with the flow" isn't as easy for me as it seems for others.

"Where do you think I should sleep and maybe find some water?" I turn to Tony, who looks like he is about to disappear as well.

"You can find water there. . . ." He nods to a spigot sticking out from the house and then pauses while a sweet expression crosses his face. "I let food and sleep find me." This is interesting but not of much practical help.

"Can't you just point in a direction to lay my sleeping bag?"

"I like to sleep near the stream; it quiets the mind." He disappears into the woods in the other direction.

I wander over to the spigot to splash water on my face and drink from my hands. I don't even have a cup to carry water in case I get thirsty during the night. I walk through the woods looking for a spot to unroll my sleeping bag. I see stained mattresses, ragged blankets, tarps strung between trees, a few tents, and a creative two-story tree house made from discarded materials. Hippies glance at me as they go about preparing their evening meal, but no one says hello. Finally, I find an open area, unroll my sleeping bag, sit cross-legged, and try to meditate. A sharp-clawed welter of fear and anger bursts into awareness. Like everything else in California, Morningstar isn't what I'd hoped it would be.

A group of us hangs out by a farmhouse, passing the time, practicing yoga, and seeing what tourists might "lay on us." Visitors come to gawk at the hippies' outlandish clothes, or lack of them, and give us food. A man with wild hair and a purple band around his forehead says, "Lou Gottlieb, Morningstar's owner, has given these thirty-two acres to God, which means anyone can live here." Lou had been a member of a singing group called The Limelighters who made their fortune in the 1960s.

Reba, Lou's curly-haired, young girlfriend, thrusts her legs skyward as she does a shoulder stand. She is naked, so her breasts droop toward her shoulders. As she gradually comes down and lies on her blanket, she says, "Winos live by the creek, but they aren't so bad."

A man wearing a leather vest, a cowboy hat, and not much

else adds, "Sonoma County is offended by our nakedness and drugs and periodically sends in Rocky and Bullwinkle to cart us off to jail." He winks at me.

I'd been uncomfortable with nudity when I first arrived, not knowing where to put my eyes. Reba's casual nakedness has encouraged me to take off my blouse as I sit warming in the sun, but I'm not ready to relinquish my skirt. I stay away from the creek, though.

Gradually, I relax at Morningstar because it reminds me of Kentucky. I toss aside my clogs and allow my bare feet to find their way on the dusty path from sleeping bag to water spigot to the orchard where I pick fruit. My mind calms; I meditate and watch leaf patterns against the sky. My anxiety and loneliness recede. Like Kentucky, time seems to stand still here. It's peaceful to the point of being boring, which is fine.

One afternoon, a group of us are sitting in the clearing, chatting—where to find free food or how to get on welfare seemed to be the biggest topics—when a car drives up. A raw-faced, middle-aged man gets out, pulls a large cardboard box out the trunk, and sets it on the ground. His wife, her hair in pink curlers, stays in the car with her arms crossed and stares straight ahead. The man approaches us cautiously as if we were Amazon natives who didn't understand English. In a loud voice he declares, "I am a baker and have a box of frozen eggs I'm giving away. Take what you want." He watches as we gather around to inspect his offering. I peer inside the box and see a liquefying mass of hundreds of yolks.

"How do we get them out?" I ask Spirit, a boy with feathers braided in his hair.

"In a pot if you got one, or your hands." He shrugs then digs in with his dirty fingers. I turn away. I'm discovering there are limits to what I am willing to do—besides, I have no way to cook the eggs.

There is a grove of pear trees whose fruit is ripening, but it is quickly stripped. Some say they give you the runs, which is our other problem. Because the toilet isn't functioning, people have to go in the woods, and I have to be careful not to walk in excrement. I don't know you are supposed to bury it, and neither does anyone else, apparently. I have to be very careful where I step or put my sleeping bag. The police have begun making raids on the grounds of unsafe hygiene and vagrancy. I've evaded one clumsy attempt to round us up. They are right on the nose about the hygiene, but we aren't vagrants. We live here.

I hitch to San Francisco and buy more bread, cheese, a canteen, and sewing supplies. To occupy my time, I embroider my clothing as I was taught at Lady Eden's. It's soothing to watch my needle slipping through cloth on the long August afternoons as we wait for the air to cool. I sew a neat chain stitch around the hem in my long denim skirt and then loop it around a hole where my knee pokes through.

Spirit nods toward it. "You're celebrating the now."

"What on earth does that mean?" I'm pleased because he approves.

"The present moment is more important than the past that is over or the future that hasn't come yet," he says. "The present is where the power is."

"Huh, the present moment. I don't know, I'm okay with it now, but there were some moments I'd rather have skipped." I begin telling him about my mother. He advises me to forgive her. This sounds right, and I begin wondering if she is worried about me. I imagine after so many months' absence she might invite me to come home again. Of course, I would sweetly decline, declaring I love the free life out in California.

One morning, after a relaxing session of yoga with the sun warming my bare breasts, I walk over to the phone booth and dial my mother's number, collect. She picks up on the first ring.

"It's me, Mommy," I say softly. "Are you wondering where I am?"

She retorts in a harsh voice, "I've had a private detective tailing you all the time. I know every minute of every day you've spent out there."

"No, you haven't!" I scream, and we both smash down our phones. I look around and put my blouse back on. Is anyone spying on me? I don't think so, yet I can't be sure. Here I am, over 2,500 miles away from my mother, yet nothing has changed. I'm shaken and depressed, as I so often am after encounters with her. I go back to my campsite to cry. Then the thought comes—perhaps my mother is showing her concern in the only way she can.

Footsteps jog past my sleeping bag, and a voice yells, "Run, the pigs are here!" As I try to sit up, my face is on fire, my head throbs, and my eyes open to narrow slits. I must have lain in poison ivy! Blue-clad policemen thrash through the Morningstar woods, their movements hampered by dangling billy clubs, guns, and handcuffs. I'm too miserable to run away. I let a female officer grab me and shove me up into the paddy wagon with the other stragglers. We are driven down to the Sonoma County jail. One by one my fingers are firmly pressed in an inkpad and onto a sheet of paper with a number, my name, date—August, 1968— and charge: vagrancy. My feverish mind screams, *Now you have a prison record for the rest of your life.*

Men and women are separated, and we barefoot, long-haired, jean-skirted females are escorted through a metal door that closes behind us with a horrible clang. Good-bye, freedom. We are told to strip and wash in a communal shower. I'm embarrassed by our smelly naked bodies, but the feeling of hot water pouring over my dirty, itching scalp is a balm. The prison matron hands us each a folded green uniform topped by a small towel. I pull on the stiff pants and shirt and realize I answer to a number now. As the group is pushed toward a cell, the matron holds me back.

"You're a sorry sight," she says, looking at my red, puffy eyelids and face. She searches in a cabinet and hands me a bottle of calamine and a cloth. The solitary cell she shows me with its painted walls and neatly made-up cot looks more welcoming than any luxury hotel I've ever stayed in. I pull back the covers and wilt onto the bed. I want only rest, but the eye of a naked bulb radiates in my face. I ask the matron if she will turn the light off. She gives a bark of laughter. I pull the sheet over my head and fall into a well of sleep.

Chapter 9

MEDITATION INITIATION

⊰⊱

In the difficult are the friendly forces,
The hands that work on us.
—RANIER MARIA RILKE

The pack's straps bite into my shoulders, and its weight almost pins me to the ground. Sharp stones poke through my mother's beaded thick-soled moccasins that had initially seemed to perfectly complement my hiking outfit. I totter up the trail in the Sierra Nevada Mountains a bit farther. Why hadn't Sara warned me that the pack is *really* heavy?

"Andrew, could we stop a moment so I can adjust the straps?" He squints his steely blue eyes in annoyance and shifts some of my heavy grains into his pack.

"Keep at it, and you'll get used to it," is all he says. I had met Andrew, Tony's older brother, at Sara's place after my night in jail. He is longhaired and sun-bleached, with tiny cheekbones that poke out beneath his eyes and a ski-slope nose. He was planning an extended camping and meditation retreat in the Sierra Nevadas.

"Sounds perfect for me," I had enthused and told him about my promise to the Tassajara monks to meditate. Also, after my disastrous stint at Morningstar, I wanted to learn the proper way to camp. Now I can tell Andrew regrets bringing me, but I shuffle along. I picture the Little Engine That Could chugging up the mountain and say, "I think I can, I think I can, I think I can."

When he helps me shrug off the pack that night, I'm literally walking on air. Astronauts bounding on the surface of the moon have nothing on me—gravity has ceased its hold. We still have to pitch a tent, gather wood, build a fire, and cook some rice. I had no idea there was so much to do before I could lay my aching body on the hard ground. We are camped beside a burbling stream. *What could be more picturesque?* I think. But during the night I'm repeatedly awakened by the rushing noise, like a toilet running over. None of this is as I expected.

The next morning we get up and do it over again.

Although I would have settled for the first available campsite, Andrew chooses a spot high in the mountains, in some pinewoods near the tree line. We have a view of a pristine lake reflecting distant peaks. The landscape has an austere beauty, which leaves me feeling like one of the pebbles that surround the water—insignificant. I miss the lush green slopes of the Appalachians.

Each evening we spend at least an hour searching for kindling to feed the flames that cook our beans and rice. Upon rising in the cold mornings, we eat warmed-over oatmeal. Then Andrew slings a blanket around his skinny naked body and walks to a boulder by the lake where he folds the blanket and sits for hours in meditation.

This leaves me to honor my own commitment. The pine trees have a comforting presence and provide shade and back support, but I also want a view of the water. I drag my sleeping bag to the outermost tree and sit cross-legged with my spine erect. I focus on counting my breath up to about two before thoughts suck me away. Questions—*What are you doing here in the middle of nowhere? Where is your life heading? Why do your mother and stepmother hate you? What's wrong with you?*—beat at my head like bat wings. I drag my attention back to my breath, but a second later, I'm again totting up my pros and cons. Soon my legs scream their discomfort. If the present is the moment of power, it isn't as wonderful as it is supposed to be—nothing is! Janis Joplin's throaty voice howls, "Why's it all so haaaaard?" over and over in my ears.

When meditation becomes impossible, I pull out my paperback copy of Christopher Isherwood's translation of the *Bhagavad Gita*. I had tucked it into my pack along with a blue and red pencil. I'd been reading the book for a while and found it surprisingly helpful. The text depicts Prince Arjuna preparing to engage in battle with his extended family. He doesn't know what to do and questions his charioteer, who is the god Krishna in disguise. The divine advice to "take the next obvious step and not be attached to the fruits of your actions" settles me down and keeps me from doing something crazy, like running away and getting lost in the mountains. As the afternoon wears away, I allow my underlining to morph into swirls, vines, and stars up and down the margins, until the paperback looks like an illuminated manuscript.

"Andrew, thank God you're back! I'm going out of my mind with loneliness." I rush to fling my arms around him as he saunters into camp, but he starts building the fire in methodical silence.

"Please talk to me. Tell me about your meditation or your courageous mother or blissed-out Tony or your pampered baby sister, Sandra. I love to hear about them." Andrew takes his time, and I try to wait respectfully since I know, unlike me, he's coming out of a deep meditation.

"Well, okay," he says after our bellies are full with lentils and rice. He launches into the story of their family emigrating from Estonia and settling in this country. Since his father died, Andrew casts himself as the wise, guiding force of the group, but

I'm more fascinated by his mother, who seems to have been the real strength. Other than that, however, I can't pierce the distance between us. He doesn't want to hear about my confusing meditations and tells me to ignore a sore developing on my lip. When we spoon at night in our sleeping bag it's more to keep warm than anything romantic. He is serious about this being a meditation retreat.

One problem is I won't wash. Andrew plunges naked into the frigid lake, comes up sputtering and races out again. I tiptoe to the water and slap it on my face, but the icy cold burns my fingertips and feet. I won't go in any farther. I yearn for hot water, a soft bed, a delicious meal, and a good novel.

One morning, after eating oatmeal sprinkled with our dwindling store of brown sugar, Andrew decides it's time. We formally lay the orange pills in front of us on our bedrolls, meditate, and swallow them down with cold water. I watch the sun climb into the clear blue sky and light up the lake as I wait for the LSD to kick in. As I gaze at the pine trees silhouetted against the sky, fine filaments of red, blue, and lavender echo their perimeters, intermeshing with echoing lines in the clouds. I look at my legs, arms, and fingers. They are pulsing with colors. The tributaries of my veins, even the hairs on my arms reach out and weave themselves into the pine branches. I hoped I'd experience oneness with the universe—now it is happening. There is a place for me in the scheme of things after all.

I lie down on my sleeping bag and watch the lake develop a fiery blaze. My filthiness and painful mouth aren't important now. Then I have a vision. I look into a tidy home through the top as if I am gazing down into a dollhouse. A mother stirs a pot in the kitchen, a father reads the newspaper in the living room, and the children study in their bedrooms. Each activity occurs in its appropriately designated room. It looks so meaningful and enticing. The significance seems to be that I should order my life and acquire the fundamentals of shelter, food, and a stable relationship.

"I've had a huge vision," Andrew says slowly when the LSD has worn off. "There is no such thing as God's favored child; we are random specks in the grand impersonality of the universe." He falls silent, as if there are no words to express what he has seen.

"You make me shiver; the wilderness is beautiful but it doesn't care if we live or die." I look around at the jagged peaks etched against the cobalt sky and wish for Kentucky's rounded green mountains. "Well, I had a vision that told me to go back to the city and look for an apartment—what do you think about that?"

His icy blue eyes look at me like he can't fathom my stupidity, and he sets about making a fire.

We haven't seen many people, so when a couple hikes through, I race up and ask the woman if she has any lip ointment. She kindly swipes lipstick on my mouth and says the sore is as good as gone, but I should get treatment back in town. She lets me keep the lipstick. Although my mouth still hurts, I feel a rush of gratitude. The next morning, several inches of snow lie on the ground. Mountains, trees, the perimeter of the lake are glistening with a cold, white mantle. We have been up here the whole month of August, and now it's the beginning of September. Andrew reluctantly agrees maybe we should go; we are running out of food anyway.

I hoist the pack, and we slip our way down the trails, which are slick with wet pine needles and melting snow. One of my mother's beaded moccasins separates from its thick sole. Andrew binds it together with string. We had nothing to eat the day before, and our circumstances seem desperate. I limp back into San Francisco with frozen feet, exhausted, hungry, and filthy. I'm amazed to see that people are wearing shorts and sandals. It's still summer, and the hippie world is in full throttle on the city streets. I have survived my wilderness meditation retreat and have a new sense of direction.

"Hiring topless go-go girls—$25 a night!" I read from the *San Francisco Chronicle* job ads. Andrew and I lounge, clean and naked, on a mattress on the floor of Sara's apartment.

"Twenty-five dollars a night!" I count on my fingers. "In two weeks I'd have enough money to rent our own pad here in the Haight. A permanent place all our own . . . say something, Andrew."

Andrew makes a sour face over *The Autobiography of a Yogi*, which he is reading. I found the book inspiring, but he thinks it's a big mistake to follow a guru.

"C'mon," I wheedle, "I'm tired of crashing on Sara's floor. Smile. Say yes." I roll onto him and try to pull his lips into a smile.

He grimaces. "Men will be looking at your tits."

I'm annoyed with his lack of contribution to our nonexistent funds. He has lost all initiative since our camping trip and is becoming a downer.

"I like to dance. We've been naked all summer, and you haven't noticed my tits. C'mon, say yes." When he refuses to look at me, I put Beethoven's *Pastoral* on Sara's record player. I let the sounds of the musical storm conceal our lovemaking and carry us into our own crescendo. This is the best lovemaking we've had so far, although I have yet to climax. The symphony's cuckoo call finds us lying content in each other's arms. Morning light streams through the paisley cloth curtaining the window and dapples our bodies with colors. I take Andrew's silence as his consent to my plan.

Tuesday morning, I try on my few remaining presentable garments. Most of my clothes are in tatters. But how does one dress for an interview to become a topless dancer? At least my body is slim and toned from eating only beans and grains and heaving around that pack. I decide to wear a miniskirt, blouse, and low heels I had stashed at Sara's. The sore on my lip has already vanished.

The bus deposits me in the nightclub section of San Francisco where I've never been before. The clubs and bars seem innocent and sleepy as a crew sweeps down the sidewalks—it's ten in the morning. I locate the bar and open the door. Inside is a dark cavern. The smell of stale cigarette smoke and booze swirls around me. It reminds me of my mother, which makes me wonder what I'm doing here.

I chew on my lip, and while my eyes adjust to the dark, I tentatively knock on the manager's office door. He shuffles out, smoking, and carefully closes the door behind him. His hair is slicked back, and he is wearing a rumpled, long sleeved shirt and green polyester pants. His fleshy, oval face is pockmarked, and his heavy-lidded eyes are expressionless.

"Strip down to your panties so I can have a look at ya," he growls.

"Here in the hallway where someone might see?" My voice rises thinly. I'm immediately aware how silly this sounds, so I do as he asks. He nods and tells me to return at eight that night.

When I check in, the manager hands me my costume and calls to a dancer with a dark pixie cut hurrying past. "Tina, show this new girl upstairs to the dressing room." It's already noisy with chattering women.

"You can sit here next to Cat," she says, patting a chair. Cat is bent over pulling fishnet tights over her legs. Other women are doing the same. Everywhere I look there are arms, legs, hips, thighs, breasts, and behinds. Some are wriggling into tights, others sliding on satin bikini bottoms or pasting glittery caps over nipples. Laugher and conversation flows around. I feel strangely at home and quickly follow suit.

I start to roll my newly purchased mascara onto my lashes as I gaze into the long mirror. Cat, after pushing her bleached bangs off her forehead, is swirling blue eye shadow around her eyes. She winks at me in the mirror.

"I'm getting a tummy tuck as soon as I've lost some weight." She pinches in a roll of fat at her waist.

"Surgery? Won't it hurt?" I ask.

"Oh, I don't care; I got big plans to be a high paid stripper.

My lover says I have the looks to do it. She'll pay for the surgery, and then I'll be pulling in big bucks and can support her and my kids in high style."

She stands and grips the saddlebags on her legs. "I'm getting thigh reduction, too. But first I have to lose some weight. If I put in enough hours dancing, it's no problem, dancing is great exercise. We got it all planned." She begins rummaging in her enormous bag.

She has her whole life mapped out, but I'm still puzzling over something she has just said. "If you don't mind my asking, how can you have kids if your lover is a woman?"

"Oh honey, I dumped the first bastard. He beat me up. My lover is wonderful to me. I would never have the confidence to do any of this without her. She tells me my breasts are my gold ticket. I cream them every night. You know? To keep them looking good. They will pay my way." She looks down at herself fondly.

I'm getting an education right here in the dressing room, and I haven't even started work. I am impressed how organized her life is, unlike me and my crazy flight from college.

Our shift starts, and we troop downstairs. Someone helps me onto a stool, and I stand on top of the bar for the first time. Music plays, and I begin moving my body. Men's pale faces swim below me. At first I feel pinned by their gaze. But the spotlight is on me, and they are shrouded in darkness, so I forget about them and relax into a dreamy flow. I watch the other dancers out of the corner of my eyes to see how I compare. Tina is energetic, so I imitate her, kicking out my foot, only to make contact with a glass that spills into a man's lap. I am aghast and sure I will be fired and call down, "I'm sorry, I didn't mean to do it" so many times the bartender tells me to just go on dancing and forget about it.

Then I notice something unusual about another dancer. Is it the starry sheen of her skin or the way her long brown hair brushes her shoulders as she weaves her hands around her head? The spotlights create an angelic aura around each dancer, but she is bathed in a special quality. My eyes zero in on the blue veins that thread into her navel. Her belly has a slight bulge, although the rest of her is in perfect symmetry. She is pregnant—a blissful, dancing, pregnant goddess. She is swimming in the divine elixir of motherhood. I'm afraid of pregnancy, and she looks as if it's the most desirable experience in the universe.

I hope our breaks will coincide, and when they do, I manage to sit next to her in the changing room. I tell her she looks beautiful, pregnant and dancing.

"Does it show? The manager hasn't said anything, and I need to go on working as long as possible." She tenderly touches her abdomen and breaths a luminous smile.

"What will you do when the baby arrives?"

"My boyfriend is in a rock band, and I'm hoping he'll settle down long enough for me to give birth and get my figure back, so I can start dancing again."

"Who will take care of it then?"

A frown flits across her face. "I'll find someone, I'm sure, or I can go on welfare for a while." She turns away to put on more makeup. Whenever I think of pregnancy, these practicalities stop me right at the start. Apparently for other women, the thrill of having a child is enough to blot them out. I wonder if there was any time when my mother felt that way.

I go back down to lose myself in moving to music. When I return to Sara's in the small hours of the morning, Andrew is pretending to be asleep. He pulls away from me as I lie down wearily, his stiff body conveying his resentment. This evening I have moved far beyond him.

During break the next night, the women pull out lunch bags or order a hamburger from the bar while I open a container of brown rice and cabbage. I've become a vegetarian and am trying out macrobiotics. I worry the women will see me as a hippie-freak. Tina had almost quit when she realized the Beatles' tune, "Lucy in the Sky with Diamonds," spelled out LSD. But the only comment comes from Cat who says, "You need more protein in your diet, dear, because the dancing takes a lot out of you." Sandy, a lovely woman with shiny hair, says something that catches my interest.

"I lubricate so much when I have sex with my husband that immediately after I take a bath and douche with vinegar and water."

"Honey, you should try it with a woman. You wouldn't have to go to all that trouble," Cat responds. Sandy gives her a cold look.

"I've heard that's not good for your female organs, squirting that stuff inside you," the pregnant dancer comments.

"Oh, a little won't hurt you, and it keeps you fresh-smelling," says Sandy.

My lips remain closed. No woman I know has ever discussed these matters, especially not my mother. Although I am no longer a virgin and have douched, I have only a vague notion of this lubrication they are talking about. I hope someday I will experience passionate lovemaking, but I suspect it won't be with Andrew.

The manager yells up, "Your shift is starting." We troop down to the cavernous, dark interior. It is early yet, and a few men are drinking—most of them wearing suits. Suddenly, I feel naked—well, I *am* almost naked. All I'm wearing is a satin bikini bottom, some fishnet tights, pasties, and shoes. Someone gives me a hand up as I step from the floor to the stool up to the bar. I stand beneath the magical spotlighted cloud that makes everyone else invisible and begin to move my body rhythmically while the music swells. I feel like the most beautiful woman in the world as my hips, shoulders, and hands move to the rhythm. I'm simply responding to an ancient flow of sound. Only vaguely aware of the bartender and customers at my feet, I am surprised when one of the girls says, "It's break time." As their warm hands help me step down, two men say they have a question for me. Once I am out of the spot light, I can see they are businessmen in gray suits. I'm drawn to the younger, baby-faced man, but he is quiet while the older man speaks. I feel vulnerable standing toe-to-toe with them in the dark bar.

"We want to know what your bra size is." I'm caught completely off guard. This has no connection to my dancing fantasy. I feel humiliated, my worth equal to the size of my breasts. I'm also ashamed because I haven't worn a bra since I've been in California. Freedom from bras was part of my liberation. I have no idea what my size is.

"That's a rude question, and I won't answer," I retort, crossing my arms over my chest and walking off with as much dignity as I can muster. Out of the corner of my eye, I can see the men looking perplexed.

As we are packing up to leave for the night, I complain about the men to Sandy.

"They didn't mean anything by it, honey. They were just admiring you. They think you're beautiful, which you are." As we walk companionably onto the street, I feel like hugging her. Her warm comment restores my self-respect. A few minutes of her presence gives me more nurturing than I had experienced in nineteen years with my own mother.

After a while, topless dancing loses its novelty. The cigarette smoke that rises in a cloud toward the ceiling where I breathe makes my head ache. The sour stench of booze is reminiscent of my mother's parties. I'm nervous about riding the bus back to Sara's alone in the early hours of the morning while the city sidewalks are hosed down and drunks sleep in doorways. My feet are sore, and I reek of smoke. To feel clean, I have to wash every follicle of hair and inch of skin. I resent finding Andrew asleep in bed. He is doing nothing, while I work for an apartment. Finally, I don't like the idea of myself dancing naked in a bar.

When I'm dancing, I can't remember to keep my feet still. The music gets a good beat, and I lift my foot and make contact with a glass. When I kick the third drink into a patron's lap, I'm afraid the manager will fire me, so I quit. But I miss the women's company once I'm gone.

❦

I coax Andrew into attending group dances led by a little walnut-faced man called Sufi Sam. Voluminously skirted women and longhaired men gaze at him with devotion and called him "Murshid." I ask one of them why, and she says Sam is an enlightened Sufi teacher. He wears thick glasses and has a long beard and an accent that belongs behind the counter of a New York delicatessen. He cracks awful jokes. I ask why his jokes are such groaners, and he says, "I used to be a scholar, but I discovered I get closer to God through laughter than through study."

Sam forms us into an inner and an outer circle, and instructs us to see the divine in our partners' faces. As we sing a simple chant, the circles rotate and we gaze at each other. At first, I am embarrassed to be staring directly into a stranger's eyes. It seems rude. But as we revolve around each other in time to the song, I dare my eyes to sink into the mysterious human being before me. Some eyes shine with joy, others with deep sadness, and some are guarded, refusing to peer back. In all of them, essence shines. We sing Arabic syllables:

Ishq Allah Mabud lillah
All I ask of you is forever
to remember me as loving you

This is the most loving idea I've ever heard. Could I possibly apply it to my mother? I imagine her in the circle with her incandescent blue eyes and vibrant smile, dressed in her chic pink-and-turquoise satin suit. But as we swirl around, she drags on my hands, pulling us all out of kilter until the center cannot hold and breaks apart. I shake my head to dispel the image. Best not to think of my mother.

In another dance, Sam stands to one side playing the part of Krishna, beloved of the Gopis, the village cowherd girls. He swoops among us, draws a girl aside, and swings her around as he thrusts his wrinkled face into hers. When he does it to me, I see a shimmering around him and feel he really is a saintly mystic. I leave feeling warm and happy.

"Sam is just a dirty old man," Andrew says as we walk back to Sara's. "I don't see anything the least bit divine about him." His doubt taints the loveliness of the evening. I'm tired of Andrew's cynicism. We quarrel and separate, and I forget about Sufi Sam.

⁂

I can't stand being homeless anymore, and my search for a family commune has been fruitless. The hippie life isn't as fun and carefree as I thought. It's time to follow up on my LSD vision, time to get shelter and a job. Time to grow up.

In a shared apartment in the Haight, I rent the cheapest room, next to the bathroom, for $25 a month. The last occupant has left a mattress, so I buy sheets and a paisley spread and tack a poster of the Indian god Vishnu to the wall. I meditate daily, seated on my mattress facing many-armed Vishnu and have an experience of seeing the golden god multiply around me into the room. The bathroom noises and the flushing toilet punctuate my serenity. But I'm so grateful to have plumbing and running water those sounds don't bother me at all. To save money, I eat only brown rice, cabbage, and lentils.

In the luxury of a hot water shower, I discover my vagina has strange warts. I panic. Where shall I go? I wait for hours in a long line of sick hippies to be seen at the Diggers' Free Clinic. It is operated in a run-down storefront. A harassed-looking, frizzy-haired guy in street clothes who says he is a doctor attends me. I am mortified to pull up my long jean skirt and show him these strange growths on my vaginal lips, but I have to do something. He gives the diagnosis of a sexually transmitted disease called genital warts. I'm horrified. To my knowledge, the only people who had sexually transmitted diseases were nineteenth-century French writers and painters who contracted syphilis. He scrabbles in a box among a few medicines and pulls out a small vial with a little wand that is used to burn warts off your hands. "This is all we have," he says, giving me a sympathetic look.

Weeping, I apply the stinging ointment, hoping the pain will cleanse my sense of defilement as well as the virus. They eventually disappear, but sex—with its worries of pregnancy and now disease—has lost its appeal. When a curly haired housemate wants to become my boyfriend, I tell him I'm celibate. He gets angry and insults me, but I don't care. His sexual need is not my problem. I apologize to my innocent body for so casually offering it to whomever. And for what? A little comfort for my loneliness. Except for Rudy, I hadn't felt much for any of those men. I wonder if Rudy still thinks of me, or if he has a new girlfriend by now. That's just another mess I've made of my life that I don't want to think about.

Next, I get a nine-to-five job as a file clerk at a large clothing manufacturer. An oppressive sensation comes over me the first morning I encase my legs in stockings and my breasts in a bra. This is definitely the dividing line between the hippie life and the squares. The dream of finding God and a family that led me to California seems flatter than my mattress on the floor.

I spend my days slipping papers into alphabetical files that fill a room from floor to ceiling. The work is boring but not taxing. My office mates are friendly and supportive. On my lunch hour, I meditate in a small church across the street. In the dimly lit sanctuary, I practice watching my breath and looking inward. What a mess my mind is! Old arguments between my mother and me rattle on while disconnected images leap up. Yet, in between, there are moments of spaciousness and a sense of settling into my body. I always come away feeling refreshed.

Included in the orientation to the company is a visit to their clothing factory. I watch as vast bolts of cloth are cut and sewed by a mostly female Asian crew. The break bell rings, and the women eagerly run across the floor for their thermoses and brown bags. Fifteen minutes later, they drag themselves back to their sewing machines. Their lives are a sobering counterpoint to my vagabond existence that seems, from this perspective, totally frivolous and privileged.

After a workweek indoors filing papers, I hunger to be in nature. On Sundays I climb Mount Tamalpais with a Tibetan group. It is led by a butterball German dressed in embroidered leather shorts, knee socks, and a little William Tell cap with a feather. He teaches us to repeat the mantra *"Om Mane Padme Hum,"* which he translates as "the jewel in the lotus," with our steps as we slowly ascend the mountain.

I enjoy simplifying my life to just these footsteps trudging up the steep slopes, the wild thyme-scented air filling my lungs, just these syllables revolving in my mind. The words became a slender raft to hang onto as doubts and questions claw at me. *What am I doing here? Why am I always alone? What is my life purpose? Where are my people, the family I seek? Where is that jewel in the lotus? Is there any jewel in the lotus?*

At the top of the mountain, the German guru dons robes over his lederhosen and performs a ceremony, initiating two men into Buddhist vows. Someone explains to me they are going to be sexually chaste and avoid killing any living beings. Inwardly, I'm ready to make a similar vow. I carefully work my way down Mount Tam, muttering, *"Om Mane Padme Hum."* I dig my boots into the sandy trail and breathe with my mantra. Perhaps I can find my way through this confusion after all.

Sara becomes like an older sister to me—she is warm but bossy. On the weekends, I hang out at her apartment and play with her son, Max, while she bakes a cake with carrots and zuc-chini in it. I tell her it is weird to put vegetables in cake, but she ignores me. One day I find her dancing around the kitchen table.

"I've got a letter from Tony, who's in New York with the guru," she says, beaming with excitement. "Sri Chinmoy says I should come there for an interview. He is going to choose one of Tony's girlfriends to be his wife. Can you believe it? I could be married to Tony!" She sits down and reverently composes a letter to the guru saying she wants to be his disciple. She slides it into an envelope along with her photograph and encourages me to do the same.

I think about it. I'm just as directionless and confused as I was when I first came to California. I've already given up sex, alcohol, and drugs, which are requirements of the guru's. The wise guidance of a teacher is something I'm longing for, and I want to become closer to God. The Beatles traveled to India for their guru—all I'd have to do is go to Queens, New York. I send in my application.

Sara and I both receive acceptance letters. We are to live a pure life for three months, and then we can come to Queens. I cry for days when I see fate is returning me to my birthplace, New York City. Part of me screams, *Don't go back there, your mother will destroy you!* Another part yearns to see how she is, and wonders if she has missed me. I still crave her love. Because they find me crying into the file folders, friends at work worry that I am pregnant, which seems ironic. I can't put words to the turmoil inside me.

Chapter 10

PEACE AND NURTURANCE

❧

Those who feel plagued by not being good enough
Are often drawn to idealistic world views . . .
—TARA BRACH

Mother is taking her time clicking back the locks and open-ing the door while I wait in the hall with my backpack and sleeping bag. She stands unresponsive. All she is wearing is a stained cotton nightgown and a hospital identity band wrapped around one child-sized wrist. To cover the silence I say with false cheer, "Hi, Mommy, how are you?"

I lean in to press cheeks and smell rank body odor. She still hasn't said a word, so I pause to look at her. White scalp shows between wisps of hair, and her eyes are gray grapes. We peer at each other across a divide as wide as a Manhattan canyon.

"You can sleep in Cecelia's room for a while," she says finally through a cloud of smoke and points her cigarette down the hall.

"Oh, thank you for letting me stay." The room contains a child's box spring and mattress wrapped in plastic next to a white and gold miniature nightstand with matching rocking chair. I drop my backpack, glad I have kept my sleeping bag. When I last saw Cecilia, she was an elfin creature who cringed when the wind blew in her face as I pushed her swing. By now she'd be a little over six years old. I wonder where she is, since the furniture looks unused.

"Yoo-hoo, I came in, the door was open," Aunt Clara calls out. I run to receive a more enthusiastic welcome. She has brought Chinese take-out, but the apartment is almost bare, and there is nowhere to set the food down. We push together some packing boxes in the living room in front of a couch. Mother and Clara sit on it while I fold myself on the floor, and we eat our meal from the cartons. Mother has never been much of an eater, and now every bone in her neck stands out. She sits silently flexing a bare big toe and puffing her Camels as if we don't exist.

Clara and I pretend everything is normal and chat about my California sojourn and her plans to return South to get her teaching certificate. Finally, I force my mouth to say what is in my mind. "Where are Cecilia and Nan?" Mother looks away.

Clara takes a breath and slowly explains, "They live in their own apartment below David and his new wife somewhere across town." This is a repeat scenario of when I first lived with David and my mother. I guess they found it worked—for the adults. Mother stands up and goes to her room. We listen to her door closing.

I move to the couch. On the phone, Clara had told me a little about the custody battle over my baby sister. Now she explains, whispering as if Mother could still hear, "It was horrible. Barbara Taylor Bradford and other friends testified against her right in court. David said he was afraid your mother's boyfriends were molesting the child. What a horrendous lie! But she keeps hoping Cecilia will be allowed to visit. And the worst part is Cecilia has been diagnosed with childhood schizophrenia or maybe fetal alcohol syndrome. She's been through all these tests and sees a child psychiatrist once a week. You have to ask David if you can visit her."

Slowly I take this in. I picture my mother on the stand in a courtroom. Her former husband and friends surround her like a pack of bloodhounds, snarling and snatching at her designer suits and coiffed hair. I am glad I wasn't there, because what would I have said? The truth is she is a terrible mother. Barbara Taylor Bradford once said about her, "A cat has more maternal instinct than you." I'd often felt the truth of this as I'd watched the cow lick her calf or the cat nurse her kittens when I was visiting my grandparents' farm. All my life I had longed for a sister, and this is what happened. Some implacable force pursued me and systematically destroyed everything I cared about. I feel bitterness surge through me.

"You know about the other stuff, don't you?" Clara asks. "David and my parents and my sister Goldie signed papers to have your mother committed to an alcoholic rehab hospital. She was there about seven months and has just been released."

This is too much. I imagine my mother as a Bowery bum, lying on the sidewalk with a bottle in her hand—wearing a mink coat, high heels, and pillbox hat. Bums are the only association I have with alcoholism, although I know without a doubt she is one. And my sister Cecelia is crazy—poisoned *in utero*. Yet Mother yearns for the damaged daughter and doesn't want me. I feel shame and rage so deep it's as if I'd swallowed acid, and it was permeating down my throat through to my stomach. What can I do? There's nothing I can do.

Mother is subdued. She paces the hallway dressed in that filthy cotton nightgown, chain-smoking. She doesn't say much, and when she does, she won't look at me. Her head hangs toward the floor. I can't get used to her without her fierceness; with a queasy thrill, I realize I'm sorry for her. I want to take care of her. But she refuses to eat or wash or dress or go out.

A sewing machine stashed among her cardboard boxes gives me an idea. I go to Woolworth's and, using the last of my money, buy a pattern, turquoise cloth, pins, scissors, needles, and thread. I spend more than a week kneeling on the floor happily occupied with stitching a becoming Chinese sheath. I proudly sew a zipper up the back. Mother tries it on but complains it is tight under the arms; she's always had a large bust for a small woman. The dress is balled in a corner of her room along with the rest of her clothes. Later I smooth it out and hang it in her vacant closet.

After about ten days, empty Vodka bottles begin clinking in the garbage under the kitchen sink. A net of red capillaries spreads across her nose and cheeks. She stands with one hand resting on her hip while the other carries her cigarette toward her lips. "All those psychiatrists at the hospital were in love with me, you know." Clearly the rehab hadn't taken. I pray that this guru thing works out, because I have to get out of here and soon.

❧

The pink profusion of a double-flowering cherry tree greets me as I climb up the subway steps to emerge into Queens. Lavender and fuchsia azalea hedges jostle my vision. Newly leafed trees shade postage stamp gardens fronting tidy houses. Lilies of the valley sweeten the air. By the time I arrive at Sri Chinmoy's peacock-blue house, my knees are shaking.

Removing my patent leather pumps in the hallway, I tiptoe into his dimly lit living room. I find a place on a folding chair. People around me sit quietly with their eyes closed, meditating. Two young women sit cross-legged on floor cushions with their laps modestly covered by shawls. Before them is an empty gold-leafed chair. I relax into the warm, incense-infused twilight and close my eyes. It's as if I am snuggling down, down into a deep feather bed. The rich silence soothes my senses that are vibrating from the long subway ride and anxiety. Occasionally someone gives an exhalation as if they are part of a herd that is settling down for the night. Slowly my body, brain, and core unclench and relax into this one place. I sigh as if I've never breathed before, as if I can't get enough of the air in this room.

Many place their palms together and I follow the gesture. Pressing my wrists into my chest helps me connect to my heart, and I imagine breathing through it. I concentrate and try not to move, not even to scratch. I breathe in unison with the others seated around me. My sense of being a separate body relaxes.

After a while, I open my eyes and see Sri Chinmoy seated facing us. He is a bald, compact, middle-aged, Indian angelic being dressed in a golden robe. The meditation begins in earnest. He appears enveloped in flames that reflect in his eyes as they flicker back and forth. His gaze beckons to us from another world. A powerful vibration like the engine of a jet plane is pushing us all upwards into a shared transcendence. I've never experienced anything like this before. I'm so blessed to have found him, so incredibly grateful.

After an endless time, Guru explains in his husky accented voice, "Mine is the Bhakti path; you come into unity with God through devotion to me. If you dedicate yourselves unceasingly to me, I will take us to the golden shores of the beyond." The words fall on my ears like flower petals. Everything I've tried has been futile. I'm more than ready to purge my child-of-an-alcoholic-mother, stepmother-rejected, college-drop-out, night-in-jail, genital-wart-infected, topless-dancing, chubby, hippie self of all that is unworthy and devote myself to him, if he will transform me into a loving and lovable woman. My long journey through England, New York, Kentucky, Brandeis, and California is over. I have found home at last. Gathering his golden *dhoti* around him, Sri Chinmoy leaves the room on naked brown feet. An urge to prostrate myself before him presses up through my heart.

People slowly begin to gather their coats and shawls to leave. As I look around, I see their eyes are shining, and their lips are wide in loopy grins. I know my face glows with the same smile. I feel a love so vast it encompasses my mother, David, and even Franca.

Sara appears and hugs me as we weep with joy. She looks radiantly happy and says she and Tony are to be married in a few months. At Guru's direction, he is going to night school to become a lawyer. They are living in Connecticut where she works to support them both while also caring for Max.

Sara introduces me to a flaxen-haired young woman who is Tony and Andrew's younger sister, Sandra. She has just arrived in New York and, like me, wants to become a student of the master. I like her immediately for her cheerful nonchalance in admitting that her older brothers spoil her. She is looking for someone to share an apartment with, and we decide we will be housemates. She needs a place to stay in the interim, so I say she can stay with me at my mother's. This is a bold step to take, considering I'm not welcome there myself.

Sara asks if we want to meet Alo Devi and I say, "Who?"

"Sri Chinmoy's divine Shakti and feminine counterpart, the Mother to his Father. The Canadian woman who brought him from Sri Aurobindo's ashram to New York. They aren't married, but they are one on the higher plane." We are brought before a petite, dark-haired woman with a high forehead and sloping cheekbones. When I place my palms together and bow, imitating Sara, Alo Devi cups her hands around mine and looks into my eyes in the kindest, most gentle way. I know then I have found my family. My people are right here where I began. My search for a different way of life from my mother's and my tribe is over. I rattle back to Manhattan on the subway in quiet joy, knowing I will return.

A few nights later, when Sandra and I are getting ready for bed, we hear Mother's drunken footsteps staggering down the hall.

"You have to leave now!" she roars, bursting into our room and, fumbling for the door, weaves her way out.

"Sandra, where can we go so late at night?" I'm humiliated and frightened.

"Hee-hee-hee," Sandra giggles behind her hand, surprising me. "Why is she walking like that? Is she putting on an act?" I look at her for a few moments as her shoulders shake in laughter. Maybe there's another way to handle this.

"We will find another place to live in a few days," I say firmly as Mother collapses on her bed. She gives no hint of remembering the incident in the morning.

Sandra and I rent a small apartment a few blocks from Guru's house. It is on the second floor of a bungalow owned by an elderly Greek couple. The Queens neighborhood is a bastion of immigrants who support the gold domed Greek Orthodox Church down the street. Racks of lamb and feta cheese squares are displayed in the grocery stores. They seem unaware that an Indian spiritual group is growing in their midst.

Early each morning, Sandra and I meditate together, gazing at a photo of Guru in God-realized consciousness perched on a cardboard box covered with a silver-threaded cloth. I fervently believe that Guru is enlightened. What else could explain those amazing meditations? Yogananda talked about this sort of transmission in *Autobiography of a Yogi*. All I have to do is completely surrender my life to him. Everything I've done so far has been an exercise in failure and misery, anyway. I happily relinquished control to this god-man.

Then we trot to the high school track and join Guru and other disciples to practice for the upcoming CKG (Guru's initials) Olympics. Guru has indicated that the body requires running, jumping, tennis, and bicycling to be purified. These are activities I loathe, but Guru wants all his disciples to participate in sports competitions on his birthday week in August. It helps that Guru starts the day by offering each one of us *Prasad*, a gift of an apple or a flower. One glance from his bright brown eyes, and I'm filled with aspiration. Guru himself jogs around the track in shorts and sports shirt while we cheer. He wants to run a marathon and encourages his followers to do the same. The idea seems impossible, but inwardly I vow to try it.

Weekdays, I shuttle down to my new receptionist's job in mid-Manhattan like a subway veteran. I put in eight hours answering the phones, typing very slowly because I'm just learning, and balancing the petty cash accounts. I retrace my route on the hour-long subway ride back to the apartment to shower, change, and race over to P. S. 86 where we often hold meditations because we are outgrowing Guru's living room.

"You're just escaping from the world following some idiot huckster," Mother says in her smoky rasp when I share my good news of finding an enlightened teacher. I have a moment of doubting Guru, and I reel away from the phone call feeling shattered, for without him, I have no hope, no future. But then I remember who I'm talking to: my mother, who has absolutely no credibility. I realize if I hope to hang onto my peace, I have to limit contact with her.

Guru tells us, "The past is dust. Forget about your parents and previous life." As it is, I think only of him: what will please him, what will make him notice me. He hasn't acknowledged me personally yet. I write to my father:

Dear Daddy,
I have found God and a guru whose love is eternal
and permanent. My days are no longer static clumps
of misery but a moving flow of bliss. I no longer feel
that I am useless and impotent in an impossible world.
How did I ever live without this? We create our own
misery—why not learn to un-create it?
*   Let me tell you about Guru. He was born in*
Bengal and grew up in the ashram of Sri Aurobindo.
He is about thirty-seven years old. He requires no
money from us but does demand attendance at regular
meditation meetings. I could tell you he is in complete
contact with God, but I don't expect you to believe
that. Guru is leading us toward spiritual enlightenment
so rapidly I can almost feel the change day by day.
Love,
Your Daughter

He types back that Grandma Blanche has died, and he has lost his Paramount job and is in a slough of despond. Maybe he will open a cigarette and magazine stand. Reading this, I can feel my father's despair sucking me down.

One morning on the way to track, I wonder out loud to Sandra when I will officially be made part of the group. Her blue eyes look at me in wonderment. "But you are part of the group." She doesn't know my background of being shunted from New York to London to Kentucky. I'm still the outsider hungry to get in. I want my spiritual name, a position in the inner circle, something that shows I'm officially accepted.

I hope Grandma Blanche is at peace. I am concerned, however, for her soul. Guru has been talking about reincarnation, and I think Grandma deserves some expert guidance as her soul makes its journey to its next rebirth. I call and make an appointment to see him.

Lalita opens Guru's door wearing a sari. During meditation, she always sits on the floor in front of Guru, looking up at him adoringly through her dark eyelashes. She tells me to come into the kitchen. After slipping off my shoes onto the empty rack, I follow her sinuous hips. As the folds of her peach-colored sari whisper, she seems to glide on skates. A cropped blouse gives glimpses of a pale, flat stomach. I'm confused, because Guru emphasizes purity, but I'm also smitten with envy. I want to look like Lalita, move like Lalita, and most of all, be as close to Guru as she is.

I look around the immaculate kitchen as she works in silence. "Do you live here?" I dare to ask.

She lavishes a smile on the lemon she is squeezing into a glass of water. "Well, not exactly, I have an apartment down the street, but I am here most of the time. This is for Guru. He likes to sip it. To keep his weight down so he can run a marathon." She yanks opens a cupboard, grabs a jar of peanut butter and a loaf of bread and begins slathering one on the other.

"Is that for Guru, too?" I ask surprised.

"Oh, no," she sniffs through her aquiline nose. "This is for Alo's mid-morning snack. And she likes butter on her peanut butter. Can you imagine?" Her delicate eyebrows rise. "It's a good thing these saris are expandable."

"I'd love to know how you get them on." I notice that she doesn't seem thrilled with Alo.

"Yes, Guru wants me to show you all how to do it, but I am rather busy. You need six feet of cloth, a long slip that ties at the waist, and a short blouse is nice so you don't look like an elephant." Her laugh tinkles gaily. I think she doesn't look like one, but I probably would.

Pouring a glass of milk and placing it with the peanut butter on a tray, she un-tucks the end of the sari from her waist and tosses it behind her. "Actually, I need to bring this to Alo. Will you take Guru's lemon water in?"

Gingerly I carry a silver tray with the glass and napkin into the meditation/living room and set it down on a table beside Guru's gilt chair. The rows of chairs are empty, but I stand, unsure where to sit. I'm still absorbing the information that Guru struggles with his weight while Alo doesn't. Until a few weeks ago, I thought Guru transcended all bodily functions. I didn't even think he peed until I admitted this to Sandra, who laughed and pointed out that sometimes Guru left the room during meditation and one could hear water rushing through the pipes. What was he doing then? Well, all right, I granted, maybe he peed, but otherwise he was purely divine.

Guru slips in, wearing shorts and a sport shirt, and sits casually on the chair with one leg outstretched and the other bent close to his chest. He motions for me to pull up a seat. I cover my knees with a scarf, fold my hands and reverently bow my head. I've never been this close and notice stubble bristling from his chin.

"Yes, yes?" he whispers in a hoarse voice.

Stumbling over my words I request guidance for Grandma's soul. I keep peeking and noticing the sour turn of his mouth. His eyes spill annoyance instead of light.

"Always, always my disciples want special attention from me," he says, rubbing his eyes and nose with his palm. "When I bless you in meditation you receive everything you need: all light, all wisdom, all love. I give you all."

His accusatory words alarm me. I explain again my grandmother has died. But I seem to be at fault for seeking special attention, since he holds the fate of the world on his shoulders.

"The world needs my light. This is my mission: to spread light. Understand? I know what you need. A mother knows what her child wants before the child knows. I am trying to arrange weekly meditations at the United Nations, to become the spiritual director. This is very, very important. Much letter writing and, how to say, pulling string? Do you know someone who can write a letter for me to the United Nations? Do you have a typewriter?"

I picture my father in England slumped over his coffee because he has just lost his job and his mother. My mother's alcoholic rants ring in my ears. Asking favors of them is out of the question. "I just got a job as a receptionist, and they have a typewriter there."

"See if you can help Lalita type up my lectures or write letters to the UN. Don't worry about the rest. Come here, good girl." He moves forward and places his warm palms on my bent head in blessing. "The Supreme is happy with you."

I float out of the room filled with happiness. Lalita gives me a tape recorder and a bag of tapes to be transcribed. If I have to type until midnight at work, I vow to finish them. I will buy several saris and sew cropped blouses. When Guru sees my single-minded devotion, I'll soon be a favored assistant alongside Lalita.

❧

I'm meditating in the front row of Guru's living room when Lalita leans in and whispers in my ear, "Guru wants you to marry that boy over there. What do you think?" I've been in the Aum Centre three months.

The light is dim, but I can see him. The boy is cute, dark-haired, and with a turned up nose like me. This is a surprise. I planned to be nun-like in my devotion to Guru. After meditation, I find Alo to ask about this marriage business. She looks as if this is a new idea to her as well and pulls me into an adjacent room where Guru is relaxing in a La-Z-Boy reading some papers. She whispers to Guru, who whispers back, gesticulating and looking annoyed. Then Alo says, "But I thought she was going to be a nun." I nod.

Guru turns to me. "This boy is your soul mate. You will support each other along the spiritual path. He will be there to bring you a glass of water when you are sick. If you don't marry him, I see you will marry at least five times." This statement gives me a moment of terror. Had someone told him about my mother? Was I doomed to follow her through her many marriages? Then he beams at me a soul-flooding smile that leaves me light-headed. "I will give you your spiritual name."

"I'm okay with it if you are," Chuck says when we discuss marriage at the next meditation. "I just want to please Guru." He really is very cute with big blue eyes fringed by dark eyelashes. I like his dedication to the path. Sandra squeals with delight when I tell her, although I still feel dubious. On the appointed day, I don a long white skirt and top it with a flowing white blouse. Chuck presents me with a bouquet on the steps of Guru's blue house, and we walk inside. Both Alo and Lalita are wrapped in saris that, I mentally note, I must acquire. We are ushered into a small room where Guru sits on the carpet. He wears a gold *dhoti* and *kurta* and looks otherworldly.

We sit in front of him. He cups his palms over our heads and steers our faces close to his. He peers into my eyes, flooding me with light until I feel filled to bursting. He does the same to Chuck. He guides our heads together, closes his eyes, and begins to chant in Bengali. Rhythmic syllables, powerful incantations peal from his mouth. Our bodies form a pyramid over which pour cascades of sound. Energy crackles around me, and

I'm infused with light. I feel the Indian gods Shiva and Vishnu dancing around us.

Gradually the chanting ceases, and the energy seeps away. As if it has rained, I am left fresh and buoyant. Dew has settled on my upper lip. I gaze lovingly at my soul mate, but Guru cautions in a rapid-fire whisper, "Sex is permitted only once a month—not on meditation nights, and only after you have bathed and meditated." Then he makes a deep bow to us with palms together, and we do the same.

Something is missing.

"What about our names?" I ask Alo.

"Yes, their names," Alo says pointedly to Guru.

He stands up with difficulty because of his encumbering *dhoti* and meditates for a moment, his eyes flickering. He walks over to my husband, places his palms on his head, and says, "Your name is Arjun or divine warrior." He turns to me and does the same. "Yours is Pujarini or devotional service." He pronounces my name as two words: puja–reenee.

Alo pounces on this and says, "I don't like it said that way, you know. It sounds cheap." She whispers something to Guru who looks exasperated.

"Yes, yes," he agrees to whatever she is saying. "We want you to pronounce it Puja-rini, with the emphasis on pujar."

I'm dismayed by this confusion. These are the people to whom I've surrendered my life, and they can't agree how to say my name? I repeat Alo's pronunciation several times to make sure I don't say my name in a way that sounds cheap. Whatever that means.

"Don't forget to see a judge and make it legal," Lalita whispers.

Since we aren't really married, Arjun continues living with his mother and stepfather in Connecticut while I stay in Queens. Weeks of bliss follow as I am enveloped in the pink cloud of Guru's approval and love. He calls me by my name, Pujarini, when he hands me a flower with special blessings at the track where we exercise. Lalita and the other disciples smile and greet me with my new name. When I jog around, my feet fall like blessings upon the cinders, my hair caresses the back of my neck. Amazed at the miracle of volition, nerves, and muscles, even my fingers throw a tennis ball reverently. I walk in beauty and am beloved of the world.

❧

Arjun's mother, Mary, calls and invites me to lunch. At the restaurant, she is dressed in a tan, double-knit suit and a creamy silk blouse with a jeweled insect brooch pinned on her shoulder. Her shoes and purse are matching honey-colored suede. A bow ties her hair at the back of her neck. But her hair must be pulled too tight, because her penciled eyebrows are high on her forehead. Mary immediately orders a scotch and water.

"Tell me about yourself, dear," she says. I do, and as she sips her drink, her face softens. When she hears my mother lives in New York, she asks for her telephone number.

"Chuck"—she can't get accustomed to Arjun's new name—"has been quite wild with the girls. He got a girl pregnant; they married but divorced after a year. Did he tell you about his three-year-old son?" She shakes her head.

"I'm not sure what to think about this guru business, but it seems to have settled him down. You look like a nice girl, and if this second marriage will give him stability, I'm all for it. We can have the marriage performed in my home by my husband acting as justice of the peace."

She grows garrulous as she moves into her second scotch. "My first marriage was to Chuck's father. Sadly, he turned out to be alcoholic. I was young and less tolerant than I am now. If I could have kept the marriage together, it might have given Chuck what he needed. I don't know." Her eyes grow moist, and she fishes a handkerchief from her bag and blows her nose.

"I wasn't going to tell you this, but Chuck has a small inheritance coming to him. I'm the executor. I'm going to see that you two are set up for a good start." She pats my hand and grasps the back of chairs as she moves carefully to the ladies room. I have passed inspection.

I like Mary and feel completely comfortable with Arjun's background; it's so similar to my own. With my all-encompassing love, I will make everything better for the entire family. Guru has seen that our souls are meant to be together. I will be a second mother to his little son. Everything is perfect.

I give notice at my workplace with relief. I hear a coworker complain loudly of all the hours they'd put in training me. She says I could be married, live in Connecticut, and still take the train to work. But I don't want to be stuck in the dull office. I want to start a new life with my husband.

I call my mother. "I'm getting married. Will you come to the wedding?"

"You're running away from life. You could do way better than that little boy, from what I hear from his mother. So no, I won't be there," she says and smashes down the phone. I don't take in anything she says. I don't want her negative presence at my wedding. But because I can't marry without her signature until I'm twenty-one, I have to wait until after my birthday in September.

Arjun and I stand facing each other in front of the fireplace of his parent's gracious Connecticut home. His stepfather, whose dandruff flakes on his suit jacket just like my father's, says the brief words that legally marry us. Aunt Clara, my only relative present, sniffles into her handkerchief.

"Your mother loves you very much; it's just hard for her to tell you so," she says. I have heard that before and don't believe it for a moment. Actually, I feel surging joy that my mother isn't here. I have a new identity, and my life is going in a direction directly opposite from hers.

After the ceremony, we have a buffet that Mary sets with a variety of vegetarian and meat dishes. She serves Arjun and me sparkling apple cider because we abstain from alcohol as well as meat. Clara sips a glass of white wine while Mary and Bill mix several strong drinks.

"I had lunch with your mother, who is such an interesting person. What a life she led! She's hobnobbed with royalty. I'm sorry Jeanne couldn't come."

We talk about the house Arjun is interested in buying. "It's a fixer-upper for sure. I wouldn't want to live in it, but Chuck seems to think it's such a good value," Mary says. Clara leaves, and as the evening sets in, Mary and her husband become very drunk. He sinks into his chair in front of the television while she scolds and becomes belligerent.

Arjun pulls me away, and we retire to the guest bedroom. "Don't pay any attention to them. It's always this way." We watch a little TV, guiltily, because Guru says it lowers consciousness, and sleep chastely back-to-back. We don't talk about the huge step we have taken. We don't know how to express the worlds we are bridging. All we have is our devotion to Guru. The next morning, we drive to Wilton, Connecticut, to look at the house whose down payment will eat up most of his inheritance.

Chapter 11

RESTAURANT TESTING GROUND

The moment you accept what troubles you've been given
The door will open.

—RUMI

"The mansion is almost a hundred years old," the realtor says as she shoves open the swollen front door. "It has tons of potential for a young couple like yourselves." We walk through rooms with cloth-covered wires creeping along the wainscoting, peeling wallpaper, blackened wood floors. Appalled, I can't find words for my reaction. Not wanting to discuss this in front of the realtor, I wait for a moment to be alone with Arjun.

He sees nothing but possibility. "I've done some carpentering," he says, sketching in the air with a forefinger. "I can refinish the floors, paint the walls, and soon it will be as good as new." The kitchen, however, silences him. The walls are bare of cabinets. One painted sink with a tin drainage board stands in the corner, and a refrigerator is plugged in the light fixture on the ceiling.

Arjun quickly regains his enthusiasm, "The linoleum is easily replaced." Here he pulls up a section that looks as if water has leaked from the ceiling and reveals a hole rotting in the floorboards. The realtor gasps and jots down something in her notebook with a tiny brass pencil. She mutters about lowering the price, and we move on.

I hold Arjun back and whisper furiously, "You can't be considering this place. It's an absolute wreck!"

"You don't understand finances." He shrugs me off. "The house is large enough that we can rent out rooms to disciples, so the mortgage will be covered." The words *finances* and *mortgage* cow me. I've never been good with numbers, and anyway, it's his money. *Maybe we can stay with his parents until it's fixed up?* What is most upsetting is how far from Guru we will be living—no more seeing him every morning at the track or trotting over to his house for special meetings. Living in Connecticut is the spiritual equivalent of Siberia.

We gaze at the large, unattached garage, the cliff and acre of woods behind the house.

"This is a fantastic value!" Arjun says, "A nine-room house, a huge garage, and an acre of land. It's great." I shake my head and glare at him. Behind the realtor's back, he hisses at me, "Guru wants us to help Sara and Tony start a Sri Chinmoy Centre in Connecticut. Don't you want to further Guru's mission?" This shames me, so I grudgingly agree. We sign the papers and a week later move in with our bed and a chest of drawers. We already have a tenant, a hippie woman named Margie and her two young children who've just driven from California in a VW van to check Guru out.

We are alone, although I can hear Margie thumping around with her kids on the other side of the house. The last I'd seen, they were putting up a tent and hammering the pegs into the floor. But I don't want to think about that now. Arjun and I have never even kissed. There are all those rules Guru has laid down. Shyly, we take separate baths in the rust-colored water that slowly trickles into the claw-foot tub. We change into fresh pajamas and meditate on Guru's Samadhi picture set up on a box. Then we sit side by side on the new bed his mother had ordered for us.

I can smell soap from Arjun's body, and his short brown hair is still damp. He looks as innocent as a choirboy, but the heat from his body is decidedly masculine.

Arjun looks away. "I've been a wild man," he confesses, "drinking too much and screwing anything with boobs. I dropped out of college after a semester. I totaled my Karmann Ghia during a drag race with a friend and didn't get a bruise." He snorts with rueful laughter at the memory. "I knew my first marriage was a mistake as I was walking up the aisle. Now I have a new start."

He turns to me and touches my hand. "I hope to be worthy of Guru and dedicate myself to his mission. But I need your help. I have to work on purity, and I don't want another baby. Maybe we could put sex off for a while and see how long we can go without." His face shines as he reveals his aspirations.

Now I turn away as I fumble for the right words. I love his yearning to transform himself. My fingers itch to brush back the dark cowlick from his forehead. I want to be the spiritual soul mate his first wife hadn't been. But all the songs, movies, and books I had ever heard, seen, or read have told me this is the moment when my betrothed should declare to me, "You are lovelier than I could have imagined. If Guru hadn't put us together, I would have searched the world for you." Then he'd peel away my flowered pajamas and exclaim, "Your body is perfection itself. What a gift you are!" And kiss me in all condemned places: my stomach, thighs, too-large breasts. With his mouth on me, he'd murmur my juices tasted so sweet he couldn't get enough of them. Most of all he'd say over and over, "I love you."

I don't have words for any of this, so I cautiously suggest we follow Guru's rule of sex once a month. We can always taper off later. Reluctantly Arjun agrees and gives me a few closed-mouth pecks on the cheek. He squeezes my breasts, achieves an erection, sticks it in me, and with a few shoves is done. He turns away from me on his side and falls asleep, making little *pfft* sounds with each exhalation.

I lie on my back in a puddle of semen and grip the side of the mattress. The sheltering darkness that was cocooning us recedes to a flat horizon in the interminable distance. I am floating, unmoored, in the middle of a vast ocean. The path I'd been so intent on following, the goal I'd achieved has disappeared, leaving me not knowing which way is up or down, right or left. My union with the soul mate Guru selected seems over before it has begun. Nauseous with vertigo, I hear my breathing and racing heartbeat and focus on them. Gradually, my exhalations slow and Guru's beaming face rises before me, radiating peace, and I fall asleep.

"Jennifer?" I hear Arjun's voice through the pasteboard walls the next morning. I sit up and listen. There is a conversation, and he hangs up. He repeats this several times. I listen to him talk to Susan, Dianne, and Brenda and grow increasingly suspicious and upset. Is he telling all his old girlfriends what a mistake he's made? Are they laughing at his joke of a marriage? Angrily I shove open the door and look in.

He is sitting in his underwear cross-legged on the floor in front of the phone and his address book. He looks up, surprised, as if he'd forgotten me.

"What are you doing?" I demand.

"I'm telling my friends about Guru," he says with dignity.

"Well stop it! You're not supposed to talk to girls, especially now that you're married to me."

"That's ridiculous, you're behaving like a baby," he says and stomps into the bedroom to yank on some clothes.

Margie's stocky figure appears at the door. "Me and the kids are going out to grab some breakfast; you want to go, too?"

I do, but I want Arjun to apologize and coax me to go, so I say I'm not hungry. Arjun gives me a hateful look, and they leave in Margie's van. I notice for the first time he has one gray front tooth, and I'm glad it makes him look ugly.

My rage turns to despair as I sit alone in the empty house. If I were in Queens now, I'd be at the track, receiving blessings from Guru, who might call me "good girl" and put his hands on my head. I'd be jogging around laughing with Lalita and the other disciples. I miss Sandra and our hurried breakfasts as we rushed to work. I even miss the crowded subway and my job. Here I am stranded without a car—not that I can drive one—without money, friends, but what is much, much worse, without Guru.

When they pull into the driveway, I watch through the window as they haul out a monster machine between them. The kids scream in glee as the two struggle. Arjun yells up the stairs that he is going to start sanding the lower floors right away. I think he could have tackled more important problems like the dangerous wiring, the trickle of bath water, or our marriage, but I stuff my words down.

Margie slips me an egg sandwich. "You must be hungry," she whispers. I'm angry with Arjun for not thinking of it and ashamed Margie has. I've judged her as grungy hippie with her frizzy hair and peasant clothes. But she is kind, while I, who have an avatar for my spiritual teacher, am petulant and angry. The roar of the sander is deafening, and the bitter taste of the dust and grit of hundred-year-old floors fills my mouth. I write a note to Alo that says, "The marriage isn't working out. Arjun doesn't love me. Can I come back to Queens?" If Guru and Alo put this union together, they'd better well fix it.

We all drive to Queens for meditation at Guru's house. Arjun and I aren't speaking. This time I'm even more grateful to see the sanctuary of the peacock-blue house and want to kiss the sidewalk in front. I need Guru now more than ever to lift me up out of my misery. Breathing through my heart, I gaze at him until I merge with his blazing eyes that look directly into mine. As we gather our coats at the end, I slip Alo the note. She pulls me into the room where Guru performed the marriage ceremony and reads it slowly in her sweet voice. Her gentle brown eyes look at me with surprising fierceness, and her hands clutch my folded palms.

"It's not important that Arjun loves you or you love him. Be single-minded in your focus on Guru. He is your Divine Lover. Think only of him. Breathe him in and out of your heart with every breath. Never let him out of your mind and heart for a moment. And keep busy. We have many more of Guru's talks to transcribe. Lalita will give them to you." I bow reverently to this wisdom from the Divine Mother and begin immediately focusing on Guru.

"How can you be so clumsy?" demands Arjun the following week as he teaches me to drive his stick shift Volvo. We are sitting side by side in what I hoped would be a loving lesson. But each time I fumble the clutch and stall the car, he slaps his forehead and acts like my ineptitude is beyond belief. I defend myself by explaining I lived in the city and have never sat behind the wheel of a car before. He shakes his head. How can anyone not have driven a car? Despite my attempts to focus on Guru, I flat out hate Arjun. After a month, however, I manage to pass the driving test.

At the end of the next meditation, I wait outside in the cool autumn air for Arjun, whom Guru has called in to have a talk. Imagining Guru is lecturing him about being more caring toward his new wife or maybe letting us move to Queens, I'm hopeful when Arjun emerges grinning.

"Guru wants us to open a vegetarian Indian restaurant. Isn't that amazing?" I blink several times before I take this in. This sounds ludicrous. "A restaurant? Are you sure? I don't even know how to cook."

"Neither do I. But we're gonna learn!" he says enthusiastically.

Lalita calls and tells us Guru needs to make a trip to Mount Tremper, New York, to see the sponsors who helped him come to the United States. Would we like to drive him and Alo up there?

Would I? Once off the phone I squeal and twirl around in joy. I'll be with Guru and Alo for a whole weekend! When I look at a map I notice that Mount Tremper isn't too far from Waltham, Massachusetts, where Brandeis is located. I've received notices from Brandeis that my trunk has been there for over two years, and they will get rid of it if I don't collect it. I shyly mention this to Alo who say, "Yes, we will definitely get your old belongings. They symbolize pulling together the past with the future to make you more solidly into Pujarini."

Arjun and I scrub a borrowed VW van into a shining condition, even burning incense in it to cover the smell of oil. We drive down to Queens on a bright but chilly October morning. Alo looks smart in a wool suit and sits in the back seat with a pillow to cushion her and a book on her lap. Her many bags and suitcases are piled close by. Guru clomps out of the house flat-footed. He is wearing Western clothes: lace-up shoes instead of sandals, slacks instead of a *dhoti,* and a heavy jacket. His movements are as encumbered as a child's in a snowsuit. I am enchanted when Lalita cozies a shearling hat over his head and ties it under his chin. "He suffers from the cold. This is until he gets comfortable in the van," she explains, laughing when she sees me watching. We place pillows on the middle seat, help him in, and tuck a wool shawl around his legs. Arjun drives while I sit beside him. We are on our best behavior and are prepared to be pleasant to one other, even if it is through gritted teeth.

Once warm enough to divest himself of his hat and coat, Guru hums to himself and looks out the window while Alo dozes in the back over her book. He asks us if we know the Indian national anthem, and since we don't, he teaches us. Alo joins her high voice with ours and then teaches us the Canadian national anthem. We sing joyfully as golden autumn scenery unfolds along the highway. I'm in rapture. *This is what a family feels like—you take drives and sing and love each other.*

We take a break at a rest stop where the aroma of cinnamon fills the air. Arjun and I try to place ourselves between Guru and

Alo and the low vibrations of the hippies with ragged hair and dirty bell-bottoms. I look at them, knowing that was me not long ago. Now I'm sure of my path, while others stumble in darkness. Gratitude to Guru washes over me. We make sure to wipe the seats and table before they sit down. Guru has never tasted a cinnamon bun, so Arjun buys one and offers it reverently. We watch as Guru nibbles it, and his round, tan face breaks into a huge grin. I feel like a mother seeing her baby try solid food for the first time. No one knows we have the light of the world traveling incognito with us.

When we are back in the van, Arjun asks Guru to talk about the restaurant we will be opening. I had almost forgotten about it. Guru says, "Your soul's qualities will be fulfilled through feeding the divine in human beings. I want the restaurant to be in Connecticut, because I want a Sri Chinmoy Centre there. Sara and Tony will buy a house and have the Centre in it. Many more Centres will be all around the world. There will be many more divine enterprises. All the disciples will participate in my CKG sports day, birthday celebration, and Madal Circus. I always loved the circus when I was a boy back in Pondicherry. I will be spiritual director of the United Nations, and my light will spread to all humanity." He sits back humming to himself. I am awed by this revelation and feel privileged to be part of it.

At Mount Tremper, our hosts look fondly at Guru and listen with fascination to his achievements since arriving in America. They had known him as a young man in Sri Aurobindo's ashram in Pondicherry, India. Guru proudly introduces us, and when we say Guru arranged our marriage, Sammy and Eric glance at each other. We don't wait on Guru quite so obviously in front of them; we don't place our hands in prayer position when we speak to him. I have the delicious sense of hiding our secret. I express my devotion through my eyes.

Driving into the Brandeis campus is a culmination, a coming full circle since I'd flown to California two years earlier. I look in the trunk and see the miniskirts, the high boots, photos of Rudy and myself kissing, and my grandmother's quilt. Except for the patchwork quilt that symbolizes my fragmented life that is now being made whole, I plan to purge everything else. I look around the campus at the coeds sprawled on the grass. *How far I've come since I was here. I'm not floundering around taking drugs and searching for my vocation. I'm a married disciple of Sri Chinmoy about to open a restaurant.* I return home with a renewed dedication to my marriage.

❦

Arjun decides to buy the diner beside the Westport, Connecticut train tracks because it has an owner who will teach us how to cook and an ongoing customer base in the commuters. He takes me to see it. The windows are weeping with condensation, the steam table stinks of day-old stew, a brown vinyl seat in one of the booths is torn, the countertop is cracked, and the linoleum floor is worn thin with use. And these are the best parts, up front where the public sees them. In the back, the cement-floored kitchen has all the charm of an army barracks—except it is filthy.

I struggle to find words for how awful it is and finally come up with, "This diner can't possibly be made vegetarian." He says we will do it slowly. *Tablecloths and flowers will pretty it up,* I encourage myself. I'm ready to transform the place into the Taj Mahal, if that's what Guru wants.

Guru arrives dressed in blue robes and performs a lovely ceremony. Alo, Lalita, and a few other disciples accompany him and walk through the diner. Lalita looks at me with pity. They bring a big bouquet of flowers that makes the shabbiness of the diner only more evident. I'm ashamed of the place and almost hope Guru will say it's not acceptable. But instead he says, "You shall call this divine enterprise Love and Serve Restaurant. Arjun is the heart with a vision. Pujarini's path is to feed and serve the divine Guest. This is a vegetarian Indian temple to the Supreme." He cuts the ribbon that crosses the battered door and then leaves us to transform it from filthy diner into shining temple.

Charlie, the former owner, looks like a fireplug with his bald head and stained apron. He'd experienced one mild heart attack and feared that flipping burgers in front of a grill all day would cause another. Since neither Arjun nor I know how to boil an egg, Charlie agrees to stay on for a month and teach us everything he knows. His grin is ecstatic when we walk in—we are so green and enthusiastic.

I'm relegated to the role of waitress, while the men go into the back to get on with the cooking lessons. A customer comes in, and I freeze. I've never served anyone before and don't know how to cook a burger or what the cost of anything is. Luckily he's just a commuter who only wants a cup of coffee that I can smell burning. He wants it black, which is good, because I don't know where the cream is, and he doesn't complain about the coffee being hours old. He hands me change. I struggle to open the ancient cash register with brass curlicues by pounding the dusty keys until it finally slides open to reveal a few crumpled bills and some coins. I sling the money in. From then on, I'm the front person, while Arjun is in the back being cook as well as a free agent who drives around buying supplies. I immediately begin scrambling to find help, because this is more than a two-person job.

My dear friend Sara becomes our first employee. She is already an expert in cooking and cleaning while I'm still learning. She shows me tricks such as putting vinegar and water in the coffee carafe to get it clean. Her motherly presence gets me through the shock of those initial months as I reel in exhaustion from long days on my feet. When Arjun charges in, dragging a crate of smelly broccoli and yells at me for running out of hamburger rolls or change or a hundred other things, Sara intervenes and calms him down.

I awaken at 4:30 a.m. to meditate and am down at the store by 5:30 to turn on the hot water machines. Wearing my pink-checked cotton sari covered by a white apron, I quickly learn to be short-order cook for commuters who come in with a rush while Sara scribbles orders on green slips. I know to focus, breathe, and methodically work the grill flipping, scrambling, toasting, and handing out full plates until finally the last suit catches his train, and we are left staring at each other in relief. *We made it!* Quickly, I discover I can breathe Guru into my heart until I'm in bliss right here in front of the grill.

Around noon I cook hamburgers, hot dogs, and melted cheese sandwiches for the lunch crowd. Arjun is out early driving to Hunt's Point Market to buy produce and arrives in the afternoons to cook. Often he starts pulling out a broken refrigerated display case or other equipment with dust flying everywhere while I serve customers. We try to close after the evening rush around 7:00, but there is always a straggler begging for one last bowl of soup or cup of coffee. Arjun prepares roast beef, chicken noodle soup, and chili in the evenings for the next day. He spits out the meat after tasting it. Once in a while, I attempt to fulfill Guru's vision of Indian cuisine by preparing green lentils and sprinkling them with curry powder. I offer the green glop to a cute construction worker with beefy forearms to try after he finishes his hamburger. He politely takes a few bites and says he is full.

We work eighteen-hour days. My feet scream from standing all day, and every pore and hair stinks of food. My fingers are stained brown with vegetable juices. My weight shoots up because I snack on broken cookies or bits of cheese instead of sitting down to a meal. I was raised with a cook and a maid and have never experienced this kind of exhaustion. When I sit down, I fall asleep, even mid-sentence. Arjun has to drive us home; otherwise I pull off to the side of the road and sleep. Once, I awaken cold and stiff with a police officer's flashlight shining in my face.

When Sara and I pause after the lunch rush, I notice her stomach is bulging beneath her white apron. I ask about it. She starts wiping down the counter while she hums and looks radiant.

"After Tony and I were married, we made love. It was like making love to myself, so beautiful. Guru doesn't want his disciples to have children, but now that I'm pregnant, he says I'm carrying a very special soul. I'm not supposed to tell anyone, but now you know."

"Sara, that's thrilling, so much better than my charade of a marriage. Arjun and I never have sex—he acts like I have leprosy or something." My envy of her peers with its evil green eye. She has everything I don't: a caring husband, children, and Guru's approval.

"I didn't know about not having kids. What is the point of marrying us off? Having a baby kind of scares me but I've always hoped to have a family someday."

"Some of the married women disciples have had abortions, so maybe it's best that you don't get pregnant." I give her a shocked look. She works for us until late in her pregnancy. After she leaves, I see her only when meditation is held at her house. She is too busy with her kids and preparing special treats for Guru to talk. I'm supposed to be meditating, so we don't share confidences anymore.

One afternoon, I'm alone in the diner wiping down the sugar shakers when a commuter walks in who has familiar auburn hair and a beard. He looks around at my shabby emporium. My apron is stained, I stink of food, and I've gained weight—almost thirty pounds. I've become a female, grubby, old Charlie, only with hair covered by a kerchief.

I postpone the inevitable. Finally I say, "Can I help you?"

"My roommate told me you worked here. Don't you remember me?" my college boyfriend asks.

"Rudy!" is all I can say in shock and humiliation. He moves toward me and tries to give me a kiss.

"I—I can't. I'm married now."

"Why didn't you call me? I waited for you! I thought you had been murdered when I didn't hear from you! I worried about you!" he says angrily, his orange-brown eyes flashing.

"Yeah, well . . . things got a little crazy out in California and . . . and then I found Guru!" Smiling hugely I point to Guru's Samadhi photograph that we have framed on the wall, as if that explains everything.

"Yeah, so . . . you couldn't have picked up the phone?"

"I'm sorry, Guru married me to . . . to someone . . . and it didn't seem right to call an ex-boyfriend." I remember how Arjun called all *his* girlfriends.

"Well, at least I know you're alive and okay—if working in this dump can be okay."

"I really am sorry, Rudy. Can we kiss as friends?"

"No, not now that you're *married*," he says drawing the last word out with a grimace.

When he walks out, I slump into a booth and cry a little. My last whiff of a normal life leaves with him. Why *did* I forget about Rudy when he was the tenderest of my lovers? I lay my head on the cool table where a few hard crumbs bite into my cheek. *How did I get to this point where nobody is pleased with me?* Guru has started calling me Queen of Depression, and all Arjun does is criticize me. Could it be that letting Guru marry me to Arjun was a mistake?

I'm going to meditation tonight, and Guru with his occult powers will see my poisonous doubt. Banish it from my mind! I jump up and start dumping out day-old stew and chili from the steam table as hot steam blasts my face. Arjun will make a fresh batch tonight. As I do this, I picture Guru's infectious grin and the way he rubs his eyes with the heel of his palm like a little kid. Sparkles dance around my heart as I breathe him in and out. Soon adoration of Guru suffuses my whole aching body, and I'm in bliss right here behind the dingy counter. My doubt vanishes.

When I arrive back at the Wilton house, I discover the front door is wide open—either the tenant forgot to close it or more likely the lock is broken. Margie and her kids have returned to California without paying the last month's rent. Arjun had let them go because she simply couldn't afford it. Now a new disciple named Terry has moved in. She wants to work in the diner, and that is great, because do I ever need help!

I wearily shuck off my stinky restaurant clothes and apron and step into the claw-foot tub, but no water comes out. This has been happening with frustrating regularity. Arjun has been promising to fix the pump, but has been down in Queens helping Swadhin start a sandwich bar a few blocks from Guru's house. While I've been feeding commuters in Westport, he has also started a whole-wheat bakery in our garage here at the house. Large bags of flour are stacked in our kitchen. We never eat here anyway. The house has become just a place to sleep, wash, and change clothes—only now I can't even get clean. I call my former roommate, Sandra, and ask if I can shower at her apartment in Queens before meditation.

Hot water sliding over my head and back feels heavenly as I scrub my hair. Enveloping myself in a purple sari with blue elephants—because Guru said I had been an elephant in a past life—I'm Cinderella, freed from her scullery and going to the ball. I sit on my cushion, legs crossed, spine straight, eyes fixed on Guru's radiance. The communal meditative power surges beneath me, pushing me up. I focus on my heart, digging down until I feel a gush of yearning. Guru's golden gaze pours light all around. My heart weeps, *See me, choose me, love me.* His eyes flood mine, and I am lifted into an angelic realm shimmering with bliss. Every cell in my body is dancing with joy. Nothing matters except this—restaurant drudgery, difficult marriage, falling apart house—it is all swept away in this rapture that goes on for an eternity. But not every meditation is so rapturous. Other times my body is heavy like an anchor tethering me to earth and all my negative qualities. Then Guru's eyes become icy turquoise like my mother's. I'm seen for what I am—a repulsive creature full of envy and doubt. No matter how hard I drive myself, I can never win the Beloved.

With a sigh, I step off the scale after I've read the numbers. *I have to get control of my eating—I'll fast for a month, and Guru will be pleased with me.* I drink only broth from steamed vegetables and use coffee enemas. Fasting is a high at times. I have unlimited energy and zip about as if on wheels. But these are followed by lows where all I can do is nap on a crate in the walk-in refrigerator. At the same time, I train to run a half-marathon. Guru is running twenty-six-mile races and urges us to do the same. There is a long, steep hill outside our house. Every day I run a little farther up the hill until I finally breach the top—and keep going. Week after week, I push myself a little farther. My feet ache after standing all day at the restaurant. But as I cross the race's finish line, I weigh twenty-five pounds less than I had the previous month. I pump my arms high in victory. *At last I'm in control of my life, and Guru will bless me!* Even Lalita complements me on how much weight I've lost.

On the thirty-second morning of my fast, however, I'm picking up pies for the restaurant. Almost unconsciously I buy an extra pie, sit in the car and push the luscious dessert into my mouth until it is gone. I know this isn't how I'm supposed to end the fast—*gradually* is the constant refrain. I can't stop myself. I eat until I regain all the pounds I've so carefully lost.

"Guru is starting a weight loss club, and your name is on it," says Jagat, Guru's henchman. "You will be weighed once a month, and if you're over, you will be out of the Centre for a full week." The pressure is on. Following the advice of a new disciple who had been a wrestling champion, I buy a rubber suit that completely covers my body. I jog gasping in the hot summer sun, and when I open the elasticized sleeves, sweat streams onto the ground. If that doesn't achieve the desired result, I spit into a bottle until I am the correct weight. Then I line up with a group of mostly female disciples, and one by one we step on a scale set up on the Queens track. I always slide in just under my appointed weight. Until one time I just don't care—and let myself be a half-pound over.

"You are out of the Centre for a full week," Jagat intones with the voice of doom.

"Does that mean I can't go to meditations, do selfless service, or even work at the restaurant?" I ask, working out the extent of this terrible sentence.

"Yes, you will not receive Guru's light for all that time."

I mentally flagellate myself on the drive home. But after I've showered and am resting on my bed the thought comes: *I've got a week to do anything I want—read, write, draw, or simply stare out the window. This is fantastic!* I hide the grin on my face as Arjun scowls at me while he rushes to the restaurant.

The next month I try a weight loss program of drinking only buttermilk with cornbread dipped in it. As the warm aroma of baking suffuses the diner, I recall my Kentucky grandmother's delicious meals, my grandfather's twinkling blue eyes, and the green mountains that surround their farm. I haven't seen them since—when?—since I was in junior high. Would Guru give me permission to go down there? Arjun would never let me leave the restaurant for that length of time. It seems impossible.

A plan comes to me: I will teach meditation in the Deep South! It isn't so far-fetched. We have taught meditation to high school students in Queens, and the few kids who showed up enjoyed it. I love sharing this practice that has given me so much peace. Surprisingly, Guru gives the trip his blessing, so Arjun has to let me go. Agnes, a disciple with an underbite and an argumentative side, agrees to drive with me. "I come from a large Catholic family of all girls," she informs me. "We constantly fought among ourselves." I abhor arguing and wonder how we will get on. I make calls to my aunts Clara and Sue Ellen, who live in Louisville, Kentucky. They will let us stay with them. I set up dates in several community centers and create some posters for advertising. After that, I will visit my grandparents.

"Agnes, let's wear saris for the drive down," I suggest. "We want to be in highest consciousness to deliver our message of peace. And every hour we should stop the car and meditate for ten minutes." Agnes agrees. All goes well until the middle of the night when we start dozing off during our breaks.

"We have to floor it and drive there in ordinary conscious-ness," Agnes commands. Good advice.

"That pimply necked gas attendant is giving me a very strange look," Agnes says as we stop for gas deeper in the South. "I don't want to be ogled by every redneck we come across. We need to change into civilian clothes." The landscape is becoming more rural, and accents are thicker, so I agree. We are far from New York City, road-weary, and in need of sleep. I wonder what kind of reception we will receive.

"You can't stay here," Sue Ellen yells at us through her screen door. "You-all are idol worshippers, and my husband might be fired from his job if his boss finds out!"

Agnes's and my eyes widen as we look at each other. We see ourselves as spiritual devotees consecrated to self-transcendence and Truth with a capital T. We have never considered that the Bible Belt might not view us the same way. And we are exhausted.

"But all we do is set up Guru's Samadhi photo—well maybe we can forget that this time—anyway all we do is sit and close our eyes and focus on our breath. It's relaxing!" I explain, but Sue Ellen will have none of it and closes the door. Agnes starts yelling at me for screwing up. We drive the distance to Clara's apartment. This aunt, who came home to be closer to her roots, is marginally more welcoming, but she is in the middle of final exams to get her credentials as a special education teacher. She doesn't want her pesky niece and friend for more than a night.

We put up posters and hold our meditation sessions, but not one person attends. This is deeply disappointing. Agnes yells at me some more. At last, we can go to my grandparents' farm. My directions are minimal—passed on by my grandfather, who has lived here all his life. But the mountains are compelling me home as if I have a compass in my heart. I'm overjoyed to see the saggy cabin at the juncture of the road and the creek. But Uncle George has built a new white-sided house across from the old one. There my wrinkled grandparents sit, while Aunt Lonnie clips what's left of Grandpa's hair. I erupt out of the car not wanting to waste another moment before I embrace each dear one. But Grandpa gets to me first, grabs my arm, and walks me away a distance.

"Do you worship the devil?" he asks, looking me straight in the eyes.

Completely taken aback, I reply, "No, of course not, Grandpa. I worship God."

"Then that's all right." He nods and ushers us into the house. He has settled things for himself.

Grandma is much the same, sitting quietly in her rocker with her head and hands shaking. She bestirs herself to proudly show us the new bathroom, which has a shower with hot and cold water and a toilet. We admire a fully equipped kitchen with glass cabinets and Formica counters. She and Aunt Lonnie feed us a sumptuous Southern meal that revolves around fried chicken that, of course, we can't eat. But we do justice to her cornbread, buttermilk, and creasy beans.

"You know, Grandma, I've been wondering how you sew a quilt. It seems a lot of work." She shows me the pile of quilts she and her church group have sewn. I particularly admire a queen size quilt with the birds of each state embroidered on it. Quilts have been experiencing a renaissance in the women's magazines that I sneak peeks at. Sometimes Guru lets us embroider little images of his artwork onto bookmarks, but I don't think he'd agree to a quilt. I smooth the soft nap of the cotton fabric and run my finger over the chain stitch embroidery.

"Aw, honey, I can't make them anymore—my hands shake too much. After all the hours the church ladies spent on this here quilt—they voted to give it to me. It's most precious."

I look around the new house. Hanging on the wall is a plaque commemorating the men landing on the moon, the ornate photo of dead Aunt Judy, and a ceramic fifty in honor of my grandparents' half decade of marriage. All of these occurred years ago. Things haven't changed here—but I have. Although I consider my spiritual yearnings right in line with my great-grandfather minister's, here they look through a very different lens.

In the morning, Agnes and I go out jogging past the old home, the outhouse covered with honeysuckle vine, across the footbridge, and over to the barn. There is no cow in it, and we look around at the waist-high weeds and the rusting farm machinery. There is a deathly quiet as if an era is coming to a close, and it stops my breath. *Who will be here when I return?* When we get back, a neighbor stops by to ask Grandpa, "Why're they runnin' away when there ain't no dog chasing them?" Of course, he might be having a joke on us. Still, it's clear that I can no longer expect the open-armed welcome I received as a child.

Chapter 12

DARK STAR COMPASS

—◈◈◈—

One day you finally knew
What you had to do, and began,
Though the voices around you
Kept shouting their bad advice—

—MARY OLIVER

"How ya doing, kid? Got a job for your dear old dad flipping burgers?" my portly, white-haired father jokes as he clumsily mimes with a spatula. I laugh and shake my head a little sadly. I know he longs to be back at the newspaper and still hasn't found another job here. Arjun and I are in his London flat visiting before we fly to Paris to start a Sri Chinmoy Centre there. Guru is expanding his mission, and to my delight and astonishment, he has skipped over his inner circle and chosen us to begin a meditation center in France. I'm proud to be a married woman with a restaurant, a home, and an established self to present to my family.

"Nah, I can't even make toast without burning it." Father puts down the spatula. "I'd like to be reviewing movies—that's what I do best." He motions me closer and whispers, "Do you ever hear from your mother? No? She's been living in England and frankly looks a wreck. I was at a party, and she was sitting right across from me. Until she introduced herself, I didn't recognize her! She told me some crazy story about a charwoman stealing her clothes. Boy, she's come down in the world. She looks ill. She may be back in New York again. Write to her."

I sit down and try to write. *"Dear Mother,"* I begin but stop because that is false. She isn't dear to me—I have completely changed my identity just to get away from her. She's my negative model, my dark star by whom I'm repelled. If it meant giving up sex, men, money, alcohol, and pretty clothes, I've done it. I will be a loving, divine, spiritual being, no matter what. I crumple the paper and throw it away.

My father fills his empty hours with a motorcycle that he shines to a mirror-like finish in a garage nearby. He seldom rides it, and I get the impression that the motorcycle is there to bolster his fragile self-esteem. He doesn't do much around the house. My stepmother works, cooks, and pays the bills. When I receive a birthday or Christmas card, it is in her handwriting. As far as I can figure out, my stepmother supports the family. Justine is a gangly teenager and only comes home to eat.

Arjun and my father bond over their love of motorcycles. Giving many cautions about driving on the left, Father allows us to borrow the machine for an afternoon. I ride clutching Arjun's waist on a noisy, hair-destroying trip to a nearby pub. We sit at a small table and after asking the waitress if there is a dish without meat, order a vegetarian plowman's lunch. We have rarely been alone together and eat silently. I'd hoped this trip might be a belated honeymoon, but we feel as flat as the mineral water we drink. Guru may have married us, but he cannot make Arjun love me. I'm willing to try, but he holds back, immovable as a brick wall.

We return the motorcycle and drive Father's car down to Bath, where we tour the ancient Roman baths. I'm impressed by the fountains, tiled rooms, and recently unearthed statue of Minerva. Arjun's face is stony, however, and he jingles change in his pocket impatiently.

"Don't you think the Romans were amazing for creating these waterworks so many centuries ago?" I ask.

"Look, you wanted to come here to see your father. This is a waste of time. We should be setting up meditations for Guru. That's what he sent us for."

"I thought it would be nice to have some time together . . . without the restaurant and Guru." But he is already heading up the street.

We stay at the White House Bed and Breakfast because it's cheap. It's also cramped and damp. I'm chilly and don't have enough pence to draw hot water for the bath. The worst part is sharing the narrow bed. Arjun turns his face to the wall, ignoring me. I curl against him and rub his shoulders, but he pretends to sleep. This Guru-mandated abstinence has gone on far longer than I thought it would. In the morning, over a stodgy English breakfast of eggs, fried tomatoes, and fried bread, we are introduced to the other guests as honeymooners. They look at us expecting radiant smiles. I manage an embarrassed wave and sit down abruptly, while Arjun only grimaces. My family has just seen me put on a show of being happily wed. Even thinking of leaving the Guru-arranged marriage is heresy. I'm trapped in lies.

I blame myself—it's probably the pounds I gained working in the restaurant, although I whittled away most of it when Guru put me in the weight loss club. Yet one day I was in the Smile of the Beyond sandwich shop, and the owner, Swadhin, said, "The boys have taken a poll to see who is the prettiest girl. You're at the top of the list—if only," he paused with a mischievous twinkle in his eye, "you lost a few pounds."

"Thanks for the back-handed compliment—I think." I replied, trying to match his light-hearted tone. I was ready to forgive him anything because he made me laugh, but this cut too close to the bone. Without ordering a veggie burger, I rushed out to hide my tears. His "if only" seemed the impenetrable barrier between myself and everything I desired. If only I were more devoted to Guru and did more selfless service, I'd be part of his inner circle. If only I lost more weight and maybe worked harder in the restaurant, Arjun might love me. If only I looked at my father with the hero worship I'd had as an eight-year-old, he would forgive me. My mother would love me if only I were— what? I was confounded as to what would make her love me. Not being prettier or losing weight—she was intensely competitive and had flirted with my boyfriends when I was in high school. Ditto being more charming. Maybe being smarter—but I doubted that would sway her. It was best to avoid her, and I'd done that by burying myself in the Sri Chinmoy Centre. And I was still as far from being loved as ever.

⁐

We fly to Paris and are met by new disciples, Olivier and Patricia, who will help us set up the Sri Chinmoy Centre. Olivier is a musician who shows us his studio in his family's comfortable home in an elegant arrondissement. He has an alive, mobile face that is very engaging. Patricia is a curvaceous blonde with wide-set blue eyes that tilt down at the outer corners, giving her a soulful, sad expression. They are friends dedicated to the spiritual path.

From the minute my feet hit the streets of Paris, I find soaking up the sights and sounds more fascinating than tacking up flyers advertising a meditation group. After we have checked out the venue and put out the advertising, Olivier and Patricia agree that, since we have come this far, we must see Versailles and Chartres Cathedral.

Amazingly, Arjun agrees, so that our advertising blitz will

have time to percolate. I'm immersed in all things French and lov-ing it: resting in wrought iron chairs that punctuate the lines of trees in the Tuileries Gardens, drinking the divine hot chocolate at Angelina's, ogling the mind-boggling ornate rooms of Versailles.

However, it's the manner with which Olivier and Patricia approach life that makes the biggest impact. With great serious-ness, they discuss the relative merits of several cafés before they choose our eatery. Then we spend leisurely hours tasting our way through elegant meals and jeweled pastries and drinking hot chocolate. How food looks and tastes is important here. In the restaurant, I eat most meals standing up because there isn't time to sit down. The most important thing in our world is to please Guru. Our emotions and bodily concerns have no relevance.

We drive toward Chartres Cathedral, whose golden spires rise above a yellow plain. After parking, we join a throng of pil-grims making our way through a medieval village that huddles around the flanks of the immense edifice. I touch my palms to the much-caressed stones—warmed by interminable suns and kissed by a thousand cold moons. Faces of saints peer from crev-ices, fingers pointing up to the one true destination.

Inside is a hushed silence that takes my breath away as hun-dreds of petitioners ask for their prayers to be answered. My eyes dance around the crushed grape, royal blue, and chrysanthe-mum yellow of the scintillating stained glass. I kneel before the gold-robed Virgin Mary with an earth-colored face. *Please make Arjun love me*, I pray.

"Your cares are God's Grace," she whispers. I bow and feel Mother Chartres' hands caress my head. Her little scepter waves away my burdens.

That night we stay at a lovely inn with red velvet curtains covering the windows, roses twining over the balcony, linen sheets on the bed, and a bidet in the bathroom. How much more romantic can it get? They only have a double bed, so Arjun and I sleep together. I hope my prayer will work. Although I curl against him, he says he is tired from the long day and falls asleep.

I roll to the opposite side of the bed and squeeze myself into a ball. What have I done wrong?

My petition has been too small, I realize. Pressing my hand against my heart, I call on a compassionate Divine Mother to grant me unconditional acceptance as I am—without an "if only." But she still seems so far away. I visualize her earthy face like the one on the Chartres Virgin—a care-worn face, whose furrows attest to her understanding of my pain. But she isn't wearing gold cloth; she wears a cotton dress and knitted shawl like my grandmother. I imagine myself placing my head in her commodious lap. Her gnarled fingers smooth back my hair, and my hands do the caressing instead.

"Everything will be all right. You are my beloved child," I hear her say, or I whisper the words—who can tell where she leaves off and I begin?

Patricia arranges for us to stay in her family's country cottage. We arise at dawn to meditate, and then I walk out, seeing a man scything the field in the morning mist. My senses—so shut down in the Centre—are alive here. I don't want to return to the stultifying atmosphere around Guru. Back at the cottage, Patricia is boiling water. Sitting at the rustic table, I ask, "What drew you to Guru's path?"

Sipping her tea, she confides, "I love Olivier, but he can't return my affection in that way, because he isn't attracted to women. I was in a lot of pain over this, but I attended a meditation given by Sri Chinmoy in Paris and felt peace radiating from Guru and his disciples. Now Olivier and I are friends on the spiritual path and want a meditation Centre here."

I empathize with her journey and long to open my heart to her. I want to say, *I love Guru, and know my dedication is sincere. But I'm having misgivings. My marriage is a painful sham, but beyond that, Guru's path is changing. At the beginning, we were a small group dedicated to highest realization of the Supreme. Now Guru demands male and female disciples not speak or look at each other. He wants Centres in every country on the globe and constantly harangues us to*

do more for him. Disciples compete to see who can come up with the
most extravagant way to publicize him. . . . But I can't share my misgivings with Patricia, because I don't want to derail her journey.
She has to make her own discoveries. So I add my untold truth to
the web of lies. I pray for the Divine Mother's guidance as we say
grateful good-byes for their gracious hospitality.

⧼⧽

"Do you have any greens for the turtle I found?" I hear a deep
voice say. I'm once again behind the grill at the restaurant.
Bholanath smiles sweetly when I turn around. He's a squat, bar-
rel-chested man who, Guru said, had been Arjun's brother in a
previous life. I go out to his car carrying wilted lettuce for the
brown-shelled creature scrabbling in a box behind the back seat.
His four small boys giggle and poke at it, while his pint-sized
beauty of a wife complains that Bholanath is always finding rep-
tiles beside the road when he should be looking for work.

"Also, I could really use a job," he adds with a hopeful
expression. Although he is scatterbrained, I'm happy to hire him
because we never have enough workers.

Arjun has become an entrepreneur with a passion for starting new businesses. From the large garage of our house, his bakery
delivers whole wheat bread to stores throughout Connecticut. He
carries cash from the bakery and restaurant in every pocket, pulling money from one side to pay bills of the other. We always owe
money because our ageing equipment needs to be replaced. Often,
I'm up front telling creditors that Arjun has just left, while he disappears out the back door. When I complain, he airily dismisses
me with, "I'll handle it." So it makes sense, at least to Arjun, to
borrow money from his mother and buy the moneymaking hand
laundry next door to bail out the restaurant and bakery.

Arjun puts Bholanath in charge of the laundry instead of
working in the diner. I'm frustrated and point out, "It takes a
cool head to take in the clothes, label them, put each batch in

a separate bag, and place them in the noisy washing machines. Then they have to be dried, ironed and folded, and an appropriate bill written up. The previous owner has been doing the work of three people for years."

"Why do you shoot down all my ideas? You have become heavy in more ways than one. I'm doing this." He walks away and I look after him, knowing it's true. I've become the nag, because someone has to put a brake on Arjun's unstoppable momentum. But that isn't what I intended. I want to be supportive and say comforting words—as unlike my mother as possible. Any criticisms that start to erupt from my mouth I bite back.

The first day, Bholanath gets rattled and starts throwing clothes into the washers willy-nilly. He comes into the diner and admits, in a dejected voice, "I put my own family's clothes in and now can't remember which ones are theirs. My wife will kill me!" A little later on, he comes in and says he can't figure out the mangle iron. I go in and don't have a clue how to work the ancient contraption. Commuters come by after work to pick up their clean laundry and discover a wrinkled heap of strangers' garments under their name. They soon stop coming, and the successful hand laundry fails. I don't say a word.

But where I see disaster, Arjun sees an opportunity to enlarge our diner into the Indian restaurant Guru had originally envisioned. He closes the laundry, sells off the equipment, and smashes the wall dividing the diner from the laundry. He drapes white plastic around the flying debris, and I keep right on serving coffee, bacon, and eggs to the commuters. They are what keep us (barely) solvent; they are our bread and butter. What keeps me going is my focus on merging my being with Guru's. As I scramble eggs and fry bacon, my heart is full of blissful longing. Every customer who walks in the door is the Beloved.

One afternoon Arjun proudly ushers a slender, middle-aged, Indian man with a wisp of a mustache into the diner. "Look who I found wandering the streets of Westport looking for a job! Pujarini, meet Prakash, a trained Indian chef who has cooked for Europe's finest hotels. Someone promised him work and didn't show up. This is the guy who will transform our diner into an Indian vegetarian restaurant. Can you believe it? This is Guru's divine intervention. This is a miracle!" Arjun starts slapping his back while Prakash coughs and smiles shyly. He looks around at the taped seats and cracked countertop and starts to pull out a cigarette until we tell him he can't smoke here. He shrugs and stuffs them back in his shirt pocket. "When do I begin?" he asks in a soft voice.

The men go in the kitchen, but this time I make sure Arjun doesn't banish me to the front. I get someone to cover for me while I watch Prakash's tan fingers efficiently chop an onion, break up cauliflower into florets, toss a handful of mustard seeds in hot oil until they sputter, add ground cumin seed and turmeric, and coat the cauliflower. He sets rice to boiling and goes about the deft maneuvers of creating chapattis. Within a half hour, the aromas of India fill the kitchen. Prakash insists we sit down at a booth and dine properly while we rhapsodize over this ambrosia. Over the months I learn how to make raita, biryani, raisin chutney, cauliflower curry, chapattis, samosas, mint sauce, puris, and sticky, sweet, gulab jamun. I still get sidelined into the lesser roles of sous chef and waitress, but I cook curry when necessary.

Our Indian cuisine becomes the finest in the area. Prakash lives in our house but declines to see Guru, living among us but not really one of us. He doesn't socialize outside the restaurant. I suspect he is lonely. He has only been with us for eight months when he gets word that his mother is ill. He returns to India to see her but then is refused reentry into the United States. We receive heart-breaking letters from him asking for help. Finally, he finds a job in an Austrian hotel. His letters stop, and we realize we are on our own. But he has taught us all we need to know.

We begin experimenting with imaginative vegetarian combinations. "Infinite Blue" is the name of our most popular entrée and contains sautéed zucchini and mushrooms ringed with salad and covered with blue cheese dressing. We also make fresh vegetable juices, sprout mung beans for salad, and bake carrot cake. We discard the meat dishes Charlie featured when we first bought the diner. We are changing into a temple of Indian vegetarian cuisine. Arjun uses his carpentry skills to build low, ethnic-style tables that he installs where the hand laundry once was. The final transformation comes when a disciple paints a life-size mural of Krishna playing his flute and Radha worshiping him. It graces the restaurant from above the counter where the long mirror had once been. In return for the painting, the disciple gets one meal a day for his lifetime.

Disciples Mahavishnu, John McLaughlin, and Carlos Santana volunteer to play a concert at the diner. Customers crowd in until there isn't space to breathe. I've been at work since 5:30 a.m. and leave as the music begins. The next day I count the money in the till. There still isn't enough to pay our bills. On the surface it looks as if we're doing really well, but I know this isn't true. Arjun opens another Love and Serve in Larchmont, New York. We are even more popular there and have lines around the block to get in. But we have the same financial deficit, and at the bottom of the tally sheet are a husband who doesn't love me and a mother I never see.

❧

Arjun drags slowly into the diner with a somber look on his face. This is so unlike his whirlwind energy that I stop in the middle of handing a customer a plate of curry and ask, "What's wrong? Is your mother ill?"

"Come in the kitchen when you're through, and I'll tell you." Wiping my hands on my apron, I follow him back. "The bank wants to foreclose on the house and on several loans I have on the restaurants. Everything is collapsing like dominoes. I don't know how to save it." His face crumples as if he wants to cry. "All my hard work, just when everything was going so well . . . I can't believe this is happening." I have an itch in my throat to yell but keep my mouth firmly closed.

Preparing to move, we begin cleaning out our house, starting with the bags of bakery flour in our kitchen. As I reach down to lift a bag, my hand touches cold flesh. A dead rat! I scream and realize I've been sleeping in the next room while vermin invaded the house. The well runs dry, and we all move out. We sell the house, then the Westport and Larchmont restaurants, too.

But where Arjun sees disaster I see opportunity. Guru has been encouraging disciples to work at the United Nations, thereby giving him an in to become the spiritual leader of many lands. I get a job at the United Nations gift shop and enjoy handling the beautiful ornaments and giggling with other shop girls. I commute by train and attend the powerful United Nations meditations that Guru holds every Friday. Once again I hobnob with Lalita and other disciples close to Guru. I'm empowered holding my own paycheck. Then I'm let go for the slower summer season, but I use the time to teach myself to type so I can become a secretary.

Arjun scrapes together the money to start another Love and Serve, this time in Greenwich, Connecticut. With the help of other disciples, we throw ourselves into making this the perfect Divine Enterprise. I design a charming green-and-white lattice décor with enormous Boston ferns hanging from the ceiling. The kitchen is state-of-the-art stainless steel with pots large enough to feed an army. We hire a responsible staff, and the restaurant is a success from the start.

⁂

"You're beautiful, you know. Such shining blue eyes and so quick on your feet. Why are you stuck in this place? You deserve tenderness from someone," the man whispers as I stand beside him taking his order. He is slender with keen dark eyes and a thatch of brown hair. I'm unnerved and exhilarated by his attention.

"Are you kidding?" I snap back, "I'm married, you know."

"Yeah, I've seen how your husband yells at you. I see what you are. You're a rose blooming in the dessert."

I hurry into the kitchen and prod the dishwasher to come out and take his order. But he keeps returning with his murmurs. "You are so lovely, you're buried in here."

He is annoying and unsettling, but in the sunlight of his gaze, something blooms inside me. When he is there, I move more briskly, laugh more quickly, and feel something like happiness. As Arjun makes his dashes into the restaurant to deliver produce, my admirer falls silent, observing. Arjun sticks his nose in a pot of food and yells, "There's not enough for dinner—what have you been doing all afternoon?" Which proves the truth of my suitor's observations.

As soon as Arjun leaves, more enticements follow me around the room, "You deserve to be loved. You're wasted here."

I can feel myself yielding to him. *What if we walk out of the restaurant and leave everyone with their mouths agape? What if we go to a forest and, among dappled leaves, he unwinds my sari and licks every orifice of my body? What if we fly to Tuscany and live among the ruins of an ancient winery? What if my body grows round with a baby, and I paint in exuberant colors?*

But I know nothing about him. This is insane. He could be a serial murderer! argues another voice in my head. After a few weeks I confront him. "You have got to stop this. You're driving me crazy. Don't come back here again." Sadly, he obeys, but as I clean his table I notice his scribbled phone number on the bill. I crumple it up and throw it away before I can find out which of my fantasies is true.

A few days later, Arjun screams at me during the lunch rush, in front of the staff and all the patrons. All eyes are on us. I untie my apron, throw it on the counter, walk down to a placement firm, and apply for a job as an administrative assistant down in New York.

Chapter 13

OUR FAMILIAR WAY
OF RELATING

❖

When another person makes you suffer,
It is because he suffers deeply within himself
and his suffering is spilling over.
—THICH NHAT HANH

Arjun and I, with some other disciples, now rent a beautiful old manor called Old Mill Farm in Mamaroneck, New York. It has a barn that is home to two donkeys and an ancient mill that dates back to the Revolutionary War. In the large kitchen are many windowsills cradling glass jars greening with sprouts. Inside the oven, milk curdles into yogurt. The cupboards are laden with the granola, adzuki beans, brown rice, and sesame butter of our healthy, vegetarian diet. We mark every shelf so we know what food belongs to whom. I tack seldom-followed schedules of duties to the walls and collect the rent. Although there are the usual tensions among people who share space, I am happy here.

Arjun and I sleep chastely on twin beds that were the low tables from Westport topped with foam. We live in a spacious master bedroom with ax-hewn beams supporting low ceilings and a private bath. Comfortable window seats overlook a wisteria-covered arbor, an overgrown garden, and a stream beyond. I feel at last I have a home. I no longer have to get up at 4:30 a.m. to serve commuters in Westport. Sometimes I waitress at our other restaurants or work as an administrative assistant in New York. I write a book of poetry and several musical plays dedicated to Guru, until he says that I must stop because he is the only writer here.

I've been getting letters from my father urging me to contact my mother, who is back in New York. I haven't seen her since before I joined the Sri Chinmoy Centre in what seems a lifetime ago—about eight years. I shove Daddy's blue aerograms in the back of my desk drawer and try to forget them. One day I'm in the town library where I sometimes hide out because disciples are only supposed to read books written by Guru. I pick up a book about a man who loses his career, family, and health due to drink. He is able to arrest his alcoholism only with the support of a group called Alcoholics Anonymous. They say that alcoholism is a disease that family members didn't cause and can't control or cure. Crystal clear is the fact that my mother has this alcoholism disease. Something impels me to call her, although as I do so, my voice shakes.

"Hi, Mommy, one of the bedrooms at the farm has been vacated recently, so I was wondering if you would like to stay with us for a week. You know, as followers of Sri Chinmoy we don't drink or smoke. So you would need to honor our commitment. Uh, what do you think?" To my surprise she agrees to come.

Before I dress that morning, I worry how she will react to seeing me wrapped in Eastern garb. But I decide to enfold myself in a pretty summer sari. I pick her up at the Port Chester train

station. Although it is hot and muggy, and the cicadas are singing, she is wrapped in a bulky mustard-colored sweater. The reek
of alcohol coming through her pores hits me as soon as I hug
her. I'm shocked by the long-forgotten smell. She seems smaller,
inwardly focused, as though she were a bird protecting a fragile
egg held inside. Puffy bags hang beneath her eyes, and her hair,
pulled back in a greasy knot, shows several inches of mixed dark
and gray roots. She is forty-five.

With my heart pounding, I ask her how she is as I carefully
drive. Sticking out a fragile wrist with a bony knob, she says, "I
broke it in Hong Kong. I was standing on the deck of a cruise
ship, and a large wave knocked me over the railing onto a Chinese junk. They put me in the hospital in China. Cecelia came to
England last Christmas for a visit." A poisonous dart of jealousy
pierces me at hearing my sister had been invited, but not me. I
still hunger for my mother's love.

She falls silent. I glance over at her and ask, "Do you want
to stop at the restaurant and get something to eat?" I hope she
will be impressed by our new Greenwich business.

She shakes her head. "I need a smoke."

"Please wait until we get outside at the farm. Remember the
house rules: no smoking inside and no drinking." I feel strange
directing her, she who always controlled me. She lights up as
soon as we arrive and seems to relax after she has her nicotine.

I show her around the large kitchen, where I have painted
the dining room chairs cherry red and covered the seats with
bright fabric. Eagerly I offer to show her the mill house and sta-
bles with the patient donkeys. *These might remind her of Kentucky and give me a chance to walk off my nervousness.*

"I'm tired; just show me to my room." She seems grateful
just to fold onto the narrow bed I made up for her.

I make her a cheese sandwich. "Just put it on the nightstand."
She nibbles a corner while I sit beside her. "I need to rest." Feeling
concerned, I quietly slip away. I am glad to escape to the restaurant.

When I come back in the evening, I find her sitting calmly

on her bed, smoking. I'm not surprised but say, "If you have to do that, please go outside." My voice is surprisingly firm. She stands in the vestibule that leads from the house to the large garage and nervously puffs. It is a warm summer evening with wisteria scenting the air. Swallows have made a nest in the light fixture and are trying to swoop in and feed their young. I move her to one side so they won't be spooked and point out these lovely fork-tailed birds as they catch insects on the wing, but she has little to say. In the kitchen she eats a little salad and then says, "I need to go back to bed." I am crestfallen, but this is our familiar way of relating: me longing for her attention, and she withholding it.

I knock on her door the next morning and ask, "Do you want some breakfast?" She calls from inside, "I need to sleep." I go to the restaurant.

That afternoon I open her door and find her lounging on the bed in a smoke-filled room, a clear glass of vodka in her hands, drunk. I feel almost physically ill at the violation of our way of life. I am also embarrassed that my housemates might have seen or smelled her. In a firm voice, I say, "You cannot smoke or drink in our home."

She responds with her old fire, snarling. "You think you can control me, Miss Holier-than-Thou. Well, this leopard isn't going to change her spots, and under all those yards of cloth, you are still hiding from life."

With words that belie the terror pounding in my chest, I explain, "Not smoking and drinking aren't just *my* rules, they are the basis on which we live. We aspire to have a clear consciousness. I'm driving you back to the train station right now." She goes, leaving me shaken and distraught, her criticism ringing in my ears. She will never be the loving mother I so desperately crave.

I walk around the farm, trying to calm down and think this through. If she has a disease, then she came here like a wounded cat seeking a quiet place to heal. But craving for vodka was clawing at her. Only her ability to manipulate me gave her a sense of control. So she attacked me to distract us both from the fact that her life has become a self-destructive plunge into the abyss. The book said alcoholics often have to bottom out before they reach for help. But these rationalizations don't help the despair I feel about never being loved by Mother.

I try to discuss her with Arjun, but he is scornful and dismissive. "We don't talk about our families at the Sri Chinmoy Centre. Remember 'past is dust.' Focus on Guru and forget her." We have learned not to call Arjun's mother, Mary, after six p.m. when she begins her nightly drinking. Her pattern is to change from a kind, maternal woman into a raging harridan in the space of a few hours.

I receive more tissue-thin airmail letters from my father, saying my mother has Hodgkin's disease. Now I'm fairly certain that my mother hasn't changed. I still want to understand her, so I come up with the excuse that I want to write about her life. We meet at a friend's high-rise apartment in New York and are seated on a vast gray modular couch. I'm at the far end looking through the wrong end of a spyglass; she is small and far away, her ranting voice a shrill squeak of a chess-sized queen. As soon as I mention writing about her, she screams, "You are only trying to uuuuse me," the syllable drawn out like the wail of a siren. I flee from her presence as if she is wielding a knife. I'm weeping, shaking, and barely able to manage the train ride back to Westchester. Seeing her isn't worth the damage she inflicts on me.

She starts appearing in the entryway of the office building where I work, sending up messages and demanding to see me. The first time I go down to see her, she rants abuse. The next time she comes, I don't go down. I can't. I resolve not to see her again.

I get calls from my uncle George saying I need to see my mother because she is very ill. I relent when I hear he will be there also. We meet in Mary's apartment in New York City— Mother's friend and former employee. They are both drunk, having a gabfest in the kitchen, and ignoring George and me. A bowl of peanuts sits on the coffee table. I pick up a handful, but one slips to the carpet. I think, *Oh, it's clean*, and pop the nut in my mouth. On my tongue is a revolting mass of hair and dust that epitomizes my relationship my mother. I spit it out onto a cocktail napkin.

※

When I am twenty-eight, everyone in the Sri Chinmoy Centre is celebrating our country's bicentennial by bicycling. The only problem is that I'm a city kid who has never learned to ride.

I had one experience of bicycling when I was ten years old, and my father rented a bicycle built for two in Central Park. Father instructed me, "Pedal as hard as you can, this thing weighs as much as a tank!" After a few false starts, we were up and slowly wheeled away. Then, magically, on a slight downhill we were flying as Father's legs went around in a blur. My feet couldn't find the pedals so I held them up. Then we slowed to a crawl on an uphill, and Father saw I wasn't pedaling.

He stopped, put his feet on the ground, and yelled, "I can't do all the work. You have got to keep pedaling." We went through this agonizing flying/crawling/yelling a few more times until I just wanted to get off the goddamn bike. My bottom and feelings were hurt, and Father was sweating and winded. We returned the bicycle in less than an hour. I never wanted to ride again—until the bicentennial.

As housemates acquire bicycles, I beg them to help me learn to ride. Various people hold the bike upright while I get going, and they run behind. I can maintain my balance, but stopping has me stymied. Invariably, the only way I can get off is to fall off. This doesn't deter me from loving cycling.

One day I have no car to get to work at our new Greenwich restaurant and decide to cycle the twenty miles. I ask to borrow Peter's new ten-speed bicycle. I'm in too much of a hurry to adjust the hard racing seat. As the miles add up, the seat becomes intolerable. When I awaken, I'm on a stretcher being placed into an ambulance with the bicycle beside me.

"You fell off that two-wheeled death trap," the gray mus-tached doctor at the hospital barks. "You have a fractured skull and blood in your spinal fluid. Can you spend the next two weeks in bed?" This is my second head injury—the first was the car crash with my stepmother.

"Oh, no, I need to work at the restaurant and go to meditations," I answer groggily.

"Then it's bed rest in hospital for two weeks," he retorts. "You're not supposed to sit up or walk to the toilet, you have to use a bedpan. Keep your head still!" Abruptly life changes to sleepy days waiting for hospital food on trays. I haven't had quiet time alone since joining the Sri Chinmoy Centre. Ironically I'm put in a room in the maternity ward, the only space available.

As the silent hours slowly meander by with nothing to read and nobody visiting, I stare out the window, and my thoughts fly free. It's as if my soul perches on the windowsill and gently shows me where I have gone astray. She says in a kind voice, "Sweetie, you want love so you throw your roses under people's feet to trample on. This doesn't work, and you aren't happy, are you? The restaurant is a chore, and Arjun isn't appreciative. And while we're at it, dear, let's talk about Guru. I know you adore him, but he's changed hasn't he? He keeps yelling at all of you to get him a Nobel Peace Prize or the Prize for Literature. When he doesn't get it, he blames you. He's like a cannibal eating you alive, dear."

I listen, amazed at the truth of this. The part of me that used to stamp out doubt doesn't utter a word of protest. "And a couple more things," my soul continues. "You're not getting any younger; it's time you started the family that your heart longs for. Remember how much you loved to paint? Do that, too." She smiles but doesn't say how to accomplish her instructions before she disappears.

Alo surprises me with a visit. Her lovely face with its high forehead and sloping cheekbones tenderly gazes at me while I try to lie still in bed. Arjun told me Guru said Alo had lost her realization, and we are supposed to remove her photograph from our meditation altars. But I would never do that. I have paddled clear lakes on a canoe trip in Canada with Alo and other female disciples. I learned how to balance my weight in the canoe, dip my paddle into the water at the correct angle, and portage over long distances. It was heavenly to meditate while mists drifted over the water, and a pearlescent dawn pinked the sky. Great blue herons lurked in the shallows around emerald islands and lofted up at our intrusion.

Alo wasn't in favor of running marathons or lifting weights to push the body to its limits, as Guru was. When we were tired, we lolled in our canoes and snacked on fruit, M&Ms, or peanut butter and jelly sandwiches. We were a harmonious group of women without any male authority dominating us. There wasn't the infighting to be among her inner circle that characterized everything that was done in Guru's presence. When we grew tired, we sang a song Alo invented that floated through my mind, "Paddling, paddling on a deep green lake in the Canadian wilderness." If I have to choose between Guru and Alo—I choose her.

There is just one embarrassing problem. I've been eating well at the hospital—any food that I don't have to cook is fine with me—and have used the bedpan to deposit a large turd. The nurses are much too busy delivering babies to take it away. I'm not supposed to get out of bed. So there sits Alo with her delicate sensibilities, blessing me, while inches away is a very smelly bedpan. Discreetly, without lifting my head, I try to shove it far under the bed while remaining in highest consciousness. Alo doesn't seem to notice, but I'm relieved when she leaves. Sometimes it's just too hard pretending I don't have a body.

◌◌◌

In the mid-sixties, when Guru first came to this country, Devadas was one of his first disciples. The white-haired, older man always sat in the front row chair closest to Guru during meditation. After Guru carried us to transcendent peace, he would ask

Devadas to play his violin. He unfolded his tall, thin body and tucked his instrument under his chin. With his eyes closed and eyebrows arched in yearning, he played music that he wrote for his Beloved. Guru's eyes danced and flickered. I gazed at them and felt raised to a world of tender union. Guru said in another life, Devadas was the Buddha's closest attendant, Ananda. I was deeply moved.

When we were first married, and I complained to Guru about Arjun's coldness, Devadas was sent in to give us marital therapy. He told us to stare into each other's eyes for ten minutes after our morning meditation. My heart opened to Arjun as I gazed into his innocent blue eyes. He wasn't trying to be mean—just managing the best he could. Then we took over the diner and forgot about Devadas's instructions.

Guru began leading meditations in a church near the United Nations, and I finagled a way to get out of the restaurant and go. After making breakfast for the morning rush, I changed into a clean sari, caught the train from Westport down to Grand Central Station, and ran to the church. Guru was always in highest consciousness at these meditations, and I'd experience deep peace and spaciousness. For me it was doubly blissful because I got to sit down, which my tired feet craved. I'd never appreciated how good sitting down felt until I worked in a restaurant.

I notice Devadas's tonsure of white hair in the front pew. Afterwards, we meet on the sidewalk. "How are you, dear? It's been a long time since we've spoken. Do you want to join me for lunch? I go to Ratner's, a wonderful vegetarian restaurant." Of course I want to eat someone else's cooking besides my own.

Ratner's is as vast as a ballroom, and the tables are graced with linen tablecloths and napkins. Hasidic men in black suits sit opposite their bewigged wives. An army of waiters trundle around with dishes balanced on their arms. We start with their famous mushroom barley soup and onion rolls and move on to potato knishes. For desert, I can't resist an apricot rugelach.

"Tell me what brings you down here? How is Arjun? How

are you feeling?" Devadas asks kindly. Tears wet my eyes. Kindness is in short supply at the Sri Chinmoy Centre—we are too busy fulfilling Guru's demands. I blink a few times and catch my breath. Do I, myself, even know how I feel? And what level of emotions is it safe to reveal? In the Centre, there is a stereotype of serene, unruffled spirituality that I try to adhere to. And we never admit doubts about Guru—we would be kicked out for that. But Devadas seems beyond such concerns. Our conversation feels—dare I think it?—normal.

"Arjun has been opening new businesses on our block in Westport, so I asked him to buy the shoe boutique there. I know it's crazy, but now I need to go down to lower Manhattan and buy some more shoes and things for the store. Really, we don't have much business—I just go in there to nap."

"Maybe I could go with you. How would you like that?"

"Would you? I was wondering how I was going to carry the shoes back on the subway and the train. Thank you so much!" I'm overwhelmed with his non-Guru-focused generosity.

Not too many United Nations meditations pass before I'm aware that lunch has become as much of an attraction as being with Guru. Devadas takes such tender care with me—just the way he opens the door for me with his long violinist's fingers, inquires if I'm warm or cool, is salve to my battered self-esteem. I inhale Devadas's kindness; it soothes the bruised, small part of me that hides in my chest. In his tender regard, I unfold like a spring flower in warm rain.

Sometimes I end the day in Queens where Devadas shares an apartment with his aged father, upon whom he lavishes an annoyed care. Sometimes, all three of us visit his artist sister in New Rochelle where he frequently spends the weekend. I discover that he eats meat, that he has been married twice and has no children. I feel like part of his family.

Devadas invites me to his musician's hideaway, equidistant between Carnegie Hall and Lincoln Center. It's his refuge between performances and also close to Grand Central Station where I can take the train home. We step off the busy street, through the door, and up dingy stairs, the roar of the traffic diminishing. Devadas unlocks a door in the dim hallway, and we enter a room so tiny it is almost possible to touch the walls with my outspread arms. The toilet and the tub are across the hall. The room is suffused by twilight from the one window that opens onto an airshaft. One of the walls has built-in shelves crammed with sheet music, books, and Tibetan sculptures. A doorless closet is stuffed with black suits for performances. The largest furnishing is a single bed made up with a red coverlet partially concealed beneath a pile of music.

"I know it's a mess," Devadas says, brushing music papers onto the floor, "but why don't you unwind your sari and lay it over the music stand so it won't become wrinkled."

"I-is this all right?" I ask hesitantly. We Centre girls aren't supposed to even make eye contact with males, so I know what we are doing is a huge breach of protocol.

"What do you think?" He pauses, and his concerned avuncular look reassures me.

"It's just between us," I say and nod. We curl up on the bed with him pressed against my back. Feeling the warmth of his body against mine is immensely comforting. We sink into oblivion as if we are in a hushed Himalayan cave free from all cares. After our nap, we sit on his bed. I can feel his thigh against mine through my thin cotton sari slip. Devadas unlatches his mandolin from a case, sets up his music stand, and teaches me how to read music. I sing the tunes he writes for Guru.

Devadas's saintly reputation comes in handy later when Arjun demands, "Where have you been? Meditation ended at one o'clock and now it's six p.m.!" I don't care, I feel rejuvenated. So Friday, United Nations meditation day, becomes my permanent day off to spend with Devadas.

On my next visit to Devadas's cave he asks, "How is your marriage to Arjun going? I know it was a problem in the beginning. Is it better now?"

"No! I'm just so frustrated, we never have sex, and he yells at me in the restaurant. It's really not a marriage at all. I try not to nag him, but he's always rushing around, he never stops to look at what a mess our finances are in. If he would be a little—I don't know—more considerate, I could bear it. But he's not."

After I remove my sari and he his suit jacket, we curl up on the little bed. Devadas gently unhitches my bra. "You will be more comfortable, dear. I'm simply helping you relax, making up for your husband's lack of attention." He massages my neck and shoulders and works around to my breasts. Starved for human touch, there is no way can I turn down Devadas's gentle ministrations. We turn around, and I offer to massage him. He allows me to soothe his neck and the tops of his shoulders. They are soft and white like kidskin gloves. There is a forty-year difference in our ages.

"Let me draw you a bath in the bathroom across the hall," he offers one summer afternoon when the city's humidity weighs on us, and the water pump is broken again at my house. He unlocks the door, gives me a clean towel, and pours bubble bath into the claw-foot tub. I'm luxuriating in the hot water when Devadas knocks and enters.

"Do you want your back scrubbed?" Of course I do. I sigh with pleasure as he massages my neck, back, and then moves gently down between my legs. I protest, but I haven't had sex in so long. Parts of my body that I'd forgotten about come exquisitely alive.

"You need this to be content with your marriage," he murmurs. Afterwards, we have our usual music lesson. But I feel an edge of distaste, of self-disgust. I let this happen once more and then stop coming to New York on Fridays. I avoid him at meditations. Life becomes a wasteland of restaurant drudgery and Sri Chinmoy Centre functions. I've been given a life sentence without parole—for what? I certainly feel no closer to God.

Around this time, I notice Guru is placing Devadas's seat farther away from himself at meditations. He is no longer invited to play his violin for us. Also, Devadas no longer wears the requisite white shirt and pants Guru demands of his male followers. When, in the safety of a Centre function, I break my silence and ask him why, he answers, "Guru's path is ninety-nine percent nonsense and one percent sense."

I'm roiling with rage and confusion over my arranged marriage, Guru's control over my life, and my strange relationship with Devadas. I want to untangle myself from all these webs. But I'm so thoroughly tied up. The only tenderness I've received came from Devadas, but who is he? Is he the saintly disciple, or is he a dirty old man preying on needy females? For that matter, who is Guru? Recently he has begun a search and destroy mission to weed out impure female disciples. Several women, including Agnes, from the Kentucky trip, are devastated when they are ejected, even though their lives are inviolate.

"My father has finally died," Devadas's soft voice tells me over the phone. "He was always very fond of you. Would you mind sorting through his things? They're meager, but he'd want you to have a memento." I know it means going to his Queens apartment, but I can't refuse.

Climbing up his building's stairs, I'm full of trepidation. *Should I say something about what happened between us? Can I tell him how much I miss him?* As I pause by his door, I hear an unexpected sound—female giggling. I knock hesitantly. Agnes opens it, laughing, and with a sweeping gesture says, "Welcome to the harem!" She is dressed in shorts and a T-shirt, as are several other women ex-disciples. They sit massaging Devadas's bare feet while another brings him tea. They are all laughing as I stand there with my mouth agape.

"Come in, dear," says Devadas, beckoning.

"W-what is going on here?" I manage to splutter.

"If Guru can get massaged by disciples, why not Devadas?" answers Agnes.

"Uh, can I have a moment in private?" I ask him. When they withdraw giggling to the tiny kitchen, I ask for an explanation.

"I'm supporting them. You know how upset they were when

Guru threw them out. Be especially kind to Caitlin, she had a breakdown and is fragile. Here's the gift from my father." He hands me a souvenir shell with *Greetings from Coney Island* written on it.

Vibrating with rage and jealousy, I look down at the shell in my hand and up into his guileless pale eyes. *You are predating on another innocent,* I want to scream; or *You can't love her as much as you love me!* But what is the truth? The words clot in my throat. In utter misery and confusion, I walk out the door. The truth is I can't believe how easily I have been replaced.

❧

I'm brushing my hair when I catch sight of my breasts in the mirror. They have become pink-nosed setters, continuously pointing. No amount of clothing covers them up. I'm speaking to my boss and glance down to discover them etched against my sweater, pointing. One week, I'm filing in a small cubicle when my boss, an older man with a Lincoln beard, enters asking for a carton of files. It is heavy, and I clutch it to my chest. Reaching for them, his large hands unwittingly grasp my breasts. I instinctively press my horizontal mountains into his palms. My animal hunger envelops both of us like crackling electricity and we stand staring at each other, mouthing meaningless words. Finally he backs out of the room. He recovers enough to treat me with a certain humor and deference, whereas I feel helpless.

Something must be done! The only person I can morally do it with is Arjun, but he is so devoted to Guru, God-realization, and the restaurant. He meditates punctually every morning at 5:30 when it is pitch-black outside. If he is tardy, and sunlight is creeping into the room, he curses himself. But even though he is busy, he feels that if anybody asks for help, he should do it. Friends have caught on to this, and they ask frequently. Arjun is handy: he can fix a faucet, build shelves, start a restaurant— his biggest problem is that he underestimates how much time such projects take and can't keep up with them all. But he always says yes. People wait for months, and he still hasn't gotten there. When they complain to me, I shrug my shoulders. *If the guy doesn't have time for sex, your problem can wait.*

I devise a plan, and the window of opportunity finally arrives when Guru is out of town. When the alarm rings, I pretend to be asleep. This is not unusual, as my spiritual impetus has taken a nosedive. Arjun rouses himself from his mattress, strikes a match, lights his incense and candles, and sits crossed-legged in front of our altar where Guru's photograph is enshrined. As he meditates in silence, I bide my time. Arjun blows out the candles and relaxes back onto his bed with a sigh of ecstasy. We both drift back to sleep. An hour later, I creep over to his bed and begin to caress him. He wakes up groggily.

"What are you doing?"

"Just enjoy this. We both need it, relax and lie back."

"Oh, my God. What would Guru say?"

I carefully unbutton his pajama tops, stroking as he lies there blinking. His inborn helpfulness assists me as I slide down the pajama bottoms.

As I began to kiss him, he asks, "Do you think Guru will be calling?" My answer is silence as I focus on the task at hand. I am massaging, stroking, hoping his natural body responses will take over. While I nibble his ear, Arjun whimpers in apprehension because his body is responding.

I'm out of my nightgown when the telephone rings. Arjun gives a little cry, but I wind my legs around him. "Let it ring, we can miss just one meditation, can't we?" I plead.

His moan is muffled beneath me. "It might be Guru. . . ."

The shrill ringing shatters the atmosphere; how can we concentrate with that distraction? "Forget about it," I snarl, my hands tangled in his hair. He struggles. I loosen my hold, and he makes a violent leap that sends him flying across the room. He lands at the foot of the telephone table and reaches for the still-shrieking machine.

"Hi, Swadhin. No, you're not too early . . . well, I guess I

228 ℓ REMEMBER ME AS LOVING YOU

sound hoarse because I just came back from running. What's up? Yes, I remember, I promised to fix that a while ago. Sure, now is a fine time. I'll be right over." He flashes me an embarrassed smile. "Swadhin's refrigeration needs fixing . . . you remember I promised to do it?" He leaves while I lie on the bed, feeling utter despair. I'm thirty years old and have been in the Sri Chinmoy Centre ten years. It's time to start living my own life, even if I don't know how.

⚬⚬⚬

My voice trembles when I call Lalita to make a private appointment to meet with Guru. I haven't been to his home in years— I'm not one of his inner circle who goes there regularly. Asking to speak with him alone about separating from Arjun is tantamount to asking the Pope for a divorce—unthinkable. But I have to do it, because I can't imagine simply leaving.

Pink azaleas are blooming in front of the peacock-blue house, reminding me of my first visit. The grass is sheared straight across to a millimeter, and the house looks bigger—it has developed more wings. I remove my sandals, adjust my sari, and ring the bell. Lalita answers the door and asks me to wait. Peeking in, I see a disciple kneeling in front of Guru, who lies on a throne-like La-Z-Boy, massaging his feet. Guru waives him away, and I'm ushered in. He gestures for me to sit on the floor, and his mouth becomes a thin line of impatience. "Yes, yes, what is it you want?"

Folding my hands reverently, I force my mouth to speak the burning words: "I want to leave Arjun and move into my own place."

Guru's beautiful golden face gives me a sideways glance. "God won't love you anymore if you do this. You will be alone in the world, and the dark forces will devour you!"

I gasp. "B-but all I want to do is separate from Arjun—I've been so unhappy. Won't God understand?"

"God doesn't want this—you will be alone in the world, and the dark forces will devour you!" Guru repeats in a low growl.

This is a horrifying pronouncement by a teacher I still consider as God incarnate. I bow again and, trying not to step on the hem of my sari, rise up and leave. But even being cursed and losing God's love cannot deter me. I cannot keep living this stunted life. The urges within me clamoring for freedom are stronger than Guru's threats.

Arjun and I find a sheriff's eviction tacked to the front door of Old Mill Farm. All of us have two weeks to leave, because the manor is to be sold. Arjun and I move to an apartment above a Greek family in Queens—a few blocks from Guru's house and the track. I've craved this for so long but now it is too late. One autumn morning I hand my husband a letter. He looks quizzically at the folded page.

> *Dear Arjun,*
> *We went to a counselor to find out what each of us*
> *sought from our marriage. I need tenderness, sexual*
> *intimacy, and a child. You asked me to stop nagging*
> *and be more devoted to Guru. I have shed too many*
> *tears over the gulf between us. I want a divorce, the*
> *apartment we share in Queens, and the Subaru. Guru*
> *says that the dark forces will devour me if I do this, but*
> *that's okay. They can't be worse than how I feel now.*
> *Pujarini*

I walk to the track where Guru is handing out *Prasad* to disciples before they jog. As I bow before him to receive the apple I say in a firm voice, "I am divorcing Arjun."

He looks at me through eyes that are slits and says, "If you do this, you will not be a part of the Sri Chinmoy Centre anymore." I nod in assent. I expected as much, and this time I'm ready.

Arjun quickly moves out, and I'm served with divorce papers. But shedding the protective cocoon of the Sri Chinmoy

Centre is not as easy. There, every aspect of my life has been controlled—whom to marry, where to live, what profession to pursue, what colors to wear, what to read, and what sport to enjoy. Now, the simplest act leaves me in a panic of indecision. My life coordinates have been removed overnight, and I have nothing in their place. I enroll in nearby Queens College, thinking that finishing my bachelor's degree is a good place to start. But I'm helpless when they wanted to know my major. I veer between art and social work.

A barrage of stimuli assails my senses on the street, on the subway, at the office. I feel as if my skin has been removed, and my body is a map of exposed nerves. I no longer have the filter of the group to protect me. I'm desperate for someone to talk to, but Lalita and the disciples whom I once considered family pass me on the street as if I no longer exist. I am shunned. This is the hardest of all—I'm so achingly alone. When I joined the Centre, I had hoped to find the love and acceptance of the tribe I never had. But I had to give up my identity and live a lie to be part of it. Reclaiming myself required leaving the safety of the pack and walking into the unknown alone. Every step away felt as if I was facing death.

I long to go to Devadas's apartment for an open talk about his true feelings for me and the other female disciples. Is he "encouraging" us or using us? Does he feel cut off in his role as a wise elder? Is that why he has crossed the boundary into sexual exploitation? I want to tell him that his tenderness gave my life meaning for a while, and I miss him. I want to say all these things, but we are stuck in a triangle of secrecy and jealousy. I don't feel welcome at his apartment that is around the corner from where I now live.

I remove the photos of Guru and Alo from my altar but have nothing to put in their place. I don't know how to meditate anymore. For years, I looked to Guru to lift me into bliss. I have no sense of how I can do it for myself. Who am I now that I am no longer Pujarini, disciple, wife, and restaurant-owner? I have no idea of what I want other than to love and be loved.

Jagat, Guru's henchman, calls me to come to his stationery store. I walk down, trembling with hope that Guru might have a kind word for me. But all he does is hand me a needlepoint pillow I had made for Guru with "Supreme I am thy glowing grace" inscribed on it.

"Guru doesn't want this anymore," he says in a dismissive voice.

Where is the grace?

⚜

"Your mother is down here in Lexington, Kentucky being cared for by family. She's pretty sick. I think you ought to come down," Aunt Clara says over the phone.

"Is she drinking?" is all I can think to say.

"Well, yeah, and she sometimes yells at us and accuses us of stealing her stuff, but I think you should come anyway."

"I'm afraid she'll curse me from her deathbed. You don't know how abusive she's been in the past years. I just left my marriage and Sri Chinmoy. He cursed me, too. I don't think I can take anymore curses."

"I still think you should come."

But I'm immobilized by fear and can't get myself on an airplane down to Kentucky.

The hospital chaplain calls. "Your mother is dying. You should come down and see her before it's too late."

I call Mother, and Aunt Lonnie picks up the phone. "Does Mother want to see me?" I blurt out.

Lonnie covers the receiver and I hear a whispered conversation. She hands the phone over to Mother who says in a harsh tone, "I'm much too ill to have visitors."

"You don't want to see me?" I ask to make sure I get this straight.

"I'm too ill for visitors." She repeats. So I don't go. She dies a week later, just before her fifty-second birthday. I am thirty-one.

Clara calls a week later demanding, "Why weren't you at your mother's funeral? Her death has hit your grandparents very hard. You should have been there for them. The family is very disappointed in you. I don't think they want to see you anymore."

I turn into ice. I don't wash my long dark hair, and it hangs in greasy snakes. Every time I look in the mirror, I pass verdict on myself—guilty. I have to get out of the apartment, and on a bitterly cold day in March, I layer up in several sweaters, a jacket, and a wool hat. When I pass disciples on the street, they cross over to the other side. I'm a pariah, the bad seed whom God doesn't love, and the dark forces are devouring me. I come back to the house, get into bed with all my clothes on, and pull the blankets over my head. This is just too hard.

The phone rings but I let it go. After the fifth call I haul myself out of bed and pick it up. It is Arjun's mother, Mary. She says, "Hello, dear, are you all right? You must be grieving your mother's death. I'm sorry for your loss, but I have to tell you something. Your mother called me the night before she died and spoke kindly of you. She said, 'I hear my little girl is going through a divorce.'"

These are words I crave to hear with every fiber of my being. Yet my mother has told them to my ex-mother-in-law. I'm baffled by this irony. Gone is any hope of closing the gulf between my mother and me. Every breath in my body says never, never, never—I will never be mothered, never have a healing between us. I will never ask about her romance with David. We will never laugh at a joke together or go for a walk in the spring sunshine. I will never ask her opinion on the best and worst aspects of ageing or of being a woman. Did she vote? Was she a cat or a dog person? I will never know.

Grief dismembers me limb from limb. I can barely drag my body out of bed, so heavy is the weight of loss. I can't cope with this barrage of loss in a few months: my marriage, Guru, Mother, spiritual and earthly family. I am utterly alone and bereft. In my bid for freedom and self-determination, I've been exiled in the wilderness.

Blackness keeps sucking at me. Part of me wants to yield, to lie down and never get up. But I have to go on. Somehow I know I have to do something with my creativity that has been stifled so long, something with my hands. I walk down to Jamaica Boulevard, past the pimps whispering, "Sexy eyes, sssexy eyesss" and timidly push open the fabric shop door. I'm dazzled by a lush display of fabrics. Bolts of cotton, silk, tulle, and metallic evening gown material are stacked everywhere. Tentatively, my fingers brush cottons in purples, magentas, and oranges, while my eyes eat up creamy whites and dreamy blues. The colors speak directly to my soul.

A sign on the counter announces the start of a basic quilting course. I sign up and ask the sales lady instructor what do I have to do? She tells me I will need a sewing machine—I already possess one—and I must choose five fabrics with patterns of different dimensions. It is an impossible task as each fabric calls, *Unfold me, stroke me, love me.* My eyes keep returning to a teal and tan paisley, its intricate swirls whisper of my years with Guru. Peach, teal, and slate gray complete my choices.

During the class that I attend on weekends, we learn how to make traditional patterns such as nine-patch, log cabin, and grandmother's flower garden. I practice measuring, cutting, and machine stitching perfect quarter-inch seams. Feeling the fabric move under my fingers satisfies me, yet I feel the urge to go beyond this traditional method. I vow that the next quilt I make won't be anything like my grandmother's. As I focus on learning the craft, I forget about my grief. Sewing doesn't demand that I attend my mother's deathbed or aspire to a higher consciousness; it doesn't ask what my college major is or that I look slim in a miniskirt. It takes me back to my childhood when I was home in Kentucky or sewing alongside Fenny. Slowly, creativity lifts me out of despair.

A few weeks after my mother dies, David, my ex-stepfather, invites me to Trader Vic's. He has agreed, once again, to pay for my college tuition. He brings his six year-old-daughter by his current wife. Marguerita is wearing a taffeta party dress with a lace collar, and her long brown hair is held back by a black velvet headband. She has invited a friend who looks almost identical. David is in his usual made-to-order navy pinstripe suit. I'm dressed in a newly bought dress whose tag scratches the back of my neck, and my legs are pinched into constricting panty hose. I miss soft saris that adjust to my size. I hope David will be consoling, although I'm nervous because that isn't his style. He isn't called "The Abominable Showman" for nothing.

We walk past the carvings of naked tikis, which flank Trader Vic's door. I avert my eyes from their erect penises. We are seated at a heavy carved table by waiters wearing safari garb. I look around at the frowning masks on the walls, the straw partitions and flaming torches. Having spent years with Guru learning how to be devoted and pure won't help me here. I feel more like a lamb sharing a meal with a lion that is about to eat her. We are handed enormous menus whose dishes all involve racks of ribs and slabs of meat. I'm still a vegetarian.

I peer at David's white face and black eyebrows and wonder why he invited me. Maybe he thought Trader Vic's would entertain the children and lift my spirits. But I doubt this. Consideration of others isn't one of his characteristics. My jaw is clenched.

We order from the enormous menus, and the girls get hamburgers and drinks with umbrellas. I order kebabs that I guess will have at least a few vegetables. We make small talk, and the two little girls grow restive and begin playing house under the table. David looks relaxed; he gazes into the distance but doesn't loosen his tie. He was always a formal man. At least his thick black eyebrows are not frowning. I gaze at my lap and try to breathe deeply as I learned in yoga class.

"Your mother was a failure, you know," David remarks. I look at him. His face hasn't changed—have I heard him correctly?

"She had so much promise, and she threw it all away." I open my mouth to defend her. But what can I say? It is true. She had clawed her way out of the poverty of eastern Kentucky, wounding a great many people as she went, and what had she gained? Marrying this man was her greatest achievement.

"Her entire life was a waste." David is looking at me as if he expects me to say something. I rally myself.

"Surely no life is a total waste. She produced me and Cecelia." This sounds weak in my ears—an ex-cult member and a severely impaired child isn't much to brag about.

He ignores me. "Hers was. And she was a whore. She used her body to leverage her way up." I think about this. I had often seen her use her wit and sapphire eyes to manipulate a man. But did she sleep her way up? She was my mother, and I both loved and hated her. To her relatives, she was a star. To me, she is a hollow in the center of my chest.

"She threw everything away on drink," David says with disgust. "And she was a lesbian." His onyx eyes watch me. I don't know how to respond. As with everything else, I don't know her sexual preferences. I glance down to see if the girls are listening, but they seem happy giggling under the table. Then waiters bring huge steaming platters of food and thump them on the table. David urges the kids to come up and eat. The smell of burnt flesh makes my stomach quiver. At least the presence of the children and food distracts David from his diatribe.

I dab with the linen napkin at beads of sweat dotting my hairline. I feel as if I might throw up and excuse myself. Simply threading my way through the crowded smoky restaurant to the ladies room is a challenge. The toilets are named Tarzan and Jane, but inside all is cool and serene. I sit on the commode and lay my head against the stall. I wish I could hide here forever. Or better still, I imagine sneaking out the kitchen door into the anonymity of the street and escaping. But instead, I wash my hands and face and walk back into the lion's den.

David has finished eating, and the girls are toying with their mountainous burgers. I say I'm not hungry, and David orders the leftovers to be cleared away. What is removed would feed a family of six. I decide to maintain my dignity. With a touch of irony I thank him for the meal as we leave the restaurant. He shows no glimmer of remorse or awareness of what he has done. I refuse his offer of a ride to the subway station. The cool touch of night air on my cheek calms and comforts me. *Someday I will find someone loving,* I vow to myself.

Chapter 14

BALM TO MY WOUNDED SENSUALITY

❧

You do not have to walk on your knees
For a hundred miles through the desert, repenting.
You only have to let the soft animal of your body
Love what it loves.

—MARY OLIVER

I slog through required courses at Queens College, putting one foot in front of the other, finishing the bachelor's degree I'd thrown away without a thought. I know I seem ancient to the eighteen-year-olds in my classes and seldom speak to anyone. English literature excites me when I write about life with Guru. Three days a week, I work as a temporary secretary filling in for the vacationing or ill. Nobody knows me, and I know no one. I sift through Manhattan's high-rise offices like a ghost. Friday is the one bright night when I stay downtown late and go to Dance Jam. In a Greenwich Village loft, a motley group of us sling our bodies around to a deejay's music. My body becomes exhilarated and alive when I dance, the music moving me hither and yon. I have no story; I'm a dust mote, an electric charge. Neither my past nor my future matters—just this music surging through my body. I feel whole as I move, the division between body and spirit healed.

Later I rediscover the Dances of Universal Peace—the same dances I had done with Sufi Sam in California. Amazingly, they have spread across the country. As we hold hands in a circle, we sing:

Ishq Allah Mabud lillah
All I ask of you is forever
to remember me as loving you.

The song raises such yearning within me. Can I think of my mother standing beside me as we dance, loving me, and my loving her? I try to recall the wonderful qualities that her friends adored in her: intelligence, humor, generosity, and fun. And what about Guru, Devadas, Franca, and David? Might I think of them as loving me? But here my imagination balks until I shrink them into children who link their trusting little fingers with mine. Only then can I believe that their original intent was not to harm.

Saturday mornings I have to be at psychopathology class at Queens College by 9:00 a.m. The class is held in an amphitheater, and I sit in the highest tier where the teacher won't see my head drooping and lids closing. By early spring we have a test coming, and I know I'm in trouble. I notice a dark-haired, bearded man sitting in the front row, who engages in class discussion and takes voluminous notes. I maneuver my steps so they coincide with his and introduce myself. He is tall with warm, golden eyes and is older than I am, so I don't become spastic with self-consciousness the way I do around cute boys. I ask to borrow his notebook.

"You're welcome to it, but I probably need to explain it to you because of my chicken scratch." I glance down at his proffered yellow pad and see what looks like code. He suggests we get together to study and gives me his number. His name is Carl.

At work the next week, I keep turning his offer over in my mind. He isn't my type at all—so much older—and wears un-cool polyester pants and a white shirt. But he exudes a confidence that men my age don't have. I like his black mustache and beard with a small white stripe down the chin. It gives him a devilish air.

Oh, what the hell. What's the worst that can happen with a study partner? I rationalize.

We arrange to meet at my apartment after work. He seems eager and excited when he stands on the doorstep of my little Queens apartment. I realize I should have chosen a less intimate venue. What have I gotten myself into? After my decade in the Sri Chinmoy Centre, where the sexes weren't allowed to speak or make eye contact, I don't know how to navigate normal social interactions. I keep distance between us as we go over his notes, memorizing various categories of mental illness and their symptoms. After a while Carl says, "It's getting late and I really could use a cup of coffee." A glass of water and an apple are all I have to offer. I never acquired the caffeine habit. I'm embarrassed by the blackened stew of miso and vegetables that lies in a pot in the kitchen. Since I've left the restaurant, cooking hasn't been a high priority.

We both get As on the test, so we decide to keep meeting. We begin running together in the mornings before work. Carl is interested in doing a marathon that fall. As spring turns the trees lime green, we jog through a Queens park, sometimes following pacing marks that disciples have laid down for Guru. We have discussions about everything from the meaning of life to Carl's history.

"I've been married twenty-eight years, but my wife is an alcoholic. I took the huge step of moving out to a little apartment a few months ago. I have three children, two who are grown, and the youngest boy, Gil, still lives at home," he says.

Carl is an actuary—he explains it to me because I've never heard the word before. It has something to do with risk assessment in health insurance, and he is at the management level. He has lived a conservative life but loves to learn. This is why he is taking college classes. He is kind, courteous, and strong. Best of all, his glowing eyes tell me that he finds me very attractive.

This is such a balm to my wounded sensuality. As we bound through the woods and explore the pink and white azalea-lined paths of the Queens Botanical Gardens, I find myself reciprocating. Carl has a great body for a soon-to-be-fifty-year-old. He is tall, athletic, and has intense golden brown eyes. When he kisses me, I feel an electrical thrill that goes all the way down to my feet.

After four months of dating, on his birthday in May, I grab his hand and lead him up to my bedroom. "This is my surprise gift for you," I whisper in his ear, shucking off my running clothes and twirling around naked. He looks a little stunned but then falls to his knees and presses his face against my belly. Suddenly self-conscious, I say, "I'm trying to whittle my weight down."

Carl stammers, "I-I wasn't sure of how you felt about me. I'm older than you . . . but don't lose one pound of your gorgeous woman's body." We lie on my new double bed as he kisses my forehead and lips, hides his face in my breasts and sucks on them, then kisses his way down my stomach and vagina. I expect him to focus there but he keeps pressing his lips down my inner thighs until he nibbles very gently on my toes and ends with a bite. I'm gasping with excitement, but when he tries to enter me, his penis wilts! Again he starts kissing me, and I am so ready, but Little Mr. Man bends over, disqualified.

Carl lies back on the bed, covering his eyes with his arm. "This is mortifying. I'm humiliated beyond belief. I've imagined making love to you, but I've had only one partner for twenty-eight years, and now . . . you probably never want to see me again. I'm leaving." He yanks on his pants and heads for the door. But I grab him and pull him back.

"This isn't easy for me either, you know. I feel like a virgin after years of sexless marriage. Let's take it slowly. Just hold me."

Carl nods miserably and enfolds me in his arms. We lie there looking at the ceiling and I begin to explore with my fingers his craggy face, course black beard with the white stripe, nipples with a few sparse hairs, smooth flat belly, curly pubic hair, and muscular thighs. He relaxes a bit.

"Why don't your recite Dylan Thomas, and I'll brush your hair?" I know that Carl has committed his favorite poet to memory. I get my hairbrush and start sweeping it through his glossy, thick hair.

"'Now as I was young and easy under the apple boughs. . . .'" His sonorous voice, similar to Thomas's, falls into the cadence of the poem. I'm entranced by the language and hand the brush to him. He slides it through my hair, giving my scalp a massage that sends ripples of pleasure through my body. By the time he has recited several poems, our equilibrium is restored. He gently slips into me and I cradle him with my legs and arms. We are one body in tender communion. As he rocks gently, we both climax in gentle waves.

"This is the first time I've ever trusted anyone enough to come," I whisper. He reverently kisses the tears on my cheeks. I lay my head on his chest, and we sleep.

We drive out to Jones Beach. In all my years with Sri Chinmoy, I had never explored the end of Long Island. Carl takes along a bottle of champagne, and we sit on the sand and watch the sun plunge into the ocean while sipping our drinks. After dark, a band plays on the boardwalk, and as we dance under the stars, I press my ear to the steady rhythm of his heart.

Then we are starved, and Carl drives us to a little pizzeria run by blue-eyed Ernesto. Carl orders baked clams—an illicit food because it isn't vegetarian. I get spinach lasagna but end up eating Carl's clams. They are delicious. He loves the guilty expression on my face as I step across another forbidden threshold. It feels utterly fantastic to be wooed and desired. Finally, I am the chosen one. I'm flying on top of the world.

I'm also scared of Carl. What does he want from me? At times his ardor feels engulfing, especially when I find him devouring me with his golden brown eyes. And our backgrounds are so different. He comes from an immigrant Italian family where he was the sole male among many sisters, the adored prince. He expects adulation as if it is his due. Yet he seems capable of taking on my chaotic, crazy family.

We drive up to New Haven to visit my half-sister Cecelia, who lives in a special school. She is now an overweight, angry teenager. We take her out to lunch where she crams lasagna into her face until tomato sauce drips down her cheeks. At the same time she asks, "What's for dessert? Can I have ice cream?" When we return her to school, she throws a tantrum on the steps, screaming, "When will you come visit again? Don't leave me here! I know you won't come back!"

I'm shaken and appalled. It's as if my mother has been reincarnated in Cecelia. The biblical phrase about the sins of the parents being visited upon the children floats through my mind. But Carl is unfazed and calm. With him I have an ally.

Our relationship shifts when Carl's wife, Norma, goes into an alcoholic rehabilitation facility. He moves back to his split-level ranch farther out on Long Island to be with Gil, who is in his last year of high school. Carl invites me to his house for dinner. While he cooks, I look through his cupboards, which contain more types of pasta than I knew existed. I feel the presence of Norma, to whom he has been married almost as long as I've been alive. I wonder if she can sense another woman standing in her kitchen. Carl's sons, Nelson and Gil, eat dinner with us, and I see their shock as they register my presence in their father's life. He comes with a lot more baggage than I do.

One night when we are at a restaurant, I notice a metallic gleam on Carl's left hand.

"Are you wearing a wedding band?" I ask, not believing my eyes.

"I went to see Norma, and she gets so upset if I'm not wearing it. I forgot to take it off. It doesn't mean anything." He slips it into his suit pocket, embarrassed.

"It means a great deal to me. I'm seeing you clearly for the first time—a married man with children, a house, a yard to mow, a mortgage, and a long history with Norma. What am I doing in this picture? When I met you, I thought you were as free as I was, but this obviously isn't the case. And I yearn to have a child of my own. I'm thirty-one, and my childbearing years are slipping away."

"I haven't been the best father. I was fine diapering the kids when they were babies, but it was tough going as they got older. Gil has a drinking problem, and my daughter is on welfare. I don't want to go through that again."

Back in New York, we separate. I try a dating service while he vacations alone in the California desert. We speak to each other on the phone and laugh at my experience dating a Basque old enough to be my father. Where do these matches come from? I also tell him I am getting to know an adjunct professor at Adelphi who is divorced and my age. A few days later, he is banging on my door.

"I can't bear to think of life without you—I might lose you!" He bursts into my apartment roaring, "I must have been insane to let you go. You are the best thing that ever happened to me."

He flashes his eyes and asks, "Will you marry me when my divorce comes through? We will try for a child if that's what you want."

I'm stunned and consider his offer. "I care deeply for you, Carl, but the difference in our ages and backgrounds seem so huge. And I have dreams of living in an intentional community—dreams you don't share. But you are offering commitment, while my other prospects aren't going anywhere. If I'm thirty-five when we have a child, you will be seventy when she graduates from high school. Have you thought of that? When I'm sixty-five and retiring, you will be eighty-two. These are big age differences. Do you think we can make it work?"

"I've figured our age differences right through to my death at a hundred and four. If I can give you thirty good years, I think we should grab it. I want to share my life with you."

"All right, I accept. Between my sense of adventure and your life experience, maybe we can make a go of it. Also, I want to be a healing influence on you and your children." He holds me in his arms while I shed a few tears over the lovers and lifestyles I will never know.

The spiritual aspect of life is very important to me, and I want Carl to share in this. We attend Guru's public meditations, but as I look at his eyes showering blessing, I wonder who he is. How could he say God doesn't love me? It's clear I can no longer tie myself to his coattails and ride them into enlightenment. Nor do I want to. I have to do it for myself, no matter how imperfectly.

Carl and I attend a Zen Buddhist meditation in Manhattan. We place our shoes on racks at the door and don black robes. When I tie the sash and smooth the black cotton, my spine straightens and I feel as if I've worn this all my life. The bare wood floors, white walls, and black cushions on the floor are appealingly spare. As I sit on the *zafu*, my senses quiet down to just this moment. We face the white wall and close our eyes—there is no teacher to look at. I realize that my alcoholic mother, controlling Guru, and all my crazy relatives have led me to just this moment facing this wall and myself. Waves of gratitude wash over me. I'm not breathing but being breathed; I'm not meditating but being meditated, floating in the lake of silence. When the bell rings, I feel like a skin diver who has been deep and surfaces for air.

A blonde, graying woman says, "Roshi is on a trip to Japan and has asked me to give a talk on the Buddha's Four Noble Truths." I'm glad the teacher isn't here, although she looks a little nervous. "This is a daunting task so maybe I'll stick to the first truth. Life is suffering. Old age, sickness, death, and impermanence are intrinsic to life."

This strikes me as so obviously true. Why had no one had ever talked about this? We were all too busy chasing something—money, fame, love, enlightenment—to see what was in front of us. This is the elephant in the living room that we all so carefully stepped around.

"Let me tell how this has helped me with the death of my brother. We weren't close, although I worried about him constantly. He was a drug addict and may have taken his own life." She looks down at her hands.

"I wanted my brother to be different—that was a major form of suffering. Can I accept him just the way he was? Can I accept how I am? If I blame myself for not preventing his death, then I'm just adding to the suffering. Life is constantly changing and evolving, and we have little control over it. Life is about how we relate to everything. As human beings, we want security, love, and happiness, but these can't be guaranteed. The best and only response is to offer compassion to myself, my brother, and everyone, because we are all suffering to some degree or another."

She bows, and I feel as if I'm a bell that has been struck. In many ways, her story is my story. There was no way I could control or change my mother, although I tried. I wished we'd had a different relationship, but we didn't. She was suffering from a disease, and so was I by trying to escape her. I begin to understand that, far from being over, our relationship will evolve as long as I'm alive. I dearly hope compassion and forgiveness will be a leavening ingredient in the mix that has so far been bitter.

A few weeks later, while walking to the subway after Zen meditation, I see in an antiques shop window the sculptured head of an Asian woman wearing an elaborate crown. I stand before her enraptured. Her lowered gaze and smiling lips bring forth emotions I can't explain. Going inside, I ask the shop owners who she is. They aren't sure, but after checking in the back, they return and say, "She is Kwan Yin, the goddess of compassion who hears the cries of the world." I happily write a check for $75—a huge amount on my tiny budget. They box her up, and I lug all eighteen pounds of her back to Queens with the string cutting into my fingers.

At home I set Kwan Yin's head on my vacant meditation table and add a flower. Her compassionate smile infiltrates my meditations. I imagine her sitting on a lotus throne with diaphanous garments wafting around her, regal yet at ease. When she sees me, tears of happiness shine in her eyes. I place in her lap those parts of myself I most want to hide: craving for love, grudge holding, and guilt over my inability to attend my mother's deathbed. Then I crawl into her arms, and she tenderly strokes my hair. "Give me your suffering and confusion and leave them with me," she whispers with motherly tenderness. Her radiance, strength, and peace merge with me, and I surrender to her love.

⧉

Eight months after leaving the Sri Chinmoy Centre, and in the process of divorcing my husband, I get a call inviting me to a party for former disciples. I invite Carl to the bash and buy trendy Jordache jeans and take them in at the waist to accentuate my hips. My blouse is blue mesh through which you can see my red bra. I'm displaying my body after a decade of shrouding it in saris.

Swadhin answers the door, and my jaw drops in surprise. He has left Guru? He had been a favorite comedian and owned a popular sandwich shop a few blocks from Guru's house. I look past him into the room booming with loud music and writhing bodies. I had only known these people dressed in white during silent meditation. I drag Carl in by the hand and keep looking around. "You have left the Centre? And you and you?"

Swadhin offers me some wine that I refuse, unsure after ten years' abstinence how it will affect me. Swadhin smiles. "Come on, we're dancing to lower chakra music," he says as the steady beat of "Louie, Louie" blares over the loudspeakers. We jump into the center of the group while Carl sits on the side. I swing my hips and perform all the moves from my nights as a topless dancer. I can feel Carl's eyes admiring my ass, and I enjoy it! I laugh as Swadhin and I dance around the room feeling free and whole.

When there is a break, I ask Swadhin, "Why did you leave?" He stares into his wine and drawls, "I was tired of putting on a show. It isn't easy always being the funny guy, you know." Then he smirks. He always made me laugh.

"Yeah, we had to put on an act of 'perfect, happy disciple,'" I agree.

Two boys whom I know to be brothers and who still have clean-cut disciple haircuts say, "We slept with prostitutes and then went straight to meditation. Guru didn't notice anything different about us."

The older brother says, "He even placed his hand on my head and told me, 'Good boy, good boy.' So much for Guru's occult powers and ability to read our thoughts. That's all crap."

My mind scrambles to take this in and can't decide which is more mind-boggling: that the disciples went to prostitutes, or that Guru didn't *know*.

Another man says, "I think Guru is sleeping with some of his female disciples." But I can't accept this. Guru's place in my heart is still sacrosanct.

"Guru told me if I left the Centre, lower forces would devour me, and God wouldn't love me anymore." I finally blurt out my awful secret.

Regina says casually, "That's only a power play. He's trying to control you and prevent you from leaving the Centre. Don't believe him. You're valuable to him. You're among the first disciples he married. I sent him a letter saying I wanted to leave the Centre and go to college, and he didn't even answer. He didn't threaten me. He didn't care if I left."

I gape at her as a new perspective on Guru dawns on me. He is a manipulative human being trying to control us; a vulnerable person greedy for fame and recognition, lapping up all our adoration and always wanting more. We aren't so different. Can all the transcendental powers I attribute to him be in me? Perhaps I can experience peace and bliss without him. Perhaps God is in me as well as well as him. The light flooding in through all the doors

I'm opening makes me giddy. For a few days, my feet barely touch the ground. I feel light, as if Guru's weight has been lifted from my shoulders. I'm free to be me—whoever that turns out to be.

***

I'm still living in my apartment above the Greek family in Queens when Franca calls from Mexico. She and my father had moved to unpronounceable Oaxaca when his asthma became acute. She wants to visit her daughter Justine—who has just had her first baby—in England. "Can Father stay with you while I'm over in England?" she asks. I say I will check with my Greek landlords, just to give myself time to think.

Downstairs, twelve-year-old Olympia turns her dark pony-tail to one side and decides it will be okay. I pay rent to her black-garbed mother, who speaks no English. Anything more complicated has to go through Olympia. She is fuming at the moment because, although they gave her brother a bicycle, they won't let her ride one because she is a girl.

I have switched to Adelphi University and am majoring in social work and learning about psychology and feminism. I'm near the end of the term year, and my plate is full. I have classes to attend, term papers to write, field work at a home for schizophrenics, and temp work to augment my income. But Father has never learned to cook, not even to boil an egg, so he needs to be left with someone who can care for him. The obvious person is me. Also, this is an opportunity to heal our relationship. So I call Franca back and say, "Bring him up."

They drive all the way from Oaxaca in an old Ford LTD named "Big Red." This is an amazing feat, considering their incessant bickering. Father is sporting a jaunty Colonel Sanders mustache and beard. But his gray eyes surrounded with white lashes look askance at my makeshift furniture. I let them sleep on my new bed, while I use a low table topped with foam rubber. He does not look happy about Franca's trip or his stay in Queens.

"She has no right going off and leaving me," he says when we drop her at the airport for her flight "across the pond," as she likes to call it.

Although he is amenable to fixing his own cereal in the morning, he expects me to serve him two meals a day as Franca does. I make a sandwich for his lunch in the morning before I go to school and prepare dinner each evening. I will not cook him meat. He is all right with this if I prepare curried vegetables, which he enjoys. The most taxing duty comes after dinner, when I am expected to sit and listen to his hours' long recitation of movies he has covered and stars he has known.

He stares with unseeing eyes and rains a cold torrent of words and recites memories as if they are a life raft that keeps him afloat in a world he understands. Without his memories, he will drown. I'm bitter with the irony of his being lost in the illusion of actors while before him is a real daughter he can't see. He never acknowledges my presence except for references to the cute things I said as a baby. It's as if I ceased to exist once I lost my unconditional father worship. Sometimes he asks, "Don't you remember?" about people and events that predate me. He shakes his head irritably when I don't.

When I feel numb and half-dead and unable to absorb one more word, I blurt out, "I've heard that story before" and flee the room to work on a term paper. I long to share with him my experience of leaving Sri Chinmoy's cult, or my mother's death, or my divorce, or my new relationship with Carl. But my father expresses no curiosity about any of this. His craving to be heard is paramount.

Social work class gives me an idea when I read about tape-recording reminiscences of the elderly. Here is an opportunity to hear about his childhood. But Father turns curiously diffident when I steer his monologue toward personal memories. There are certain questions to which he just shrugs—like, *When did you discover your father was Jewish? Why didn't your father have life insurance to leave Grandma when he died, to prevent your becoming destitute?* I do discover Father never finished high school, yet went on to write for a newspaper. He is a self-taught man. I try more questions.

"What attracted you to my mother?" I'm startled when he slowly spells out S-E-X.

"Jeanne was like Holly Golightly in Truman Capote's short story, 'Breakfast at Tiffany's.' But not Audrey Hepburn, whom Capote didn't think had enough sex appeal to play the movie role. Jeanne was so vibrant and charming; then I found out she was married to an older man she'd left back in Kentucky. Read the short story." He shakes his head and closes the subject.

I withdraw Capote's book out of the library and read it. With great poignancy, it depicts a naïve country girl who expects her wealthy dates to hand her a $50 bill when she goes to the ladies room—presumably to tip the bathroom attendant with a lot left over—and who then goes to bed with the man later. She hopes to marry one of them. If Holly Golightly had a daughter, she would turn out just like me. This is just the way it was. From another perspective, I marvel at my mother's adventurous spirit and Venus-like allure. She seemed to cast a spell over everyone who knew her. Flawed, she could be cruel and self-deceiving. It wasn't her fault; it was just the way she was made. I have to make peace with her legacy.

Finally, I screw up my courage to ask a question that lurks in my heart.

"Did you and Franca ever discuss why I left Huntington?'

There is a totally uncharacteristic silence, and then he gives me a sidelong glance. "No, we never talked about it, but she lost several teeth in the car accident. She was wracked with guilt. . . ." So he never asked and was never told about the accusations that I was destroying their marriage. I'd been turned into the scapegoat. It came down to Franca or me. He needed her more. The pain of this revelation feels as if a hundred-pound weight has been dropped on my heart. Thank God I'm in therapy and have someone with whom to discuss it. She tells me I have to start parenting myself, because I'm not going to get it from my father.

Then Franca's transatlantic phone calls take a disturbing tone.

"Maybe while I'm in England, I should take a short trip to Italy to see old friends," she says in her piping British accent. "I want to visit my sister Anna in California now that Daddy is happily ensconced with you." I have visions of months sliding by before she returns to collect him.

"One month is all I can stand Daddy. You have no idea how close this arrangement is to falling apart."

I ask Father how he feels about Franca's wanting to continue her travels. I'm learning about emotions in my psychology class.

"Feelings?" he splutters, "I have no feelings!" But his face is red and his tone explosive. "Look at this," he says opening up his wallet. "I had your *New York Times* birth announcement laminated the day you were born and have carried it ever since. Maybe it's time I handed it over to you."

As I turn the yellowed card over in my hand, I'm touched that he has held onto it all these years. But the fact that he no longer wants to keep it makes my heart plummet.

When Franca returns after a month as planned, I'm relieved. We stack her suitcases in the bedroom and take her to a nice restaurant. Afterwards, Father is reading the newspaper in what passes for my living room when she shares some personal information.

"You were lucky to leave us when you did back in Huntington. We had a hard time when we lived in England. Your father can't seem to find himself. On this trip I discovered it was really such a relief not to quarrel with him all the time." She is looking more relaxed than I've ever seen her. "Maybe it's time we should separate. I hoped I could just keep traveling and leave him here with you."

This is a jaw-dropping concept. In my mind they are a fixed entity and have been so since I witnessed their marriage before a judge when I was eight years old. I want to move beyond our painful past, however, and be supportive. After all, I have read *The Women's Room* by Marilyn French and subscribe to *Ms. Magazine*. I'm a feminist.

"Well," I say, "you can leave Daddy if that's what you want, but he can't stay with me. I have my own life to lead." Father comes in at the end of our talk and hears my words.

He begins yelling at me. "You can't desert me again! I'm not a helpless child. You can't decide my fate." Again, it is easier to turn on me than to confront Franca.

Somehow, in the midst of all this, Franca begins criticizing my stained toilet bowl. She prides herself on her housekeeping. I know I should let this go and focus on the real issues, but I get deflected by my need to show her the porcelain is clean. We three assemble in the tiny bathroom around the toilet as I scrub, but the rust stain on the cracked bowl doesn't lighten at all. Clarification of Franca's intention to leave Father is completely lost.

The next morning I have classes, and when I return, "Big Red" is not in front of the little Queens house. Maybe they have gone out for a drive? I climb upstairs, and my apartment is empty of their belongings. They have gone, leaving no note, no explanation. A week later, I received an unsigned postcard from Amarillo, Texas. I turn it over, studying its back and front. What the hell is going on? Finally I get a card saying they are in Albuquerque drying out Daddy's lungs. It is like so many unresolved incidents in which I feel at fault. My relationship with my father is as ruptured as ever. Nothing I do seems to change that. But I wonder how long they will stay there. I've always wanted to visit New Mexico.

Chapter 15

BECOMING KWAN YIN

Last night as I was sleeping,
I dreamt—marvelous error!—
That I had a beehive
Here inside my heart.
—ANTONIO MACHADO

My mood is buoyant as Carl drives us westward through the lush summer landscapes between New York and Kentucky. I admire his Roman nose and devilish black beard. I have done something right! After meeting him, Father had given his seal of approval. We consider ourselves engaged, although his divorce still hasn't come through. During the last three years, I have accomplished so much: slipping Sri Chinmoy's noose, getting my bachelor's and master's degrees in social work, and soon a new marriage. We are driving to Chicago, where Carl has a new job. A wonderful life awaits us. But first, with Carl's support, I plan

to mend the rift between Mother's family and me that occurred when she died three years earlier.

I find my grandparents' house in Knott County, Kentucky, by recognizing the sagging shack across the dirt road from their new house. My Chevette rolls to a stop in front of a hill of coal that takes up most of the front yard. Carl and I sit in silence, looking around at the rusting machinery littering the lot as the car ticks and cools. My mouth and hair are filled with road dust. I'm hot, car sore, and wondering why I have come to this end of the earth. My gaze lights on a mimosa tree in full bloom, its powder-puff blossoms covered by swallowtail butterflies. This cheers me up, and when we step out of the car, a white duck rushes up to give us an enthusiastic greeting.

An old man in a straw fedora emerges from the lumpy shack across the dirt road. As he slowly walks closer we eye each other. Finally I ask, "Is that you, Grandpa?" He nods and holds himself stiffly while I peck his cheek. He looks older, his cheeks sunken and the fragile skin under his eyes puffed out. My Aunt Lonnie had warned me that burying my mother had been a terrible strain on them. I introduce Carl as my fiancé, and we walk into the house.

Grandma is slouched in her cracked vinyl glider. She looks much the same: white hair pulled back in a wispy bun, head sunk on her chest, hands quivering over her soft middle. In her laconic way she says, "Look who's here." She stands up with a thrust of her arms on the chair and shows us to the kitchen, where she has been cooking all morning. We sit around the table and eat food with tastes I associate only with this woman and this place. We don't say much as we gorge on fried green beans, corn bread, fried chicken, coleslaw, biscuits and gravy, and banana pudding. There is enough welcome here for several prodigal granddaughters. As I eat, I look around at the kitchen and living room. It is all as I remembered: cupboards open showing piles of mismatched crockery, an ancient '50s radio, leather couch, and pile of handmade quilts. Time stands still here.

I ask to see Mother's grave. When Grandma hears this, she scolds Grandpa, "I asked you to pay the neighbor's boy to pull the weeds from the grave, and it's never been done." Her mouth turns down like a horseshoe, and although I know this is partly due to not wearing her false teeth, she just always seems so sad. A while later, I find her alone rocking in her glider and ask how she is feeling. She is surprised at the question. Eventually she says, "I miss my mother." A cold weight falls on me. I miss the mother I never knew, as well, and probably my mother missed the nurturing she never received. Grandma was raised by relatives, and who knew what happened to her mother? Where would this generational lack of mothering end?

Grandpa picks up a cane his brother whittled and says, "Don't worry, woman, I'll use this to push the weeds away." He is eighty-two, but in good shape. He talks endlessly about houses he rents out and deals he is going to make. We walk past the old house where my mother was born. The people sitting in rockers on the porch wave and say, "Hey" as we pass. We cross the rickety little bridge over the creek where I used to make mud pies with my cousins Gwen and Sonny. The barn where I remember milking the cow is filled with weeds. Everything looks smaller than I remember. "I plan to clear it out and rent it," Grandpa says. He points in the distance to a house built in "nineteen and ought five" that he rents. It has no electricity or indoor plumbing. My grandfather is a slumlord.

We have to bushwhack our way up the steep hill to Mother's grave. At the time of her burial, Grandpa had it bulldozed, but now trees have toppled, and weeds grow waist high. Grandpa thwacks with his cane, creating a path, while explaining how "the dozer pushed the earth this way and that." Finally, we reach the top of the hill and the stone monument. On it is engraved "Jeanne Gibson Merrick, March 18, 1928–March 9, 1980. The Lord is My Shepherd." She was not quite fifty-two when she died.

I'm moved to think of her ambition stilled, her sapphire eyes closed, her small body wrapped in a mink coat six feet under the earth. Tears lie aching inside my eyes, but Grandpa keeps talking while he stares at me, and they refuse to fall. He tells of his plans to clear the path and how difficult it was to dig the hole. Then he says he hasn't told "the woman" this, but he wants to be buried here in the jacket and slacks Mother gave him.

I want to weep and feel the release of forgiveness. But tears won't come. There is too much here. Too much hidden, too much left unsaid, too much pain, too much anger, too many missed opportunities. I never went to see my mother as she lay dying. Now I have to remind myself why. I was afraid of her cruel sarcasm, biting wit, and slicing tongue. I was afraid of her alcoholic rage, her need to annihilate me, her oldest daughter, the only child who wanted or was able to understand her. And everyone here worshipped her and judges me. My grandfather keeps on talking and watching me as if assessing this daughter who didn't attend her mother's deathbed. It's an impossible situation.

Back on the porch, we are grateful for the gradual cooling until mosquitoes drive us inside. Grandma rhythmically rocks in her glider. Then she suddenly stands with surprising vigor and trudges into her room. I peer in and see their clothes hanging from nails jutting from the walls. She brings out several albums and a box. We sit together on the Victorian leather couch, and I absorb photos of a young, confident, happy Jeanne. Although I look through many photographs, there are none of my mother and me, other than a few when I was a baby. There she is with her sisters, with David, and Cecelia. I feel cut out, and it hurts. I wonder where I was when the photos were taken. I can't ever recall my mother being in Kentucky when I was there.

Carl whispers, "Your mother's rags-to-riches story is fascinating. I wish I'd met her."

"I'm thankful you didn't, because she seduced everyone. She was closer to your age—you'd be dating her instead of me!"

I give Carl a chaste kiss and go into the little bedroom Grandma insists upon. Carl and I are not permitted to sleep together until married. I lie down on the cool sheets and listen to the locusts drone. A mist rolls through the valley, bringing with it a luxurious coolness. I pull the quilt over me and turn off the light.

The darkness and creak of crickets is so familiar and close. I sense my mother's body lying buried up the hill in the soil where she was born. My fingers stroke the quilt, remembering the silky feel of the earth when I made mud pies near the creek. The perfume of honeysuckle stealing in on the cooling night air lingers in my nostrils. Both our lungs have been infused with the oxygen from this moist air. My mother will always be a part of me. Her courage and creativity are in me. I fall asleep, at home at last.

The next morning, Carl comes in to see if I want to go running. We talk about my mother as we jog along a dusty road hugging a mountain. A coal truck rumbles by, showering us with black stones. Dogs bark as we pass shacks with washing strung out to dry. A man is sitting on the edge of the porch putting on his boots. Carl and I wave hello, but he only grunts. I'm relieved the dogs don't chase us. My mother sure came from rough country.

We jog back and sit, sweating, on the porch. Grandma is fussing in the kitchen, so I offer my services. I'm quickly put to work scrambling eggs while she cuts biscuit dough circles with a jar, stirs up gravy, and cooks sausages. We sit down to a mammoth breakfast that includes fried green beans, honey from the comb, and cornbread. I think about my usual diet of miso soup, curried veggies, and brown rice and wonder what Grandma would make of it. When we are through, I offer to clean up. "Irene will do it, leave them for her." Grandma said the same thing last night. Who is Irene and why is she expected to do all the cleaning up?

I hear a truck drive up and run out to greet my Uncle Elwood and his huge black Rottweiler. I kiss his grizzled cheek and repress a cough from the reek of alcohol while his dog growls. Elwood has become a bleary-eyed redneck with a beer-keg belly, who is already sweating in the morning's humidity. I discover Irene, Elwood's wife, in the kitchen attacking the pile of dirty dishes. She is brisk around me, cool, and I figure out why.

"Irene, I understand you were close to my mother at the end. Tell me about it?"

The words in my mouth are stiff, hard to form, and I am afraid they are going to bounce off her rigid back. But she turns around and leans against the stove. She is shorter than I, compact with a bush of curly brown hair, an intense little person in jeans and a loose shirt.

She is formal. "That last year Jeanne was in constant pain. She said it was like walking on hot knives. Every day I shone a heat lamp on her groin, bathed her, gave her enemas and massages. Me and her were like twin sisters." Irene turns her back and continues scrubbing the stove to hide her tears.

"She needed nutritious, expensive food, and I'd drive across Lexington to buy fresh oysters, oranges, and the best steak. When I had to work, and other family members cared for her, they bought frozen food, and she lost seven pounds in one week. I cooked what Jeanne wanted at any time of the day or night. Her sisters wouldn't help her bathe, and when I returned, she hadn't been washed in a week." I feel as if I'm being beaten by her words.

"Jeanne told them, 'As soon as I put my feet on the floor at night, I hear Irene's feet hit the floor, running to help.' We slept in the same bed after a while.

"We had a last fling—a night at the Lexington Hyatt Regency. Jeanne had her hair and nails done. She looked young and well. We ate dinner and planned to spend the night between crisp sheets and have breakfast in bed the next morning. But during the night, she couldn't breathe and had to be propped up with pillows. In the morning, I put her fur coat over her nightgown and took her to the hospital. Her kidneys had failed.

"When Jeanne was in the hospital, she shared the room with a woman with cancer who wailed that she was going to die. Jeanne raised up on her skinny elbow, this big around, and chewed her out. The woman went home and is probably still alive today. Jeanne talked about Cecelia frequently and asked that her jewelry be saved for her."

"Did she ever talk about me?" I finally interrupt and ask what my heart is crying to say.

"No—oh well, you want the truth?" Irene turns around to face me. "She was very angry at you because you told Cecelia that she was an alcoholic." Oh. She was angry with *me* because I told the truth. For a moment I have a guilt pang—how could I have said such a thing? But what do you tell a kid whose mother is always late or not there or sleeping? I had tried to save my sister the confusion that had dogged my early life. No one else was going to tell her.

Then I remember the Buddha's First Noble Truth about suffering. I'm not alone in the pain—we are all grieving Mother's death. Blaming myself, Mother, or anyone else isn't going to help. I have to be larger than that. I have to become compassionate Kwan Yin. Pausing to take a few deep breaths, I speak from my heart.

"Irene, thank you for being my mother's faithful companion when she was sick and dying. I wish with all my heart it could have been me sharing those intimate moments with her. But we didn't have that kind of relationship. She was brave, and you stood by her. Thank you so much. We are all grieving her loss." Tears began flowing from my eyes like a balm. Miraculously, Irene's face softens, and a moment later I feel her arms around me. She is sobbing as well. We comfort each other for a long time before we collapse into chairs, exhausted but relieved.

The next morning, as we are getting ready to leave, Irene comes over with some gifts. "This here little metal teapot your mother used to make tea. Jeanne hated using a tea bag in a cup." Irene had been using the teapot to store bacon drippings and when she hands it to me, it's still greasy. She also has a crate filled with mason jars of sauerkraut she's pickled. She offers me some. I'm not crazy about cabbage, but to be gracious I accept two. Then she insists, "Take the entire box and return the empty mason jars," although there is no way I can do this. I am flustered and annoyed at having to cram the crate into our already full little car. I remind myself that this woman cared for my mother and gave me the gift of forgiveness. I can put up with a few jars of sauerkraut.

Irene and I kiss and hug. Grandma and Grandpa stand on the porch and wave as Carl and I fold ourselves into the Chevette. The duck waddles over and is the most demonstrative, quacking and running around. With a sigh, I remember I have Aunts Lonnie, Sue Ellen, and Clara to visit before I reach my new home in Chicago. This is going to be a long trip.

⚬⚬⚬

I dream that Mother is on a Greyhound bus on that fateful journey from Kentucky to New York City. But this time I'm with her. Our shoulders bolster each other as we giggle like girlfriends. She is eighteen. Her blue eyes sparkle, and her face is bright with vitality. She smokes unfiltered Camels with quick puffs. She is excited and nervous—more anxious about her mother's reaction when she finds out Jeanne has run off—than what she will do when she reaches that mecca, New York.

We slide open the bus window, and the humid night air rushes in with its scent of honeysuckle. Occasionally, as we slow around a torturous curve, gears grinding, sweet gum branches scrape the sides. She reaches out and grabs a star-shaped leaf and slaps it in her lap.

"That's gonna be me!" she drawls, and we scream with joy at her audacity. But we know what she says will come true. She is a rocket streaking into the blue, shaking off dull gravity and Kentucky clods.

We lean our heads back against the seat, taking forbidden pulls on our beers. In silence, we soak in this endless night, certain we will forever be held in the lap of Lady Luck, who smiles at us so warmly. No one was impervious to Jeanne's charm in Kentucky, and surely she'd reach into the hearts (and pants) of the big shots in New York.

Somewhere in the night, a mockingbird wheedles a few notes. We hum our favorite tune and then sing the words, the anthem of our bound fates:

> *"I'll give to you the key to my heart,*
> *That we may love and never part,*
> *If you will marry me, me, me,*
> *If you will marry me."*

EPILOGUE

I have arrived, I am home
In the here and in the now.
I am solid, I am free
In the ultimate I dwell.
—THICH NHAT HANH

Carl and I move to the Chicago area and marry in the exquisite Baha'i Temple on the shores of Lake Michigan. We live happily while I become a psychotherapist and an art quilter. Neither Carl's body nor mine cooperates in creating a child. Tippi, a toy Shih Tzu–Poodle rescue, becomes my baby. His sanctuary is a dog carrier bag that I take everywhere. He is content as long as I'm near.

As Carl approaches his late sixties, we begin plans for his retirement. We look for a home near but not too close to my parents, who now live in Albuquerque, New Mexico. Choosing a spacious cabin perched on the side of the Jemez Mountains, forty-five miles from Albuquerque, we have it renovated into my dream home. Fiery hummingbirds zoom across the decks each morning while I delight in views of golden cliffs, black volcanic

264 ℓ REMEMBER ME AS LOVING YOU

peaks, and deep ponderosa pine forests. The towering thunder-clouds look like galleons sailing across turquoise skies. I relish inhaling dry air scented with pine and vanilla. Every night a billion diamonds gleam across black velvet skies while coyotes' yips and howls echo across the canyons. In the high desert drought, I save precious water from my showers and pour it on irises that display dancers' frilly skirts of purple and saffron. When summer monsoons sluice down gullies, I collect pottery shards painted with designs made by ancient Pueblo people. I feel these peoples' presence as I dye fabric and create layered art quilts in my spacious studio. Outside my door, a wind chime weighted with bear fetishes and a feather tinkles in the breeze.

Because Carl has yet to completely retire and is often away still working in Chicago, I take long hikes alone through the silent pine forests, high into the inverted vanilla cones called tent rocks. I am trailed by apricot-furred Tippi who, when I stop to let him drink from my water bottle, gives me a look that says, *Woman, where are you heading to?* I start a reading group and make good friends. I consult with a few therapy clients over the phone. In the village of Jemez Springs I practice Zen Buddhism at Bodhi Manda Zen Center, where we bathe in sulfurous hot springs after four a.m. meditations.

It is a magical yet anxious time, because I'm so far outside the familiar. Jemez Springs feels like another country, where Spanish is the first language, the sound of hunting rifles crack out, and we are warned to keep our cars fully packed and headed down the driveway in the event of a wildfire. A few months after we move to this enchanted place, a savage event occurs that changes my life forever.

꧁꧂

Shadows loom and shrink, dancing in the flicker of votive candles. Hosen, Abbess of Bodhi Manda, sits immobile with her shaven head sunk forward on her chest, her palms still cupped in a meditative *mudra*. The blond hair of the young man opposite me gleams in the dark. His breathing is regular, his back slumped against the wall. I seem to be the only person who notices a mouse scurrying across the floor where we sit on our black cushions. I gasp but relax when the end of its tail disappears beneath the white-clothed altar.

The drowsy silence is thick and portentous. I follow my breath, or try to, and notice smoky plumes coming out of my mouth in the chilly September air. How can Hosen go barefoot when my feet are freezing in wool socks? I wonder what I am doing in a Zendo in the Jemez Mountains on a cold morning. I worry if Tippi is warm enough in his nest of blankets in the car out in the parking lot.

At last, shards of sunlight break over Guadalupe Mesa, streaming into our wooden cell. A moth, trapped inside, batters its wings against the screened window, rattling it like a snare drum. My eyes fly to it. The winged creature is, like me, searching for the ever-elusive freedom from suffering that the Buddha promised.

After morning meditation and breakfast, I walk to the car and feed and cuddle Tippi, who seems warm and content. Then Hosen and I shuck off our robes and bask naked in the hot springs. The warm sulfurous water washing over my face, shoulders, and back smooths away the tension that has accumulated since moving here. I gaze up at the pinion-clad mountains sharply etched against the clear blue sky, and my doubts about our move slough away.

"I saw a mouse during meditation in the Zendo," I murmur to Hosen.

"Because Frost killed the cats, probably." She furrows her brow and rubs hot water over her shaven head.

"The cats can't tolerate cold?"

"No, Frost is a pure white wolf–dog mix that I raised from a pup. She thinks they're prey animals."

"Oh. I've never heard of such a dog."

Later, a group of us assemble around vans readying for a day trip with Hosen. I hold Tippi in my arms for a while but as we continue to wait, I set him down with his leather leash wrapped around my wrist. Suddenly, there is a sharp tug on the leash. It has snapped. Tippi is in the jaws of an enormous white German shepherd that is shaking him back and forth. I scream—someone punches the dog until Tippi drops to the ground. I open his carrier bag, and Tippi crawls in. My head is both frozen and on fire at once. I can't think of what to do. Hosen promptly says she will pay all medical bills. The vet is twenty-two miles away down curving Route 4. They ask if I need someone to drive me, and I say no. I place Tippi's bag gently in the car and pull out onto the twisting road, careening around the lanes.

The moments in the car stand etched in slow motion: the serpentine road, the blood red gullies from a recent downpour, Tippi's gasps that make me unzip his bag while still driving, the froth dripping from his mouth staining the car seat red. Every moment lasts forever.

When I pull into the vet's parking lot, I just sit. I've gotten us here and can't think of what to do next. The vet, a tall Jemez Pueblo Indian, opens the car door, reaches in and gently plucks Tippi up into his muscular arms and disappears into the building. After a while, I walk in and ask to use the phone. I called Carl in Chicago, and, gasping for breath, explain what has happened. He says he will get a plane back as fast as he can. Then I go into the bathroom and begin to cry. I weep, sob, and when I think I have no more tears, cry some more.

All my hopes of creating a new life here are destroyed. I've been living in extreme anxiety since we moved to Jemez Springs, and now I know safety is an illusion. Over the years I have been betting everything in a specious bargain: that if I meditate and am a good person, I will be protected from life. Today I realize the true meaning of impermanence—anything can happen at any time in any place. We are in a vast universe of constant change, subject to forces beyond our control. I can't keep from harm the one creature that loves me unconditionally. How am I to live in such a world?

My broken heart also grieves that no one in my life has loved and protected me the way I'd hoped: not my mother, father, husbands, or spiritual teachers. Carl, who seemed such a bulwark of strength when we first married, isn't here when I need him most. Hosen has raised a violent dog at the Zendo. I have betrayed Tippi by not holding him in my arms and protecting him. My life seems shattered and over, as my fur baby's life is probably over.

But Tippi isn't dead. Two vets work on him for many hours, closing the punctures in his lungs and chest—a hundred stitches, they say. They have experience sewing up small pets savaged by larger dogs. They keep him for a month in a veterinary clinic that usually tends farm animals. Tippi learns Native American commands from the Jemez Pueblo vet as they check the cows together. My little dog will over time completely recover, so that not a scar or discoloration will betray his wounding. For me, it is a different story.

In the following months, my blinks become longer until my eyelids clench closed, effectively blinding me. Then my voice hoarsens and deepens until I sound like a man with a bad chest cold, and eventually speech becomes unintelligible. Carl and I search for answers for what is happening to me. We discover I have two rare neurological conditions, blepharospasm and spasmodic dysphonia, that cause my eyelids and vocal cords to spasm. Botox shots in the eyelids ameliorate the first condition but do little for my voice. I write what I need to say on yellow legal pads that litter my house and car like police crime scene tapes.

While I take refuge in my studio creating art quilts, Carl becomes my voice and liaison with the outside world. He, however, has lost his direction in retirement and becomes resentful of my vocation. He uses loud, angry words as weapons against me when I have none. We embark on a long, circuitous journey away from each other, only to reunite decades later.

Seeing we need to get away from isolated Jemez Springs to a more familiar environment, we move to Asheville, North Carolina, a vibrant community nestled in the Appalachian Mountains.

There, I begin practicing Zen with a meditation group in the tradition of Thich Nhat Hanh. When I discover that an integral part of retreats is taking naps (they call it "deep relaxation") while lullabies are sung, I know for certain this is the path for me. Thich Nhat Hanh's philosophy emphasizes interbeing—including the fact that "your parents are in every cell of your body," and slowly I begin the process of healing my relationship with my mother. I also find support through Alanon and rediscover the healing body prayer that is Dances of Universal Peace. But above all, I crave expression through the words that are now so elusive. I join a women's creative writing group led by Peggy Millin and pick up the process of finishing the life story that I began so long ago when my mother gave me a five-year diary.

One day, a friend places binoculars in my hands and has me focus on a Great Blue Heron. Immediately, I have magic powers to observe the miracle of interlocking feathers, scaled feet, and shiny wild eyes. For a few moments, I forget my voiceless torment and *become* the heron. Quiet, observant birders are my favorite people, as birding becomes a passion.

Yet feelings of exclusion and painful isolation circumscribe me: people forget I'm here because I don't say anything. An invisible little girl again, I'm back at my mother's parties with the adults holding forth while I'm forgotten. Or I'm a disciple unable to express my anguish at being excluded from Guru's inner circle. Feeling alone in a crowd is so painful that I pursue solitary activities: creating fiber art in my studio, bicycling long, lonely stretches of road, and meditating as if my sanity depends on it—which it does. At the same time, I crave connection.

During a group hike, I listen to others chat, and suddenly my heart cries out. I want so desperately to be heard and to engage. All I can do is press my palm, this very hand that is the same as Buddha's, against my cracking heart. I ask myself, *What if everything is perfect just as it is? What if there is nothing to change, nothing to search for? What if silence is the best gift I can be given—how it brings me back again and again to the present moment—the only moment I have? Can I drop the need for others' attention? Can I call this palm pressing its warmth against me love enough? Can I drop the story that I am unloved, unnoticed?* There is so much to absorb in this moment with women happily talking while one woman is silent—can I drop the story of lack and focus on the plenitude?

Falling to the back of the line, I grow quiet within myself. I follow my breath and feel my feet kissing the earth. I let my ears open to the softest, most distant sounds: the staccato clatter of a woodpecker's excavations, the soughing wind in the trees, and the muffled sound of my own footsteps. At one point, I see the flash of a scarlet tanager, and with every step I become increasingly aware of my old friends, the trout lilies, bloodroot, and violets. As I see, I am seen—and I am comforted. I am home in the here and the now. I meet each moment in kindness and learn the lessons that only loss can provide by appreciating the small, sacred moments of everyday life.

It has taken me a long time to appreciate spasmodic dysphonia's many gifts. Only when I could no longer speak do I begin to listen to what a person is saying without planning my response or being impelled to carry the conversational thread. I'm free to step outside social norms and enjoy the intimacy of the moment; the light caressing your hair, the joy in your tone, simply being *with* you. When I do speak, I limit my words, and that gives them power.

Listening is a path to the present moment. My ears are highly receptive as I focus on hearing. Every day sounds I never noticed before accompany me: breathing, footsteps, the tinkle of a spoon in a cup, the rush of water through pipes, my dog's snores. When I meditate, I invite spaciousness by listening to the farthest sound I can hear. I experience how silence surrounds and gives birth to sound. In pristine silence is the potentiality for all being. With deep listening, my heart cracks open, self-absorption blown away by seeing how much everyone suffers. My mother, father, grandparents, and all my ancestors have suffered and passed it on to me. I'm not unique in my pain, yet from the compost of our suffering comes our joy. Without this voice-loss journey, I'd never have looked so deeply at speech, listening, and interconnection. I feel full now and no longer hunger for love. I'm living a life I enjoy with people who care about me. I feel such inner abundance that it spills over, and I want to share it with all. My strangled voice helps me learn that I am not this body. I am life without boundaries in a vulnerable human container.

⁂

Years later, I read Internet accounts by female disciples of Sri Chinmoy's coercing them to having sex with him. I'm appalled and disbelieving—yet these are written by longtime devotees whose dedication had been unparalleled. Why would they write these detailed accounts unless they are true? I wonder if Devadas's sexual license with me had been in imitation of his teacher.

Both men's deceit and betrayal of their high ideals is staggering. I can't put together the radiant Guru whose meditations lifted me so many times with the man who bribed his spiritual daughters into incest with promises of higher consciousness followed by threats of expulsion if they revealed their secret. The only explanation that makes sense to me is Sri Chinmoy believed he was above the morality he so strictly enforced with his students. That he justified his predation by his sense of entitlement because of his "self-realization." And yet . . . and yet . . . I don't regret my time with him, because I was given amazing inner tools and bonds with the family of former disciples that last until this day.

Meditation teacher Jack Kornfield suggests that the fiery gate of teacher betrayal can be an opportunity to examine where we have given ourselves away or hoped to be saved by another. These are core themes that run through my life. He also says, "Forgiveness is one of the greatest gifts of spiritual life. It enables us to be released from the sorrows of the past." And this is what I work on daily.

I see my mother dressed in mink, pearls, and a pillbox hat as she hunches over her cigarette, flicking her bare big toe. She whispers sympathetically into the phone, "I hear my little girl is getting a divorce." Father is beaming affectionately at me and saying in his deep voice, "Never forget you are my firstborn child." Franca is writing me the birthday card that she sends every year. David is wearing rags—he's a young Oliver Twist in the orphanage asking, "Please, sir, may I have some more?" "Food, Glorious Food," the other boys burst into song around him. Grandpa is dressed in denim overalls and a straw hat, while his blue eyes dance with humor before he delivers a joke. Grandma Tishie smiles shyly to herself as she rocks, her eyes closed in a moment of private peace. Grandma Blanche stands on stage, dressed as the Little Quaker Maid, the spotlight illuminating her lovely features. Sri Chinmoy is garbed in a golden *kurta* and *dhoti,* his eyes flickering in bliss. Devadas rises and tucks his violin under his chin. His eyebrows arch as he bows a tender tune of adoration. Both my husbands jog in, wearing running shorts and T-shirts. Frost pants, her long pink tongue contrasting with her gleaming white fur. Tippi nestles at her side, his peach fur adorned with purple hosta blooms he's been sniffing.

And me? I'm a flower child wearing a red gown with blossoms twined in my long brown hair. I admire the incredible cast of characters my life has been blessed with. I beckon to them, and we form a circle holding hands, Frost and Tippi in the center. We beam at each other and laugh in sheer incredulity at the roles we played. Now it is time to move on to a new dance: one of compassion, harmony, and joy.

AUTHOR'S NOTE

Memory is a creative thing and I have been writing this memoir for many years in absence of others' corroboration. Please forgive me if my rendition of events doesn't match yours. Also, I have changed the names of most of the people who were with Sri Chinmoy in order to honor their privacy.

ACKNOWLEDGMENTS

Deep gratitude to all those who offered support along the way: my husband, Carl, Peggy Millin and Clarity Works writing groups, my many editors, my friends who read the early pages (all 420 of them!) and have given precious words of encouragement along the way, and the lively family that is the former students of Sri Chinmoy.

ABOUT THE AUTHOR

K imberly Childs graduated from Adelphi University with a
master's degree in social work. She has worked as a psychotherapist and fiber artist, and is a former small business owner.
She lives in Asheville, North Carolina with her husband and dog.

Author photo © Cat Ford-Coates

SELECTED TITLES FROM
SHE WRITES PRESS

She Writes Press is an independent publishing company founded to serve women writers everywhere. Visit us at www.shewritespress.com.

All the Ghosts Dance Free: A Memoir by Terry Cameron Baldwin. $16.95, 978-1-63152-822-4. A poetic memoir that explores the legacy of alcoholism and teen suicide in one woman's life—and her efforts to create an authentic existence in the face of that legacy.

Don't Call Me Mother: A Daughter's Journey from Abandonment to Forgiveness by Linda Joy Myers. $16.95, 978-1-938314-02 -5. Linda Joy Myers's story of how she transcended the prisons of her childhood by seeking—and offering—forgiveness for her family's sins.

The Sportscaster's Daughter: A Memoir by Cindi Michael. $16.95, 978-1-63152-107-2. Despite being disowned by her father—sportscaster George Michael, said to be the man who inspired ESPN's Sports Center—Cindi Michael manages financially and heals emotionally, ultimately finding confidence from within.

The Butterfly Groove: A Mother's Mystery, A Daughter's Journey by Jessica Barraco. $16.95, 978-1-63152-800-2. In an attempt to solve the mystery of her deceased mother's life, Jessica Barraco retraces the older woman's steps nearly forty years earlier—and finds herself along the way.

Scattering Ashes: A Memoir of Letting Go by Joan Rough. $16.95, 978-1-63152-095-2. A daughter's chronicle of what happens when she invites her alcoholic and emotionally abusive mother to move in with her in hopes of helping her through the final stages of life—and her dream of mending their tattered relationship fails miserably.

Motherlines: Letters of Love, Longing, and Liberation by Patricia Reis. $16.95, 978-1-63152-121-8. In her midlife search for meaning, and longing for maternal connection, Patricia Reis encounters uncommon women who inspire her journey and discovers an unlikely confidante in her aunt, a free-spirited Franciscan nun.

www.ingramcontent.com/pod-product-compliance
Lightning Source LLC
Chambersburg PA
CBHW021502090426

42739CB00007B/421